THIRTEEN IN AUSCHWITZ

MY GRANDMOTHER'S FIGHT TO SURVIVE

LAUREN MEYEROWITZ PORT

ISBN 9789493418158 (ebook)

ISBN 9789493418134 (paperback)

ISBN 9789493418141 (hardcover)

Publisher: Amsterdam Publishers, The Netherlands

info@amsterdampublishers.com

Thirteen in Auschwitz is part of the series *Holocaust Survivor True Stories*

Copyright © Lauren Meyerowitz Port, 2025

Cover photo: Ruth Krautwirth. April 1, 1943. Frankfurt am Main, Germany. Photo taken by the Gestapo. From the collection of Ruth Krautwirth Meyerowitz.

Photos from the collection of Ruth Krautwirth Meyerowitz and Lauren Meyerowitz Port.

CONTENTS

Preface	vii

SHARING MEMORIES: A CHILDHOOD IN NAZI GERMANY

A Story for my Granddaughter	3
Early Years	18
Persecution	43
Rescue Efforts	61
Photos	81

SURVIVING THE SHOAH

Arrival at Auschwitz Birkenau	89
Inhumane Conditions	101
The Selections	117
A Tribute to Loved Ones	129
Ravensbrück and Malchow	151
Liberation and return to Frankfurt am Main	162
Photos	175

LIFE AS A HOLOCAUST SURVIVOR

New Beginnings	183
The Fate of Our Friends and Family	201
The World Gathering of Jewish Holocaust Survivors	228
Perspectives	243
Photos	265

POSTSCRIPT

The Final Years	273
Photos	289
Acknowledgments	293
About the Author	295
Amsterdam Publishers Holocaust Library	297

This book is dedicated in loving memory of my grandmother Ruth Krautwirth Meyerowitz and her mother, Chana Krautwirth.

It is dedicated to their loved ones who were murdered in the Holocaust and whose names will now carry on in this memoir.

In memory of Ruth's best friend from childhood, Irma Stern.

In memory of Ruth's companion in Auschwitz, Mimi Benmayor.

And in memory of Ruth's father, Yitzhak Krautwirth.

In all that we do, we remember them.

PREFACE

Thirteen in Auschwitz: My Grandmother's Fight to Survive is a memoir containing stories told by my grandmother, Ruth Krautwirth Meyerowitz. I have formatted the book as a series of first-person letters written between us. Ruth narrates her Holocaust experiences in letters to me, and my responses pose questions and provide additional details for the benefit of the reader. The letters do not physically exist. Instead, the content of each letter is based on various sources and are a composite of Ruth's written and oral testimonies.

Ruth was an active Holocaust educator, and she gave lectures to schoolchildren and to groups at synagogues. She also wrote articles and letters to the editor for publication in Jewish periodicals and newspapers. She provided oral testimony to the United States Holocaust Memorial Museum and the USC Shoah Foundation. She was featured in Walter Cronkite's documentary *The Holocaust: In Memory of Millions*. She also wrote many short stories, and she began an autobiography that was never completed. These sources were used to develop the letters featured in this book.

I have only edited Ruth's words so that they are in a readable, publishable format. I have not changed her testimony, and I have retained her tone and original words. The story is told the way she remembered it, without changing her description of the events of the Holocaust.

However, I removed my grandmother's use of the word *Gypsy*. The term *Gypsy*, and the German equivalent *Zigeuner*, are derogatory terms meant to exclude this group of people from society by connoting antisocial criminality. The term was commonly used in the concentration camps and throughout society after the war. Rather than using the term *Gypsy*, I refer to this group as Romany or Roma.

Although much of the content is horrendous, gruesome, and graphic, I have made no attempt to make it less so. I recommend this book only for mature audiences; it is not for children.

Neither the names of the perpetrators nor the names of the victims have been changed. The names of the victims were submitted to the Shoah Victims Database, a compilation of names of people who did not survive the Holocaust, so they may be remembered in perpetuity.

Ruth felt a mission to ensure that the victims were not forgotten. After Ruth attended the 1981 World Gathering of Jewish Holocaust Survivors Conference in Jerusalem, Holocaust remembrance became her purpose and work. I have written this book to ensure that her story is never forgotten.

Family tree 1 – Ruth's immediate family before the war

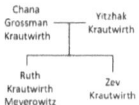

Family tree 2 – Ruth's maternal ancestors

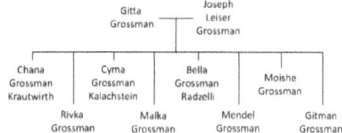

Family tree 3 – Ruth's paternal ancestors

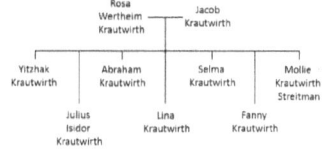

Family tree 4- Ruth's immediate family after the war

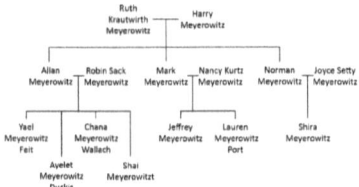

Family tree 5- Zev's immediate family after the war

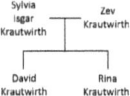

SHARING MEMORIES: A CHILDHOOD IN NAZI GERMANY

Frankfurt am Main, Germany
1929–1943

As told through letters to Lauren, 1986–1988.
With letters from Lauren to Ruth, 2006.
New Jersey, United States

A STORY FOR MY GRANDDAUGHTER

A Promise to Remember

March 25, 1986

Dear Lauren,

Your mommy, daddy, and big brother Jeffrey welcomed you into the world today, March 25, 1986, at 5:54 p.m. You weigh just over seven pounds! Your father, my son Mark, called to tell me the good news of the birth of a healthy little girl. He says you will be named, in Hebrew, after my mother, Chana, who passed away just six months ago. You have a strong namesake, and you should have a bright future. I am overjoyed to welcome you, my newest grandchild, into our family. I cannot wait to meet you!

I've decided to keep a journal for you of all the things that are happening, so you can catch up with them as you grow older. I've done the same for your brother and your older cousins. I will hold onto these letters and give them to you once you have the maturity to understand them. I will also tell you some of the things that happened long before you were born. If there is a bit of homegrown philosophy mixed in, I know you'll forgive your doting grandma.

You are too young to understand right now, but one day you will learn that there was once a thing that happened to our people, the Jewish people, called the Holocaust. You must read and study the war years, 1939–1945, when the fate of European Jewry played such a tragic part. As you get older, you can reread my letters, and you will understand.

Let's call it by the Hebrew name, the Shoah. It was one of the most tragic of human events. You will hear the number six million. That is how many Jews were murdered. Do not forget that the life stories of six million individuals stand behind that number.

In learning of the Shoah, you will hear similar tales repeated: We came home one day, the German troops had invaded, we were deported, we never saw our parents and our little sisters and brothers again, we nearly starved, we were beaten, we never bathed, and finally, blessedly, there were other soldiers who liberated us, and we tried to find the remnants of our families.

Even when you hear about Auschwitz, you will hear the same stories of lice and rats and filthy clothes and beatings. Every day was the same for everyone, and yet not. Every survivor has an individual story of his own tragedy. So yes, it was all the same. We were all the same. We didn't even have a name – just a number. We had our hair shaved, which was lucky because lice teemed by the billions. But we also had individual things occur that we can remember and talk about.

Do not forget that each story is unique. Each one deserves to be remembered. For if we erase the individuality behind each person, each story, then we erase our personal and collective identity. Keep in mind that while the ghettos were burning, Jews were teaching their children how to live and die with moral strength and courage.

Out of all these stories, I promise to tell you the story of one little girl and what she went through during this catastrophic time in Jewish history. I'll tell you of the city where she was born: Frankfurt am Main, Germany. It was a wonderful city that once held a grand Jewish community with much learning and study, great people and great striving. It is the story of one city like many others that had been home for us Jews; it could have been any one of the thousands of communities that once held vibrant Jewish beings. I'll also tell you of the friends this little girl made, and the aunts and uncles and schoolmates she had – and lost – along the way. This is the story of one particular person: me, your grandma, as I saw it and as I lived it.

I will tell you, but not because I want you to feel maudlin and overwhelmed with pity. Not at all. We are past that. I want you to feel proud that you belong to a strong people who have gone through some terrible things and have come out of it with steadfast ethics and unimpaired morals.

I must tell you my story because, if not, it would be as rabbi and philosopher Emil Fackenheim says, to hand Hitler and his cohorts a final victory – the obliteration of the Jewish people. That was exactly the aim of the Nazi government in Europe during those terrible times.

I promise to tell you my story of surviving the Shoah, from the very beginning to the end, with the vivid imagery that remains in my mind to this day. What I would like to reinforce is that, yes, there was cruelty imposed upon us by others, but even in my worst days and nights, never did I ever lose pride in my people. The more the Nazis wanted to degrade us, to dehumanize us, the more I felt the humanity of the Jewish people. I will tell you the story of my fight to survive in Auschwitz.

Forgive me for my morbid sense of return. I keep going back to the events of my youth. It is dismal to speak of children dying in a world made by adults. But how else can we remember those who died?

How can we learn not to repeat? What does it take? Where do we get the wisdom? How can we attempt an explanation of such inhumanity? I will try my best to convey all my thoughts and memories to you even when my questions have no answers.

Never forget that there was such a place as Auschwitz, but also remember that Jewish culture and tradition and all that is beautiful in Jewishness were not killed there.

You've been born into a strong family with a rich Jewish heritage. Please ask me all the questions you can think of. That is the Jewish tradition. I will answer them as openly and honestly as I can.

Promise me in return, my granddaughter, that you will remember my story.

Love, Ruth

Your purpose and mine

2006

Dear Ruth,

I want to thank you for always sharing your story with me and answering all my questions. I will always cherish the letters you wrote me when I was a baby and which you gave me when I became a Bat Mitzvah. Now that I am grown, I realize how much your words have impacted my life.

I did not realize it as a child, but I know now that my generation is the last to hear the stories from survivors directly. Future generations will go to the Holocaust museums of the world and will learn the historical lessons in class from teachers. Yet, they will not get the chance to meet survivors who visit their classrooms to tell their stories. They will not be able to discuss Grandma's story over dinner with her. I am fortunate enough to have you in my life, always teaching me your lessons. You have been so vocal in answering my many questions over the years.

We, the children and grandchildren of survivors, have an important role in not letting the world forget what happened. The historic memory of the Holocaust must be passed from each generation to the next in the hope that the world will learn from it and one day learn not to close its eyes to genocide. You stress the importance of the second generation, the children of survivors, in actively playing their part to remember the Holocaust. As part of the third generation, I too feel the great responsibility to remember your story.

When all of us grandchildren were little, you did not hold back from sharing your story, but you did filter some of the most atrocious details so that we would not have nightmares. We always knew about how you met your best friend, Irma. We knew Irma did not survive, but you spared us some of the details.

Whenever you spoke to groups in schools or synagogues about the Holocaust, the beginning did not start with your birth. You felt the story could not be understood without the historical background and context of the country, the city, and your family. You described for us what German society was like before the war, the history of Jewish settlement in Germany, and what life was like for the Jews of Frankfurt from the establishment of its Jewish Ghetto to Emancipation in the 18th century and to the rise of Hitler. You spoke about the history of medieval Jew-hatred and how that hatred shifted to the pseudoscientific racial hatred of the Nazis' antisemitism. You would then explain what life was like in the camps. You concluded by telling the story of your liberation and coming to America.

What you didn't speak about much was the loss of your father. It was the most painful part for you. After hearing your stories, I would always give my parents a hug and kiss and tell them I loved them. Even at a young age, my cousins and I learned that we are very blessed to have our parents. We knew that while no question about the Holocaust was off-limits, we should be mindful of your feelings when asking about your father.

Your story must transcend your lifetime. Just as you have lived each day of your life with the memories of the past, so too must your children and grandchildren always remember. For this reason, I have decided to preserve your story by writing your biography. Will you help me?

Thank you for passing your story on to me. I promise I will remember it always.

Love, Lauren

Chana – my mother, your namesake

1986

Dear Lauren,

I now have four grandchildren. There are your cousins, Shira Lee and Yael Aviva, and your older brother, Jeffrey. Your Hebrew name is Chana, for my mother, whom everybody called Mutti and who died this past December 11. My children, your father and uncles, called my mother Mutti because that is what I called her in German. (*Mutti* means "mommy," since *Mutter* means "mother.")

When your Uncle Allan was a student at the Jewish Theological Seminary, he used to come home for Shabbat but would first stop at her apartment and fill up with chicken soup, gefilte fish, stories from the old country, and words of wisdom. There is a special relationship between grandchildren and grandparents, and Allan had a great share of it. He was especially close to Mutti.

For the last two-and-a-half years of Mutti's life, she lived in a nursing home in Fair Lawn. Almost every Friday, his day off, Allan would visit her in the nursing home, bringing little Yael with him.

Little Yael would crawl on Mutti's bed and kiss her and sometimes share ice cream. Mutti enjoyed this immensely. I love your uncle and your cousin so much for it. Sometimes your aunt went with them, too, and that was a great mitzvah. For the last several months now, Yael has not gone into the nursing home, but she passes it in the car on the way to our house.

Today Yael is almost three years old. As young as she is, she asked one day what happened to Mutti. You children are too young to know about death, but then again, we all are, and it is tough to speak of it or make any sense of it. I suppose that, by now, she must have heard of this unexplainable, horror-inspiring thing called death. Her father is a rabbi, so funerals and unveilings are part of his spiritual work.

A few days ago, passing by there, Yael turned to her mother, saying: "This is where Mutti lives. Do you love Mutti? I love her." I guess this was her tactful way of saying that we should go in and see her and ask why her parents were not taking her. Now you know that death takes those we love and those we do not care for too much at the same rate, and without questions or answers. How can we explain death to you children? Let's always love one another so that we never have any regrets. I love you, your cousins, aunts and uncles, and your mommy and your daddy, and everyone in the family.

Mutti was very sick. She was 85 when she died. She was in unbearable pain, constantly medicated and losing ground. People say that it is for the best, that she did not have anything left out of life, only pain. But to me this loss is terrible. I cannot ever have another mother.

I stood at my mother's bedside on Erev Chanukah [The day before the start of Chanukah], a few days after the doctors had told us that there was only a short time left. Unable to use coherent sentences, I resorted to small talk: "Tonight is Erev Chanukah." "Oh," she replied, "you must pray for a good year for me." Jews had always believed that at the time of a *Yom Tov* [Jewish holiday] the heavens were especially receptive to prayer, more than on ordinary days. Both my parents died in the week of Chanukah, 42 years apart and in different parts of the world.

You will sometimes hear your uncles and dad talk about Mutti. Remembering and contemplating is good for the soul. I do not want to remember her from the times when she was not well, but from earlier, when things were good. Now she is gone, and we only have memories. Not that we did not fight at times, but you'll find this is natural between the generations. Don't ever let it get to the point where someone will be hurt. People should love, love, love. It's best for everyone's soul.

Mutti did not have a happy life. In Poland, where she was born in 1900, life for Jews under the Russian tsarist regime was very bad. When Poland became independent again in 1918, the constant antisemitism really came to the fore. Jews were accused of collaborating with the Russians, the enemy. You can imagine the rest: pogroms, murders, beatings, cheating Jews out of their work and their possessions. Mutti, the oldest daughter at age 18, was reluctantly sent to Germany to an aunt and uncle. Many parents faced the same dilemma in those times. They wanted a better life for their children, and if only enough money was available for one trip, one child was sent abroad for a chance at a better life. Many sad songs were written in Yiddish about this plight. The parents and children usually never saw each other again.

Mutti stayed with this aunt and uncle until 1927, when she married my father, Yitzhak. For six years they had a happy life together. But in 1933, Hitler came to power and put an end to all that happiness and security. Not that they were not personally happy. They had the greatest marriage, full of love and devotion.

Although my father was separated from my mother and me when we were deported to Auschwitz, my mother and I remained together for the duration of the war. It was our bond that kept me going. My mother saved the lives of some of the women imprisoned in Auschwitz. She saved *my* life when I had typhus. She was a mother to many women in the camp who would never see their own mothers again. She brought hope to the hopeless and provided strength to the suffering women in the camp.

My mother never adjusted after the war and remained a prisoner of Auschwitz until her death 40 years later. She had brought the others strength and hope in the camp. Yet, after the war it was as though she existed with only enough air to breathe on the surface but not enough air to take a big, deep breath to laugh and enjoy life. Mutti only lived half a life, neither happy nor satisfied, and so her life was very tragic.

She died still mourning the loss of my father. My father was killed in Auschwitz in December 1943. She was too devoted to remarry. She busied herself with work. She did not attend many social events, since they were the type of events that she would have attended with my father.

I pray that her sacrifice will be noted in Heaven and that her descendants will not know any sorrow from now on. I pray that *Hashem* in His mercy will give a tender seat to Mutti; she suffered so much in this life.

Lauren, you will learn a lot about Judaism from your cousin Yael. This is very important to me. As you know, I saw so many of our Jewish people destroyed in what has become such a casual expression, "the Holocaust."

Love, Ruth

Learning about Grandma's life

2006

Dear Ruth,

I have so many childhood memories of how you told your story to all the cousins when we were little.

One vivid memory was right after the blizzard of 1992. It was a cold, snowy day. You came over to play with us. We put on a skit. It was to be a realistic nonfiction drama, not a comedy or a musical. We were cast as the grandchildren with you playing the grandma. In our skit, we were going to ask you questions, and you would answer them. Our parents were the audience. This was your idea to keep us entertained and still ensure passing on your story in an educational way.

I remember we sat in the living room in front of the fireplace and took turns asking the questions. Clearly the questions were not ordinary ones that little children would typically ask their grandparents, but rather our questions to you were about your experiences in the Holocaust. We asked things like: "How long were you in the camp?" and, "Was your brother with you?" We asked about what kind of food you ate and how you felt about being tattooed. I don't remember coming up with the questions. I am pretty sure that you wrote these questions for us, or at least guided us in the right direction.

Aunt Robin remembers many times you made special dates to be with us grandchildren for the specific purpose of passing on memories, often through games. Our skit was just one way that you opened the avenues of communication so that when we were older, we would be comfortable asking questions at any time.

We learned about the conditions in Auschwitz, about how you got tattoo number 42716 on your arm, and about being in the barracks with your mom. You told us about the cold, the starvation, the diseases, and the death all around.

You frequently told us the Noodle Story, of how you carried potatoes, thinking they were noodles, when you were liberated. It was a happy story compared to the rest, and I remember asking you to retell it over and over. Looking back, I realize only now the historical significance of such a story. At the time, I thought it was just a normal bedtime story.

How did you answer our question: what happened to the rest of the Jewish people? How do you explain to children what six million is? Such a number is incomprehensible. Most likely you told us about your best friend, Irma. As children, we all had a best friend we could think about when we heard about your friendship with Irma. I would have thought of my best friends from elementary school at that time, Jodi, Alisa, and Melissa, who are still my best friends to this day.

We concluded the snowy-day skit with a feeling of great appreciation for our parents. We gave big hugs to you and to our parents after hearing your story.

Love, Lauren

Teaching children about the Holocaust

1986

Dear Lauren,

You are so small and precious. You have dark hair and green eyes just like my son, your father, while your big brother looks more like your mother.

I feel a great sense of responsibility to tell you and my other grandchildren my story. You must learn about the Holocaust and, one day when you are a parent and grandparent yourself, teach it to your children and grandchildren. One of many Jewish values is to teach our children Torah. Similarly, it is of the utmost importance to teach our children every aspect of the Holocaust. Children who are exposed daily to murder in the media should be able to handle this essential part of Jewish history if it is properly adjusted to their age and maturity level.

Children must be taught the cruelty of the murderers, the indifference of the world, the bravery of the partisans, the desperate struggles in the ghetto uprisings, the courage of the Righteous Gentiles. They must acknowledge the rage of the resisters and the nobility of those who accepted death with dignity. They must hear the emotional impact on the soldiers of all the armed forces who came as liberators. They should know the acceptance or denial of guilt by the German people and their collaborators.

They must study Jewish history, which is replete with persecution, with ridicule and betrayals. They must appreciate the miracles of survival and be witness to the successes of the State of Israel and the vitality of new Jewish communities in the postwar world. This and so much more makes us the Jews we are today, and it is our duty to teach our children in each generation.

Love, Ruth

Indelible trauma

1986

Dear Lauren,

The events of my life are very traumatic. Telling you my story makes me relive this trauma. Yet, I do so because I cannot forget what happened, and neither should you. Neither should the world.

Sometimes I think back and wonder, *Did this really happen to us? Could someone really have done what happened to other human beings?* It boggles my mind as to what could make one human do this to another human. Today it is generally known that traumatic experiences can cause a sense of disbelief and denial when we remember the events.

Sometimes I think that my memories of the war are like nail heads randomly placed along the lines of my mind. Some of them are deeply embedded; I would have to jiggle them to pry them loose. Some do not need much urging; they can be called up at will. And some will come to me, pull at me until I am totally submerged and inescapably immersed in the events.

I get anxious when I tell my story, because sometimes it is difficult to retrieve these memories from the back of my mind. Even having done it so many times, it is not easy for me to talk about the past.

I think one of the reasons it makes me so anxious to talk about it, when I do tell my story, is my belief that this kind of cruelty can be prevented and stopped before it gets out of hand. There is still genocide going on in the world even in recent times. Maybe the small contribution I can make is by learning to be brave and tell my story.

Even today, I still cannot watch any movie on the Holocaust. I was never able to watch many of the war documentaries that eventually came out. Even when the Eichmann trial was televised in 1961, other people were able to watch it on television, but I just couldn't face up to it. Sometimes a movie comes on and I think, *Oh, I'm brave. I'm going to do this now.* Two minutes into the program, off it goes. I don't go to war films of any kind of war. It is too traumatic.

I always contemplate, as I give my lectures and such, how easy it is to fall into a police state, to slide into this pattern of uncontrolled hatred and destruction. In my mind, over and over, I still try to figure out why and how inhumanity occurs. And yet, inhumanity like this continues to go on. We now know about genocides that occurred before World War II. For us Jews it culminated with the murder of six million during the Holocaust. It seems to me now that the world has come to accept large numbers of killings. Large numbers continue to be killed. People talk about it and cry about it. But then people forget about it. What can be done to prevent it?

I must do everything I can to keep the history of what happened in front of the public so eventually people will know that it really happened. Perhaps it can be a warning to the people of the world. I think all of us – the survivors – are trying in a little way to say: "This is what happened. Beware – don't fall into this sort of inhumanity."

I've seen protesters shout that the Holocaust never happened. It feels like the world never changes and will never learn. Don't ever believe them.

Sometimes I have been asked for my thoughts on the meaning of life. I shall save the answer to what the meaning of life is for the time when I do not "stand on one leg."[1] It would be presumptuous for me even to attempt an explanation. As I understand it, the question was probably meant to be, what my feeling is about the value of human life after Auschwitz. Can any meaning be derived from this suffering?

My answer on the value of life is probably the same as before I was in the camp. Survival was the most important impetus at that time. Survival personally, for my family, for the Jewish people. Survival of morality for the world at large, for whenever we give up thinking in moral terms, we, the people of the world, are enveloped in murder, betrayal, and all the other evils that came to the forefront during the time of the Nazis and only lie dormant to be awakened whenever another despot decides to grab power. But I am committed to survival

---

1. Reference to a rabbinic tale about a heathen who facetiously asked to be taught the entire Torah while he was standing on one foot.

on moral terms: the best possible life for the largest possible number of human beings.

Why do I speak about the Shoah if it is so difficult for me? It is to alert you to the revisionists, who lie in the face of historical evidence. But it is also for you to know, to imagine what it was like, so that when you are older, you can act on it whenever you see an emerging injustice.

Despite the difficulty of retelling it and the emotional trauma it brings to the surface, these are the reasons why I must continue to share my story.

Love, Ruth

EARLY YEARS

Our heritage

1986

Dear Lauren,

Now, let's start at the beginning.

My life story begins with a newlywed couple by the names of Yitzhak and Chana Krautwirth. Married in 1927, they resided in an apartment located at Ostenstrasse 18, Frankfurt am Main, Germany. They were your great-grandparents, my parents.

I was born on June 23, 1929, and my brother, Zev, was born May 16, 1933. Zev is my brother's Hebrew name, but the name on his birth certificate is Wolfgang in German. Both Zev and I were born in the city of Frankfurt. As the first grandchild, I was named after my paternal grandmother, Rosa. My father thought Rosa was too old-fashioned a name, so they named me Ruth instead, which similarly started with the letter R.

My father traced his lineage back to medieval times in the city of Frankfurt. He was descended from the Schreiber family, one of many families to emerge from Frankfurt's Jewish Ghetto. *Schreiben* translates as "to write." The family members were *sofrim* [scribes] of holy texts.

During the Age of Enlightenment at the end of the 18th century, many wanted to reform and update the Jewish masses, yet many insisted on remaining faithful to the past. A war of ideas, modern versus traditional, was fought. The Frankfurt Jewish community was deeply involved. The Schreibers did not agree with the modernists and moved to Bratislava in today's Slovakia. The most prominent member of this family was Rabbi Moses Sofer (1762–1839), who is known as the *Hatam Sofer*. He was an Orthodox rabbi opposed to the reformists, and he wrote important legal decisions and Talmudic writings that influenced European Jewry of the time and continue to be influential in Orthodox Judaism today. My paternal grandmother, Rosa Wertheim, who was born around 1875, was one of his descendants.

The Wertheim family traces its roots back to Germany in the Middle Ages. Her family stemmed from the little town of Wertheim, located southeast of Frankfurt, in a confluence of the Main and the Tauber Rivers. That's where my grandmother's surname came from. When Napoleon invaded all of Europe around 1790, he wanted to make sure that every person had a last name. Before then, in the ghetto, no one had last names. You were just "so and so, son or daughter of so and so." If you came from a small town like Wertheim, you took the name Wertheim. Sometimes people took names related to their occupations.

Rosa was married to my grandfather Jacob Krautwirth, who was born on July 21, 1868. My grandparents, Jakob and Rosa Krautwirth, were living in Bardejov (Zborrov), in what is now Slovakia, but at the time was Austria-Hungary, when they had their oldest son, my father.

Born on May 24, 1897, my father was given two names: Yitzhak in Hebrew, and Ignatz in German.

Jakob and Rosa moved to Frankfurt as a young married couple, sometime after the birth of my father. Frankfurt was an appealing place for Jews to live at that time. The Jewish community thrived. German Jews enjoyed legal equality. Once in Frankfurt, Jakob and Rosa had six more children. Isidor (his German name, although we knew him as Julius) was born in 1899. The others, whose years of birth I do not know, were Abraham, Selma, Lina, Mollie, and Fanny.

Grandma Rosa died on June 22, 1908, at a young age, of pneumonia. As the story goes, my Aunt Lina had raced across town to fetch a doctor. There was a parade in the center of town, and Lina was delayed. Rosa died. As a child, Lina never forgave herself, thinking that had she not been delayed, she might have saved her mother. What might have saved her would have been a shot of antibiotics, a treatment that was still decades away. Aunt Lina left for the United States in 1913 to try to restart her life. Many years later, on January 13, 1936, my grandfather Jakob Krautwirth died.

Although our ancestors were strictly Orthodox and anti-reform, by the 1920s my paternal line were proud German Jews. We were assimilated into German society, but we still observed the Sabbath and other holidays, and kept kosher. I still have some pictures of my aunts and uncles dressed in the high fashion of the day. They were cosmopolitan, modern, and appear rather wealthy.

My father, Yitzhak, served in the Army of the Central Powers (Germany and Austria-Hungary) during World War I (1914–1918). He had been drafted into the army. The Nazis would later say that Jews were not dedicated citizens. They said this to justify the actions they were taking to separate Jews from the rest of society and to justify eventually murdering us. Despite this twist of the truth, the German Jews were very devoted citizens. The Nazi propaganda about Jewish patriotism did not resemble anything close to what had actually happened during World War I, when Jews dutifully served in the German army. My father was a veteran having proudly served his country.

Despite our deep ancestral connection on my father's side to the city of Frankfurt, we were citizens of Czechoslovakia because that is where my father was born. Czechoslovakia had been created in 1918 out of the former Austro-Hungarian Empire. The German citizenship laws of the time considered Zev and me to be Czechoslovakian citizens, based on our father's citizenship rather than our own place of birth.

Now on to my maternal side. My mother's family originated in the Pale of Settlement, the legally authorized area for Jews within the borders of tsarist Russia. Our ancestors lived in a town called Ostrowietz, near Radom, in what became southern Poland. Located south of Warsaw, it was near the Prussian border.

My great-great-great-grandparents, the Privers, had lived in Warsaw. They had somehow, by the extreme application of their talents, managed to work for absentee Russian landlords and were able to make a very good living for themselves. During the Russian Revolution, the landlords lost their estates, and so the Privers became extremely poor.

At the end of World War I, Poland was re-created through the will of the League of Nations. It became an independent country patched together from a small core of what before had been called Congress Poland, and lands taken back from Germany, Russia, and Austria. Attacks on Jews were commonplace. At that point, some of the Privers fled to France. I do not know very much about the family, and most records were lost during the war. One of the daughters of the Priver family living in Poland was my great-grandmother, Chana Priver Feldman.

My maternal grandfather, Joseph Leiser Grossman, was married twice. Both his wives were daughters of Chana Priver Feldman. The first wife died in childbirth at a young age. The second marriage was with the late wife's younger sister. The second wife was named Gitta (Gitl) Feldman Grossman.

My mother was Chana Grossman, born on April 7, 1900, in Radom, Poland, and named after her grandmother, Chana Priver Feldman.

Initially, Gitta was not happy to marry her late sister's widower. She wanted to marry a boyfriend who had gone to the United States. However, the marriage was arranged. According to the family lore, this was done to consolidate the wealth between the families. Joseph Leiser was a pious man who owned a lumber business. The business was cutting trees down in the forest, turning them into logs, and then floating the logs down the river, where they were caught by an agent and sold in the market. Gitta told her mother that she would not forgive her for arranging this marriage. By later naming my mother Chana after her mother, she must have forgiven her to some extent.

Joseph Grossman had eight children between the first and second marriages. The three sons were Mendel, Gitman, and Moishe, while the five daughters were Rifka, Chana, Bella, Malka, and Cyma. Gitta raised all children as her own and made no distinction between the ones she had given birth to and the others. The record of which of Joseph's children were from the first wife and which were from the second wife, Gitta, is lost. The family refused to differentiate which children were from which mother and, when asked, did not pass the information on to their own children later in life.

Gitta was a traditional religious woman who dressed modestly. She had a career as a midwife, and would carry around her bag of instruments – perfectly clean and organized – which no one was permitted to touch. She used to meet with many doctors in the area, who consulted with her. She was very well respected throughout the town as a midwife. She was a wonderful person. Overall, though, she had a difficult life. In another time, she might have had a very different, easier life.

There is a family story about my grandmother Gitta. Within our family, she was reported to have been a witch! This is what happened: Gitta had taught her craft to my aunt Cyma, the youngest daughter, since Bella, Cyma's older sister, was too squeamish. In 1933, my grandma Gitta was diagnosed with inoperable cancer and took to her bed. As she was dying, her children gathered to be with her. One day, a very frightened father-to-be rushed into the house and insisted that Gitta come to attend to his wife. Something had gone wrong with the birth of his child, and the attending midwife was lost in incompetence. There was no way Gitta could attend the emergency. After a good deal of persuasion, Cyma, who was 18 at the time, very reluctantly agreed to help. She left for the man's home, where his wife was in labor.

Meanwhile Gitta seemed to be saying the oddest things: "Move it up... Arm... Lift a leg... Twist a little there..." Her daughters at her bedside thought she was dreaming or in a state of delirium.

When Cyma reached the house, she saw that this was no normal delivery. The baby was all twisted in the umbilical cord. She set to work. Then she heard her mother speaking to her, and she thought her mother had been able to get out of bed after all and was standing in the room behind her. "Turn the baby, shift the mother's body, turn the head, push here, pull that..."

Finally, Cyma had a squealing baby and a healthy mother. When she returned home, she proceeded to thank her mother, whereupon she realized that her mother had never left the bed and the instructions had come through extrasensory perceptions.

Bella was in shock at what Cyma said she had heard. Gitta's delirious ramblings suddenly made sense. Bella would later recall that she wouldn't have believed it if she hadn't seen it with her own eyes. I know that science has a precise definition for this phenomenon of telepathy, but witchcraft sounds much more comical.

Not only did Gitta's special powers make her the best midwife, but she also had the gift of prescience. Long before the *Churban*[1] in Europe, Gitta urged her children to leave.

Grandma Gitta died of cancer in 1933. Since she was so well-loved and had delivered so many babies, the entire town of 15,000 people, which was half Jewish and half gentile, went to her funeral. They talked about her like a saint. My grandfather Joseph also died before the Holocaust.

My mother had left Poland years before. Her uncle Moishe David was drafted into the Polish army for World War I, but he fled to Germany to escape serving, since he knew there would not be kosher food in the Polish army. At that time, there were frequent pogroms against the Jews in Poland. Germany was considered an ideal place to move for a better life. In 1918, Moishe David returned to Poland to visit. He wanted to bring one of the siblings back with him to Germany for greater opportunities. He decided to take my mother. At age 18, my mother left the rest of her family behind in Poland for the chance of a better life in Germany. Her younger sister Bella was five at the time and would later recall my mother leaving, but almost as though it were a dream, since she was so young.

That was how my mother ended up in Frankfurt, where she met and married my father.

By 1927, my parents were married. My father started a small leather goods business. Many Jews in Frankfurt were in this industry. His office building was originally located across the river from Frankfurt, in Offenbach.

I speak so often of Frankfurt, the city where I was born. I cannot say my *hometown*, because the city spewed its Jewish residents out like dirt. But the Jewish history of Frankfurt is rich with good people and

---

1. "Destruction," specifically the destruction of the Jerusalem Temple but also used to describe the Holocaust (Hebrew).

good deeds, fools and charlatans, charitable organizations and seats of learning. We identified as proud German Jews.

Our family unit consisted of my parents, Yitzhak and Chana, and us, the children, Zev and me. With deep historical connections to the city, my parents had high hopes that our family would thrive in the Weimar Republic. Germany was an advanced country, known for its educational system, music, philosophy, medicine, and more. We Jews had been in Germany for hundreds of years, and we were accepted into Germany society from the time of the Enlightenment.

But antisemitism lay just beneath the surface. First, the world economy crashed in 1929, the year I was born. Then Hitler rose to power in 1933, the year Zev was born.

So, little Lauren, now you know all about your ancestors and how we ended up in Frankfurt, which is where my life story begins.

Love, Ruth

Intensifying Persecution

Dear Lauren,

Here in New Jersey, in this decade, you and your cousins will have a happy childhood. You have loving parents, happy homes, and a great sense of safety and security in your communities. It was not this way during my childhood. I grew up in Nazi Germany.

My very first memory is from when I was around three years old. I remember the agitation and the worries over the election in 1933. There had been a lot of unrest in Germany from the end of World War I through the Depression due to the high level of inflation. I was too young to know anything of that, but I could sense the unrest and fear in the air. The Nazis were out to get the Jewish people, to convince non-Jews to vote for the Nazi Party because Jews, Communists, and whoever else the Nazis were against, were their enemy. Even at such a young age, I could sense this fear in my midst; it was the general atmosphere of fright that made me fret.

We lived in an apartment on the third floor. My parents had gone out and left me in the house with a nanny. I was worried because everything seemed so insecure all at once. I went onto the balcony to look for my parents. From the window I saw people marching. The next time I looked, there was a propaganda banner for the National Socialists strung across the street between two apartment buildings on the floor beneath ours. With a child's lack of depth perception, seeing this banner I was worried that my parents would never be able to cross into our house again. It seemed a barrier that no one would be able to cross, and so I was very fearful that my parents would not be able to come back. That was my very first memory of the rise of the Nazis.

We celebrated the Jewish holidays with family. I remember the *sukkah* that my parents built on the small porch and which extended into the dining room as 43 guests crowded together for *Sukkot*.[2] My mother was the perfect hostess and glowed with the assurance of having created a flawless meal. The guests alternated their seats to fulfill the mitzvah of eating in a sukkah.

Simchat Torah[3] in the city was like no other. We went to the majestic Börneplatz Synagogue in the old part of town. It was the synagogue of the Liberal Congregation of Frankfurt, which would be equivalent to a Conservative synagogue today. It was still early in the Nazi reign, and Simchat Torah was a most exciting holiday. For the whole day, my brother Zev, my friend Irma, and I participated in the marching

---

2. Jewish holiday celebrating the gathering of the harvest and God's protection for the Children of Israel when they left Egypt.
3. Jewish holiday celebrating the completion and restarting of the annual reading of the Torah.

and organized mayhem of the happy celebration. We children were usually confined to the balcony, where the women had their seats, but for the *hakafot*[4] we joined the men downstairs in the big hall of the sanctuary. At one time, goodies could be gotten from the many congregants on a grab-as-you-can basis. Outside the synagogue we absorbed the warmth, the love, the great dedication Jews feel for Torah. There were men in tall silk hats, women in their brightest fineries, and children, well-behaved and prim.

These were a few happy memories, but most of my childhood memories are of living in a police state in Nazi Germany.

The onslaught happened from the moment Hitler came to power in 1933. Hitler built on the prejudices of the many centuries that saw Jews destroyed in Europe repeatedly. By the end of the 18th century, it was assumed that the Enlightenment would bring acceptance and cause brotherhood to prevail. Germany once had philosophers and artists to equal the best in Europe, but less than 150 years later its people were reduced to sadists, petty barbarians, and sniveling fools.

There was frequent harassment of Jews, but in a city like Frankfurt, it didn't quite begin at the same time as in smaller cities. Before the war, we really weren't bothered by the average German. It's possible that I don't remember it entirely. There were restrictions, but I still remember that we could go to public places. We went to the beach and the river. My father tried to teach us to swim. I remember going to other places of interest in Frankfurt on Sundays. We went to the Cloisters, or to the Cathedral, all the way to the top, where we enjoyed a magnificent view of the city. I remember one Sunday, which must have been in spring or summer, going to the forest.

I didn't feel the intensity of the persecution until later. Gradually, however, they encroached on our liberties. Taunting and

---

4. Part of the Simchat Torah celebrations in which members of the congregation carry the Torah around the synagogue.

persecutions occurred. The evil minds of the evildoers were busy scheming up ever worse persecutions, and in their depravity, they taunted us and held us up to their stupid ridicule. I cannot count the many ways they set their sophomoric minds to the torture of the Jews. A Jewish fish store was prohibited from selling fish to the zoo so that the sea otters would not eat Jewish fish. One bus stop was approached through a small wooded area; a citizen complained that the Jews should not benefit from Aryan shade trees.

At first, we were permitted to use the same public swimming pools and ponds as Aryan Germans. Since there were reports of Jews drowning and nearly drowning, we found it safer to stay at home. My parents may have suspected that the drowning incidents were not unintentional. Later on, we could not swim in the same place as Aryan Germans. Instead, a small, segregated stretch of shore on the right side of the River Main was opened for us Jews, but it was so crowded, it was impossible to go near the water.

As early as 1934, times really were bad. Fear and paranoia swept the country like an iron broom. The Nazi government rounded up every known socialist and communist. Ideas were banished, and books were burned. Newspapers were full of ridicule for foreign governments. Talk of war was everywhere, and Jews were shot on any pretext. The voice of reason was stilled in the land.

The Depression was so intense and the inflation so high that the currency was worth practically nothing. There was a running joke that toilet paper was too expensive to buy, so you were better off wiping your *tuchus* [rear end] with *Deutschmarks*.

One day, my mother waited in one of the endless lines for potatoes to be bought on ration cards. A lot of non-Jewish people waited in the same lines. At the time, a joke was making the rounds, clandestinely of course, that Germany was making guns instead of butter for its populace. A man in line, after observing a plane cruising overhead, stated: "There goes our butter." Immediately two men pulled him out of line, flipped over their lapels where they had stickpins identifying themselves as *Gestapo* [*Geheime Staatspolizei*, the secret police], and took him away. Another voice of sanity was silenced. I am telling this because it shows that it became a duty to obey not only the Nazi party superiors but also the ideals of the Third Reich.

Once, when I was about five or six, while walking at the edge of one of the parks encircling the city, a Hitler Youth boy drove his bicycle into me, knocked me over, injured my knee, and went on his way. My parents did not report this outrage for fear that we would be punished.

In the years leading up to 1938, we were more grown up, so the actual Simchat Torah service at the Börneplatz Synagogue meant almost as much as the gifts of sweets did when we were younger. It was rumored that Gestapo spies stole into the services, so being on our best behavior and avoiding incidents became imperative. In the last few years before 1938, bags with candy were handed to us, a civilized end to the much more exciting tradition of throwing and grabbing the candy. The Börneplatz Synagogue stood until Kristallnacht, November 10, 1938.

Among our neighbors was a small Jewish family with a little girl, a few years younger than me, who was in class with my brother. Her father had done something the Nazis did not approve of. How major could it have been? They took away this little girl, had her surgically sterilized, and then returned her to her family.

As a sidenote to this, in 1977, my three sons, my husband, and I went to Frankfurt. We did selective sightseeing: our house, my school building, cemeteries, places where once stood synagogues and other points of Jewish interest. My sons were grown when we stood in front of the house of this little girl and remembered what they did to her. Four grown men shed tears for this one unfortunate child.

These were the small incidents and provocations we were forced to swallow without outcry. But they increased in ferocity and frequency. Many of the beatings, the jailings, the expropriations of property, the myriad humiliations, were not even discussed in front of us children; it was simply too dangerous and frightful.

The small towns soon became too dangerous for Jews. Therefore, many moved from surrounding areas into the city of Frankfurt. In these early years, such relocations into the city compensated for the numerical loss suffered due to emigration and later deportations out of the city.

What was our inner reaction to the impending catastrophe? At first, only the very farsighted were willing to go into exile. Those who had been arrested early on fled Germany at the first opportunity. These people knew without a doubt that there was no getting along peacefully or dealing with the Nazis or their collaborators. If only the others had heeded their warnings…

Many of us stayed and learned through studying the history of our people that persecution had always existed, but we had always overcome it. Jews had been part of the population in Germany for centuries. We had contributed greatly to the social, cultural, and economic wellbeing of many countries in Western and Central Europe. And so, the call went out not to panic, not to leave the field to Hitler, a ridiculous little dictator with his comic opera minions and his inane rituals.

When I was in school, around age 11, we studied the history of German Jewry in Frankfurt and particularly the conditions in the ghetto, starting in 1462 and ending in 1806 when Napoleon bombed the city. I literally felt ill. I learned of the medieval persecutions, about how the city council and the rulers fought over ownership of the Jews, while the poor victims were made to pay for the privilege of being abused.

Yet, the persecutions of the past were never to the point of extinction. Had they been, the well would have dried up. One historian of the city, I recall reading, described how many *Goldgulden* were paid in bribes for every occasion. Even with this study of the past, little did I imagine what horrors lay ahead for our people.

The Jewish community called on the stones of the city to bear witness to the devoted contributions of the past. Soon it became apparent that the normal dealings with a normal government were outdated rules of conduct. Like an uncontrollable robot, the twisted cross of the swastika churned and marched onward, destroying everything in its way, devouring every human interaction along its path.

When Jews were dismissed from the theater and the opera, we formed our own cultural society. We prepared winter help for those who had nothing. Our schools functioned until there were no more teachers and students in the city. The congregations of the destroyed synagogues prayed to the best of our abilities.

In Frankfurt, the *Lehrhaus*[5] prepared Jews for emigration and, more importantly, tried to instill pride in a discouraged Jewish community. By some miracle, many who had been marginal Jews accepted the challenge and proclaimed themselves proud Jews.

This does not mean to say that only antisemitism can keep us united and alive. I hope that it means we realize how fragile our long-standing humanity is and how valuable it becomes when we are faced with its loss.

As you can see, my childhood in Nazi Germany was no real childhood. Remember how lucky you are to be here in the United States. Always fight to protect your right to live freely as a Jew. You will know what this means when you are older.

Love, Ruth

---

5. School founded in 1920 in Frankfurt by the philosopher Franz Rosenzweig for learning topics related to Judaism.

The question of "what if?"

Dear Lauren,

Playing the "what if" game in history is at best an exercise in futility, nonproductive yet tempting.

A young man, Adolf Hitler, applied to the Vienna Academy of Art two or even three times. He was rejected every time. His art, which is often described as greeting card paintings, did not show the talent required. In the classic manner of the bigot, he closed his mind to his own shortcomings and looked for causes outside himself. What easier scapegoat could he find than the old-time scapegoat – the Jew? With his mesmerizing ability at rabble-rousing, he was able to raise the antisemitism that lay barely under the surface of German society. What if Adolf Hitler had possessed the talent of a Picasso or a Chagall?

As a child growing up in Hitler's Germany, I used to hear: "Don't worry, that moron will not last long," or "Someone is sure to get him out of office soon." True, his reign only lasted 12 years, but oh, that terrible damage he did to the world in those years. We had enough warning when Hitler published his *Mein Kampf*. But who would have believed it?

Often you hear that it would have been dangerous, even fatal for the German people to speak up against the Nazis. They would have been killed. Their families might have been destroyed. Yet, if in 1933, 200,000 Germans had been killed rising up against Hitler's hordes, the world would have noticed and sent help. As it was, millions of German soldiers lost their lives fighting an insane war – and losing their souls in the process. Homes were bombed; families were ruined. The cost was far higher than doing the right thing. What if prewar Germans had stood up to the Nazis?

What I am trying to reiterate is that even little, seemingly unimportant things cannot be discounted. We must be aware of everything and deal with it promptly from a position of strength. One cannot hide one's head and hope the ugliness will go away.

You must always remain vigilant for antisemitism and hatred in politics. Jewish people, because of our longtime sufferings in strange lands, have been in the forefront of the fight for equal rights for *all* citizens – regardless of race or religion. But frustrations and hatreds crop up now and again. It is almost as if we can take the *Haggadah*[6] literally: In every generation there arises one evil person (or ideology) who wants to do us harm.

I am one of the few people alive today who remembers Frankfurt's thriving prewar Jewish population with its great institutions of learning. I mourn the loss of that society and all its members. An entire world was lost with the destruction of the six million. Had my community not been decimated, what would have been the people's contribution to society? Had those six million been able to flourish and contribute to society, not "would" but "how would" the world be a better place today? Do I dare even to wonder… what if the Holocaust hadn't happened?

How different would my own life have been? The alternative is too painful for me even to contemplate.

Love, Ruth

---

6. Religious text used during the Passover seder (ritual meal).

The importance of being *Korah*

Dear Lauren,

Here's a happy childhood story from before the war: the occasion of the first time my mother called me "Korah,"[7] specifically: "you Korah, you." That Thursday, Frau Strubel had delivered to me one of her handmade specialties: a lox-colored silk dress with fluffy puckers of dark blue silk thread along the top and at the wrists, an undisputed masterpiece. That Sabbath morning my mother dressed me and, lest I smudge myself in the house, ordered me to wait in the front yard. As soon as I opened the door, I beheld a blissful mirage, as only a three-year-old can call blissful. Here stood the two large garbage cans with no one swinging from the sides. Every other time the children of the neighborhood vied for that exalted spot. I, the youngest and the littlest, was a continuous loser in the war for the handles of the garbage cans. Today, Sabbath morning, no one else was about; I had the exalted spot all to myself. And when my parents emerged a few minutes later, I was seen swinging from the cans, happiness written all over. I could not, for the life of me, understand my mother's outburst.

The next occasion I remember was the sore event of the spectacles. In the second grade, my teacher, Fraulein Hanauer, discovered that I bent over too close to the books I was reading. She immediately sent home a note enlightening my parents and urging them to have my eyes examined. That done, I was outfitted with said spectacles. Then emerged what I still call the tug-of-war between teacher and parents. Every morning my mother watched me from the window as I made my way across the triangle in the street, where I met up with my best friend Irma and a bunch of my other classmates.

---

7. A biblical figure who led a rebellion against Moses.

As I disappeared from my mother's view, the glasses disappeared from my nose. For the rest of the day, they lodged in the deep innards of my school bag, only to be resurrected when I approached the house. Soon Fraulein Hanauer lost patience with what she perceived as neglect on the part of my parents. Her notes to my parents grew in vehemence. My parents were perplexed, but not for long. A severe lecture by my father placed the hated contraption securely on my nose for the rest of my school days.

In the second grade, in 1936, we began the study of the Bible. Soon I became acquainted with the story of my namesake, Korah, though any similarity between the mutinous son of Moses' first cousin and non-guilty-me remained a mystery. In the desert, Korah had rebelled against the leadership of Moses and Aaron. He had amassed the chieftains of the tribes, indicted the governance of the brothers, challenged their leadership, and ended up being swallowed into the ground along with others who had gone too far.

All *I* did was follow my own inclinations!

Love, Ruth

The country goose in a city apartment

Dear Lauren,

A thoroughly tasteless dinner of goose with its prerequisite trimmings one recent evening brought back into my mind an almost forgotten event. The Nazi era, being what it was, produced few even remotely comical episodes. But this happened soon after the Nazis rose to power, so perhaps for that reason it is still possible to write of normal emotions and humorous occurrences.

My father's business manufactured leather goods for wholesale and export. Only at Christmastime was the shop open for retail trade.

Shopkeepers and farmers and sometimes a lawyer or dentist would stock up on gifts for their female relatives or employees. This year, 1934, a farmer and longtime customer took several belts and purses and handed my father a promissory note. Emboldened by anti-Jewish propaganda and the general air of ill will toward Jews, he stalled and finally refused to pay altogether.

My father was not yet used to accepting the whim of Nazis, and so one Sunday morning he betook himself to the farm with the express goal of collecting the debt. My father's customary, well-practiced logic did not prevail. As determined as my father was, the farmer was equal in his persistence to withhold. When nothing seemed to help, my father agreed, I am sure reluctantly, to take in payment a live goose. I suspect that lots of threats and intimidations were used on him, and when it was over, my father was the reluctant owner of a half-blind goose. An uneven barter by any standard! Perhaps he rationalized that one goose in the hand...

Now, what my father did not know of geese could fill tomes. To him, if a goose had the approximate shape of a goose, then one goose was as good as the next. That the beast was long past its prime and the loser (probably to a younger rival) of one eye in a barnyard rumble was never mentioned in the negotiations.

It will always be a mystery what form of transportation deposited the hapless goose and its handler in our house, but the uninvited guest soon was ensconced in a bathroom with a basin of water and a dish of milk laced with chunks of white bread provisioned for its comfort.

What does a country goose do when it comes to the big city? Explore! But first a goose must splash and preen and divest itself of needless feathers, soak its feet, practice its voice, try its wings. Was it the goose's limited eyesight or the narrowness of the quarters? Who knows? All I know is that its ambition exceeded the available area, and it ended up with stubbed wings; after many attempts, still no uplift.

But having been placed in a room where the family's intimate business was conducted, the fowl soon considered itself an indispensable member of the family with unrestricted access to every room. Soon it took off for the mysteries of the parlor and dining room. With decided nonchalance it paraded across my mother's precious Persian rugs and highly polished parquet floors, leaving scratches and wet footprints in its wake.

One could not tell by its feathers, but this was a goose with exquisite tastes. My mother had taken it into her heart to grow tropical plants in the cool climes of our town. There was on our porch a pampered plant, a native of Italy, tall and ungainly, possessor of the scrawniest leaves and puniest stems. There were also several lesser botanicals in various pots, carefully nurtured but anemic nevertheless, placed around the spoiled tree. Every spring and fall, the flora made its required move from the veranda to the dining room and then in reverse as the equinox bade. This being March, the plants stood in a protected corner. This being a newly urbanized goose, and obviously unfamiliar with the refinements of tropical growths, it began to think of the greens as a side dish to the bread chunks and milk. By evening, the plants showed the results of avian assaults.

What followed was the stuff of slapstick. The fowl's every venture into the proximity of the dining room was met with the end of a broomstick. It, in turn, took off over the Persian rugs, barely maneuvered between the polished buffet and the glass breakfront, and dangerously jingled the crystal glassware and Meissen figurines. My mother, with tools at the ready to collect any droppings this unpleasant guest was rude enough to leave behind, was helped by her friend Miriam, who brandished a carpet cleaner and a feather dust mop. (Any defensive weapons will do in an emergency.) There was my mother, broom in one hand, dustpan in the other, shouting imprecations at the evil fowl and probably reserving some for my father. The guest ignored the feather dust mop; any resemblance to a distant kin and its inglorious end was none of its concern. The bird's outrage only served to heighten its resolve. All this was accomplished with a maximum of noise and probably much under-the-breath cussing together with vivid thoughts of murder. Luckily for him, my father returned from work after the goose had retired for the evening. But it had retired undefeated, and the morrow brought another day of the chase. When it tired of vexing my mother, the goose nipped at my ears and pulled my hair – obstreperous behavior, which did not make for friendly coexistence!

That Friday morning, the *shochet*[8] came and put an end to the adventures of an ungracious guest!

But the goose – and the Nazi farmer – had the last triumph: the bird was way past its prime, so tough it was inedible. A perfectly well-anticipated meal fell victim to the chicanery of the old party member.

Love, Ruth

The death of my husband, your grandpa Harry

Dear Lauren,

You lost your Pop-Pop Harry last month, on August 28, 1986, before you, your brother, cousins, and he had a chance to play baseball together. He was a good daddy to your dad and your uncles. He died of a heart attack at just 65 years old.

I cannot believe my husband is no longer here. Maybe I saw it coming. He was always tired, but I thought it was from all the nervous energy that goes into running a business. I pray that he will have sweetness and light all the days of eternity. He loved life so much and wanted to do everything a person could do.

---

8. Person certified to slaughter animals for food in the manner required by Jewish law regarding *kashrut*.

I know he loved your brother, Jeffrey, very much and was crazy about you, Lauren. He wanted to take you home with him and play with you all the time.

We had good vacations this year. We traveled to the Canadian Rockies, where we did a lot of climbing and hiking. Nothing seemed wrong. We enjoyed the Vancouver World's Fair and thought about you guys all the time, how you would love the rides and all the color of the different nations displaying their arts and culture. We spoke of you on the trains and glaciers after we left Vancouver. Well, the city is there for you to see and experience when you grow a little older. Enjoy, enjoy.

And so, I tell you the things on my mind. I miss your Pop-Pop very much. He would have loved watching you grow and seeing you and your cousins develop into fine personalities.

Sadly, you miss out most, because a grandparent has a special relationship with a grandchild. We love admiring all the cute and clever things you do. We see an extension of ourselves, and we pray for the best of lives for you always.

With him gone, I think about my own mortality, and I become even more committed to continuing to tell my story.

Love, Ruth

Yom Kippur

Dear Lauren,

Today is Erev Yom Kippur. Mutti purchased a blue felt hat in 1934. She did not have much time or chance to get dressed up in it. Hitler had come to power a year before, and life for the Jews was increasingly bad. Before we were deported, the hat, along with the other dear accumulations of a happy marriage, was stored with a non-Jewish "friend" of ours. It would have been easy for him to hide us, but he did not. After the war when we returned to Frankfurt, hoping against all odds that perhaps my father or anyone else of the family would be found, we tried to retrieve some of the tokens of our former life. The expensive things were gone, but we got the hat back. The hat is still stylish today, and I shall wear it tonight to services.

The Hebrew year 5746 was a difficult one with the losses of both my mother and my husband. At least, I have my children and my four grandchildren, with another one on the way; Allan and Robin are expecting their second child in April.

I wore my mother's blue felt hat to Mutti's funeral last December. Somehow it symbolizes my parents' loss to me. I must pray that if God is merciful, He will reunite the souls of my parents in heaven, so both can have the happiness cut short by Hitler. The hat has become a memory of things past.

Today is the Day of Atonement. I wonder if those who killed our children and burned our parents are still alive today, if they ever ask God for forgiveness.

May God help me, I cannot forgive.

Have a good Yom Tov and a happy life, sweet little Lauren.

Love, Ruth

Uncle Abraham – the classical musician

Dear Lauren,

Now, back to the past with more on my youth in Nazi Germany and specifically the memories I have of my uncles.

My father was the oldest of three brothers and the only one married. His two younger brothers, my paternal uncles, naturally gravitated to the warmth of our household and the expertise of my mother's cuisine. Uncles Abba and Julius played with me and spoiled me. Abba, the younger of my father's brothers, was an aspiring opera singer and often practiced in our house. To supposedly enhance the vocal cords before each performance, he would puncture a raw egg and suck out its contents.

Soon after the Nazis came to power, they dismissed Jewish artists. Most prominent were opera singers; they were among the first to go. Jewish painters were considered "decadent" and were not allowed to show their works. Music by Jewish composers was not to be played, and when a piece of music was so well known that the public clamored for it, they simply announced that the lyricist or composer was "unknown." This happened with "The Lorelei," a staple in the German repertoire with lyrics by Heinrich Heine. Today Heine is acknowledged by Germany to be the best German poet after Goethe. The many works by Felix Mendelssohn Bartholdy, the grandson of Moses Mendelssohn, were also labeled "unknown," even though his parents had baptized him as a Lutheran and they later converted to Lutheranism themselves.

Uncle Abba was dismissed in 1933 from his job at the opera. The multitude of unemployed Germans were given the jobs vacated by Jews, and together with the shift toward a German wartime economy, unemployment ceased immediately. Given that Germans were now fully employed, it was easy for them to adore their *Führer*. It became commonplace for them to rationalize every move he made.

The *Jüdische Gemeinde* [Jewish community] created a *Kulturverband* [cultural organization] to employ these now unemployed and unemployable singers, actors, and other artists. It also provided entertainment for the Jewish public, which, especially in large cities, was reared on cultural events. With their convoluted logic, the Nazis permitted Jews to perform the works of Jewish composers. The Kulturverband was formed not only to fill the employment gap but also mainly to retain the sense of humanity and culture that the Nazis denied us. Yes, the Nazis assaulted us with the big deprivations – the arrests, the disappearances, the awareness of early concentration camps like Buchenwald and Dachau – but they also ground away at our self-esteem, our ancient rights, and our hopes, with their little annoyances played out day after day.

Thankfully, Abba escaped from Nazi Germany in time. Having experienced the callousness of the Nazi regime early on, Abba went into *Hachsharah*, the Zionist-sponsored agricultural schooling, to prepare for emigration to Palestine.

Uncle Abba sang with the Kulturverband until he left Germany. Shortly before his departure, he was to sing a small part in an opera. I think it was Mozart's *The Magic Flute*. On the morning of the dress rehearsal, several Gestapo men were present. At the end they announced that the singers and actors could not wear any costumes. Not a world-shaking order, but just one more bit of chicanery in a long line of petty annoyances.

Abba left for Palestine in 1936. The voyage lasted for six days, one of which was Yom Kippur. He conducted services for the whole ship, and it was the last time Abba sang in public. He lived for a long time on a kibbutz, where he cultivated tomatoes, a fruit he particularly hated.

Since Uncle Abba had promised to lead the service for Yom Kippur at a small congregation near Frankfurt, my father, who had a pleasing voice, was called in to take his place that year. As a seven-year-old, this did not sit well with me. I loved my uncle, but on this most beautiful of holidays, my father was off fulfilling my uncle's promise.

Love, Ruth

PERSECUTION

Uncle Julius (Isidor) – The writer

Dear Lauren,

My father's brother Julius was a writer. I remember only vaguely what he looked like, and I know nothing of his personal life, his political outlook, or his social concerns. In the early 1930s, he was a writer for a German newspaper. I do not know which newspaper or what his capacity was there. He was my father's unmarried brother, who spoiled and teased me and made my life fun.

One day in 1933, my father let me in on a conspiracy and a request, which I promised to fulfill with all the earnestness a four-year-old can muster. He said to me seriously, if anyone were to come to our house and ask me about Uncle Julius's whereabouts, I should say that he had played with me just that morning. Actually, I had not seen him that morning but had hugged him goodnight the evening before.

Sure enough, two men came to our house, spoke to my father, and left. The men came and must have been satisfied with my father's answers, for they never thought of interrogating me. This I considered a mixed outcome. I had been quite anxious to do my act, to prove my mettle, while at the same time I was petrified of goofing the whole thing and disappointing my father. I was even more disappointed that I was never asked anything and so never had a chance to show my father what a reliable child I was.

When I grew older, I realized that these two men were from the Gestapo. Apparently, Uncle Julius had written something the Nazis did not approve of, so they had come to arrest him. My father wanted to cool the trail and buy some time for my uncle's escape. Uncle Julius left Frankfurt, and that was the last time I saw him.

It was during the mass arrests of Jews in 1933 that he made his way across Bavaria and over the Czechoslovak border into nearby Pilsen, the closest large city near the German border. There he continued to be a thorn in the side of the Germans. He continued to write! He was also active in the Jewish Community Center (the Czech equivalent of the Jüdische Gemeinde) and in some literary clubs for Czech Jews. He met a young Jewish woman and soon became engaged.

My uncle kept writing, but his letters to us were infrequent. When he did send us some mail, it was usually in 10- or 15-page letters. For those occasions my parents' friends gathered around in a solemn ceremony to hear his precise and clear vision of the situation in Europe.

I remember being with my father at the post office where he mailed a letter, pointing to the mail slot and telling me that the letter was now on the way to Uncle Julius. I envisioned a rolling band that would take the letter directly to him.

In 1938, the German Army occupied Czechoslovakia, annexing the Sudetenland. By March 1939, the rest of what had been Czechoslovakia was divided into two. Bohemia and Moravia became a German Protectorate while the province of Slovakia became a semi-independent client state called the Slovak Republic. The Slovak Republic remained unoccupied, although its leader, Father Jozef Tiso, was entirely in the Nazi camp. The region of Pilsen was partly in the Sudetenland and partly in the Protectorate of Bohemia and Moravia.

At some point thereafter, the hunt for my uncle began again. It must have been around 1942. His only hope was to flee Pilsen and head east into the Slovak Republic.

Uncle Julius never made it there. His fiancée wrote us that he had bought a used motorcycle and set out for his trip. In his eagerness to make his escape quickly, he drove into a ditch, was thrown from the bike, and broke his leg. He was taken to a hospital in Pilsen. The Nazis arrested him there, with a broken leg and other injuries, and took him to jail where he was shot.

I do not know if he wrote as a socialist or a democrat, or what his political views were. He had two strikes against him: he was Jewish, and he was an independent thinker. He was my uncle, one of many of my relatives lost in the war.

Many years after the war, I wrote to the Czechoslovakian government to see if it had any information about my uncle. Did any hospital records or arrest records from the war exist? If he was shot in the hospital, could he have been buried in the Jewish cemetery? Were there any articles published by him?

They had no information for me. No records were to be found. Their replies were not particularly helpful. The country is under Soviet domination and uninterested in helping me. For several years now, I have been considering traveling to Pilsen to see what I can find. It seems the Soviet influence is in decline. Perhaps more information will be available in the future.

Before she died, I told my mother about this idea of traveling there. She was skeptical. What do you expect to find, she asked me.

Answers that do not exist? Sympathy? I am not sure, but the unknown is nagging at me.

Love, Ruth

Kristallnacht

Dear Lauren,

On November 9 and 10, 1938, the Germans went on an insane rampage. It is now known as "Kristallnacht." The front windows of Jewish-owned stores were broken, the insides looted. The shards of glass that sparkled on the sidewalks gave the name to Kristallnacht, or "Night of Broken Glass."

I remember how the Nazi hordes stormed apartments where they knew Jews lived, and then plundered everything that was not tied down – and often, even if it was – and what they could not carry away, they axed.

As an extra measure to show their contempt, the Nazis cut open feather pillows and emptied them into the open air. Since it was a wintry November, the wind caused eerie piles of feathery swirls so that my memories of Kristallnacht are enveloped in the swirl of feathers. Those feathers remained on the ground in wet clumps until the spring rains washed most of them away. But for me, thoughts of Kristallnacht will always bring back the memories of swirls of feathers.

Our beloved Börneplatz Synagogue was burned and destroyed.

It is true that many Germans came to gawk at the tragedy. Some did not approve. My brother Zev recalled hearing a German man say that the burning of books had gone too far. Some of our father's so-called friends pointed to the ravings and hysterics of Hitler's oratory and suggested that such idiotic behavior would not be tolerated for long. We would learn later that these friends just used this as a cover; it turned out they had been long-time members of the Nazi party. No one spoke up after Kristallnacht, so the Nazis were further emboldened.

Love, Ruth

The Philanthropin school

Dear Lauren,

Before my elementary school days began, I attended nursery school. Anne Frank attended the same nursery as me. The Frank family lived in Frankfurt before they moved to the Netherlands. Anne was just a week or two older than me. I vaguely remember her.

I went to a very well-known, progressive school by the name of Philanthropin. We had been so inordinately proud of our school. In 1804, Mayer Amschel Rothschild saw some poor Jewish boys. He took pity on their ignorance of both Jewish and secular knowledge and commissioned his secretary, Sigmund Geisenheimer, to gather them and see to their education. What began as a charity, as "Philanthropin" implies, soon became the most prestigious of schools.

During its span of existence, it paralleled the vacillation that German Judaism underwent. Beginning with an Orthodox outlook, yet with an eye on worldliness, it incorporated various degrees of reform as the times and surroundings changed. When my brother and I attended, its orientation could be compared to modern Conservatism. Very few parents of my fellow students did not keep kosher or observe the Sabbath.

I started school in 1934 at a time when Nazi agitation really went into full horror. We were not allowed to walk on the sidewalks or look a German child in the eyes when meeting one. Often, we were beaten for no reason by other children, and our parents were kept from reporting such things.

Our situation deteriorated after Kristallnacht, and I could feel the tension at school. I was nine years old at the time. After Kristallnacht our school reopened, but the number of students had dwindled. We stood along the flower beds in the schoolyard in little groups, frightened and lost. Some of our friends never came back. We hoped they had made their way to freedom in far-away countries. We who were forced to remain behind never returned to our former lives. The cherished routines of school and parks, of synagogue and friendships, and the many amenities of normal living that we expected to be our rights, were taken away. Instead, there was a blanket of fear, of hatred and mistrust that sat on us, heavy and unperturbed.

Then more and more restrictions were placed on Jewish teaching. I suppose the Nazis couldn't control our learning Hebrew and the Bible and Jewish history, but we were no longer allowed to play Jewish music by Jewish composers.

Sometime later, the deportations started. Jews were called, ostensibly, for "repatriation into the East" or "settlement in the East." We were under the impression that we were being relocated to communities in Poland or elsewhere where there would be work.

Among my more horrible memories are the suicides we heard of daily, though our parents did not discuss this with us and we learned of them only in whispers. Many of our teachers left, too, including some who committed suicide because they were disillusioned with what was happening and were afraid of the future.

Our school was at the forefront of educational experimentation and practice. Thus, the language department was staffed with professors with near fluency and extensive knowledge of the languages they taught. Dr. Marcus was my English teacher. I owe him my fluency in irregular verbs and accuracy in English word usage. When the order came for Dr. Marcus to be deported, he committed suicide. Almost the same scenario happened with Dr. Freudenberger, the last of the principals of our school, and his wife.

The three Jewish cemeteries of Frankfurt were not completely destroyed during the war, although the ancient one was severely desecrated. I've gone back to the New Jewish Cemetery, where those who died during this time are buried, and I recognized some of the names. I placed a stone on the graves. They all date within a certain time period. The teachers must have come to the realization that everybody would be killed, and some people preferred to die in their own beds and by their own choice. Yet, I remember the dilemma and the horror. We mourned the loss of those who committed suicide, and we wished they had chosen to try to live instead. In retrospect, I know that had they not committed suicide, they would have been gassed to death and their remains converted to fertilizer. Perhaps I should have only prayed that their deaths had come quickly and easily.

Early on, the lucky students left for the US and other safe places. New students from the outlying little cities took their places. Thus, enrollment remained even. After the deportations to the East started, some students were not in school because they had been sent out on the transports. Eventually there were only a few students left.

Soon after November 1938, the school building was annexed by the German army. Every book, every report card, every remnant of the once vibrant study body was torn out until no trace remained. Military material was installed. For the last few years of the war, the building served as a military hospital.

Our school was combined with another school. These two Jewish schools had both existed for at least 100 years. The other school's building was closed, and we had classes for a short time in an old orphanage. It was the Jewish orphanage building, called the *Israelitisches Waisenhaus*, located at 87 Roederbergweg at the corner of Waldschmidtstrasse in Frankfurt.

By this point, most students had left. A few had stayed behind. The spirit was gone. Every day more students no longer showed up. Did they try, even at that late date, 1940–1942, to find their way to a safer country? Or were they simply rounded up, disappearing into the cauldron? I only know that very few returned when the war was over. I never heard of any who might have escaped but who chose not to return to the city.

Our famous school, well-known and respected in every European country, was closed in 1942. The Gestapo finally put an end to all that "superfluous" education and stopped classes altogether. My parents were left having to keep two active kids entertained.

My brother and I had taken violin lessons. We were pretty bad. Once we were no longer allowed to go to school, my mother wanted us to practice playing to keep busy. We endlessly played checkers and practiced – what I call playing but was closer to scratching – on our violins.

In 1945, the Philanthropin building and a few other public buildings were handed back to the Jewish community. Since these were in different parts of the city and were in a general state of disrepair through bombings and neglect, the Jewish community eventually sold the structures. In their place, the community built a new central hub containing a Jewish school, social services for the aged, lecture halls, and a kosher restaurant.

I stopped by to visit the new Philanthropin School a few years ago. On the first-floor hallway is a marble plate, a tribute to Sigmund Geisenheimer. The plate had hung in the old building before the school moved to the orphanage. With its honored place so visible on top of the stairs, the history has come full circle.

Yet, there will never again be another Philanthropin as I remember it. Its spirit departed with the last of its Jews in 1942.

Love, Ruth

Irma Stern – My dearest childhood friend

1987

Dear Lauren,

Happy birthday! Today is March 25, 1987. Your first year has gone by quickly. You are turning from an adorable infant into a precious little toddler. You crawl like a little toad and will be walking in no time. I will continue to write you letters about my childhood for you to read one day. Soon you will attend nursery school at the local synagogue, where you will start to make your first friends. I have a story for you about my first friend.

I remember the day I met Irma. I was probably about four years old, so it must have been the summer of 1933.

Just as Aryan children could only play with other Aryan children, I was only allowed to play with other Jewish children. Very early on, my parents warned me not to play with non-Jewish children. They were motivated by all the problems this could cause. If children were to start fighting, it would be the Jewish child who would surely end up the loser, with bad consequences. We were not allowed to defend ourselves without endangering our family, and so we were constant targets. Better to avoid such a situation altogether. None of this was really on my mind that day. It was a nice, sunny day. I had taken a swing between two garbage cans and wove in and out of Frau Schulhei's sheets drying on the line. Tired of that, I watched the strange contortions of a worm, slimy and ugly, as it crept along the edge of the lawn, when I heard someone say, "You can chop his head off over and over again, and he'll just go on growing a new one." This was interesting news and could have used further investigation, when my mother's warning about whom I could play with made me cautious.

"Go away. I may only play with Jewish girls," I said.

"...But I am Jewish," she replied.

"Prove it!"

After some haranguing on my part denying she was Jewish, and after much negotiation, she started singing one of the central prayers in our religion.

"*Sh'ma Yisrael Hashem Elohenu Hashem Echod*... [Hear O Israel, the Lord is our God, the Lord is One.]"

I was convinced she was Jewish. Since she had learned the same prayers, I decided she was safe to play with. I should not have argued with her; after all, she knew best who her ancestors were.

I invited her for some intensive worm watching. She threw back her thick, light brown braids, screwed up her nose until her gray eyes became slits, jumped lightly in the air, and came to rest next to me.

Then the worm must have grown tired of his celebrity status and disappeared. We had time to exchange some vital statistics. Her name was Irma Stern, she was about the same age, and she lived in a house nearby. Her birthday was August 1, 1928. She had a brother, Walter. Her parents were named Sigmund and Paula Stern (maiden name Israel). We would start school on the same day.

We became best friends. We started kindergarten together at the Philanthropin, were in the same class, and had the same friends.

Regardless of the conditions, life with Irma was not all sorrow and fear. We were children, after all, and life asserts itself, no matter where or how dreary the circumstances. We were an unholy pair of cohorts, making life a small misery for our teachers. Fraulein Hanauer separated our seats in class, but I don't think it had the desired effect of breaking our cohesive spirit. Irma was the greater tomboy, and I was glad to follow her lead.

I remember a time when we were a bit older when we absconded with two cigarettes from the little box on her father's desk. Not to be seen, we locked ourselves in the bathroom and proceeded to light up. Neither of us thought we could get violently ill from that misadventure. We turned green, somehow in a shade to match the ugly wallpaper, and spent the rest of the afternoon with dual emotions – regretting our stupidity and admiring our bravery.

Just about then we reached an age when we began to realize that about half the class was not of the same sexual persuasion, and we began a rating system. Wolfgang was the cutest, next came Gunther...

We remained friends for all our years in school, and later when there was no more school. But the normal cycles of life were cut short. The Stern family was chosen for "resettlement in the East" around late 1941 or early 1942. Before she left, Irma gave me her most prized possession: a white linen suit. During resettlement, as they were told, she would not be able to give it the needed care.

I remember how my friend Irma looked on the last day I ever saw her. I watched from my window as she was taken out of that house, a small person, now even smaller, lost and frightened. She was in a small group of forlorn Jews carrying all the things they were allowed to take in one rucksack. She carried a small bundle – all the belongings she could take in order to make the sham seem real, in order to make people feel they were legitimately "resettling." Her light brown braids had been chopped off to make life more sanitary in their new places of settlement. She was a scared little person of 12 going to her death.

There is no grave for her. I have been in Frankfurt about three times since I moved away for good in February 1947. Mostly I go to put a pebble on my grandmother Rosa's grave and the graves of various other ancestors. I walk along the building that held our school and think of what should have been. Then I walk one long block to Irma's house. The house has been restored since the bombing damage during the war.

I imagine Irma coming out to greet me, carrying a tray of cookies. We enter the house and visit. We exchange news and boast of our grandchildren. The dream vanishes. It is incredibly painful not knowing what happened to her. I place a small pebble on the low retaining wall in front of the house. After the death of a friend, Alfred Lord Tennyson wrote:

> *Dark house, by which once more I stand*
> *Here in the long unlovely street,*
> *Doors where my heart used to beat*
> *So quickly waiting for a hand...*

I think of Irma frequently. I remember my friend with much love, and yet I remain tormented by what the Nazis did to her. Kill, kill, kill. What did Irma do to them? Why kill children? There is no answer.

Love, Ruth

2006

Dear Ruth,

I remember your telling me about Irma when I was in elementary school. I always loved hearing about your fond memories of her. I had three Jewish best friends when I was growing up – Melissa, Jodi, and Alisa – and could relate to the first part of the story.

I have tried to find any information on Irma's fate that might be out there in the German archival records.

The Auschwitz Death Books do not contain her name. The archivist referred me to the International Tracing Service (ITS), an archival center based in Germany that houses the documents and information about victims and survivors of Nazi persecution. The ITS originally told me they could not disclose information to non-relatives. I angrily explained that Irma had neither living relatives nor descendants. I pointed out the deplorable hypocrisy of this request. The ITS said the details would be difficult to trace and referred me to the United States Holocaust Memorial Museum (USHMM) database. At the USHMM, I found your submission of her name to the Shoah Victims Database. Nothing else. In circles I go.

This does not mean with certainty that she did *not* end up in a death camp, since often names were not recorded. We just do not have a record of the destination of the transport containing the Stern family.

I found Irma's name at the Holocaust Memorial in Frankfurt. Outside of the old cemetery dating back to 1200, in what had been the Jewish quarter, there is now a memorial with little square plaques that contain names. There are 11,000 little square tablets – one for each of the deported Jews of Frankfurt. The plaque listed her fate as "unknown," and the database inside the adjacent Judengasse Museum was incomplete. Her parents and brother are also memorialized with their fates listed as "unknown."

What we are left with – the only record that remains of her, the only tangible proof that she once existed – are her photographs that her best friend saved and framed.

Irma's life was remembered by *you*. Her life will continue to be remembered by *me*, too.

Love, Lauren

What fools these mortals be!

Dear Lauren,

When Shakespeare said "What foods these mortals be!" he must have meant Hans Schmidt and his mousy, nondescript wife, whose name I vaguely recall was Helga.

Their daughter, Erika Schmidt, could have been a model for a Hitler Youth poster. Blue-eyed with blond pigtails and delicate skin tones, she had none of her mother's mediocrity or her father's robustness. She was shy with the shyness of the edelweiss, the delicate alpine flower the German soldiers used to sing about.

She was a sweet German girl, about our age, who lived across the street from Irma. We were Jewish, and she was not. Occasionally we broke our parents' rule and played with her. She would stay with us for a short time, probably until she, too, remembered that her mother had warned her not to play with Jews.

Hans and Helga Schmidt ran a little butter and cheese store. From afar, one could smell the sausages and cured meats that were sold there. His wife could be seen, the corners of her apron tucked into her waist, her brown hair pulled into a knot, scrubbing milk pails that threatened by their mere size to swallow her up. Helga never came to the front to speak with the customers the way Hans did. He was the one who cut the cheese, ladled the milk, and weighed the bacon. Erika's favorite place was on the windowsill. There she sat, her face pressed to the glass, watching Irma and me kick a pebble or play hopscotch.

Eventually Erika began to avoid us when we met on the street, and she no longer played with us.

We had thought things could not get worse, but they did. By 1939 the war had started. Everything was in short supply. Goods were rationed, and even minimal services ceased. Then the government cracked down on even remotely suspected dissidents. Betrayals were common, everyday things. The Catholic churches were ordered to have a picture of Hitler, larger than the crucifix, hanging above every cross. War propaganda was heard on every radio and was piped into public places. Complaints were unpatriotic and punishable by death.

One day, during a snowstorm, school was dismissed early. As we walked home, our attention was drawn to the Schmidt's shop. People were gathered in front of the store. They broke up and regrouped. Irma and I played nearby, ignored by the crowd.

From bits of conversation, we heard that Erika was ill but that there was no doctor available: "...since yesterday... doctor cannot come... not enough medical personnel... all doctors are at the front tending soldiers... civilians must wait their turn for retired old doctors or interns..."

Suddenly an ancient car made its way, slowly, through the snowy street. On the passenger side of the front window was a yellow star with the word "doctor."

"There goes Dr. Levinsohn. Perhaps you should call him for Erika. He knows more than anyone..." But Jewish doctors were only permitted to treat Jews.

Hans put his chin into his hand, red from handling the milk cans and stuffing sausages, and contemplated the next move. I could almost see his mind work. The muscles under his ruddy skin moved up and down slowly, like an engine starting its pistons. His head nodded and shook like a horse at the feed bag. It did not take him long to regain his solid composure. He had made his decision.

No, not a Jewish doctor for his Aryan daughter. One does not spoil one's heritage by groveling for a Jewish doctor. The car disappeared slowly where the road met the highway.

It is the next morning, and the little store has not opened. Someone comes and a leaves a little later. More people; hushed voices. We children do not dare ask what is happening. Again, we hear parts of sentences. "Erika is dead... died last night of peritonitis... doctor came last night but too late, took her to the hospital right away, but the appendix had already spread the poison into her body."

Irma and I were sad. We knew just enough of death to know that we would never see Erika again. Her death must have moved Irma in some special way, for a few days later she showed me a letter she had written to Erika's parents. I do not remember the exact words, but the sense of it comes back to me fleetingly.

"Dear Mr. and Mrs. Schmidt, Erika was my friend and now she is dead. She died like a brave soldier. A soldier does not know when or why; he only knows that he must. The soldier is dead, but wars will always be with us to bring us grief and glory."

After she had written it, she was not sure if the parents would be angry at receiving a letter from a Jewish girl. I thought they would like *brave,* and *glory,* and *soldier.* Words of war were heard everywhere, and sacrifice became the highest order of patriotism.

I think of Erika occasionally, sacrificed to an inane theory of racial superiority. Her body died when her appendix burst, but she was killed more so by the poison that pervaded the minds of the people. She was another victim of the fanaticism that was everywhere.

How difficult it is to ignore the wisdom of Puck in *A Midsummer Night's Dream:* "O Lord, what fools these mortals be!"

Love, Ruth

The radio

Dear Lauren,

Your baby cousin, Ayelet Adina, was born on April 9, 1987. I can see how much you love her already and that you will be very close, just like your big brother Jeffrey is with your cousin Yael. When I visit my grandchildren, there is always the noise of babies crying, children singing, music blasting. It is a happy noise, even if I leave with a headache.

Speaking of noise, I remember listening to the radio programs on Sunday mornings in the years before the war. The German population turned the radio to the weekly speech by Hitler. They wanted to prove their loyalty by turning the sound up for all to hear. The streets were quiet, but the ranting came to us from all directions.

We tuned in to the German news and elections on the radio. As an aside, the first election I saw in the United States was between President Truman and Thomas Dewey. It was conducted in a calm and civilized manner, at least on the surface. I thought something was wrong. Politicians were supposed to scream and beat the podium, foam and bluster. How would anyone be elected in such a decidedly untypical atmosphere? But I soon learned that this was the norm; the other was unacceptable.

By the early 1940s, one of our real wells of solace came from an unexpected source: Radio Luxembourg, which broadcast clandestinely into Germany. Every few days we would gather around our Blaupunkt radio – a big clumsy box – valuable to us because of the clarity of its transmissions even at very low decibels. (This was a time when ordinary radios featured more static than clear broadcasts.) We would listen to its call number, the first few bars of a Schubert serenade, with our ears glued to the radio to hear news of the real state of the war and other good things happening in the world.

Soon the Nazis caught on that somewhere, not just in our house, those broadcasts were listened to. They announced the invention of a spying device that would catch the traitorous listener. Once, during the hour of the anticipated broadcast, I saw a truck with some sort of propeller turning on its roof, plying the streets. It looked officious, but its vaunted fierceness did not materialize. No one stopped us from enjoying the defeats to the German armies, which became our daily sustenance from 1940 on.

Love, Ruth

RESCUE EFFORTS

Father's ongoing rescue efforts

Dear Lauren,

There were many Eastern European Jews who had fled to Argentina many years before World War II. In the early part of the century, the imagined grievances held by the native populations in their homelands against the Jews grew in intensity and translated into acts of violence. No wonder, then, that many young Jewish men, seeing no future in these dark lands, escaped to Argentina, where they lived in freedom and prospered.

Yet, life proved to be difficult in Argentina, so some chose to return to Europe – not the Eastern Europe of their pain, but to Germany, to the perceived freedom of Western Europe, where they soon again were beset by another enemy: Nazism.

Returnees very often had held onto their Argentinean passports, which, as it turned out, would save their lives. My father was often able to restore these fallen passports, giving their owners the chance to return to Argentina.

My father soon became an expert on having passports reinstated to people who had left Argentina years before, never imagining Argentina would become their last hope for refuge, despite whatever had caused them to leave that country in the first place. My father knew his way around consulates, and he knew the corruptibility of attending officials. He learned how to negotiate with them. He knew which consular officials could not resist a bribe and for how much a Jew could be saved.

After the war, I met a man who was helped into Argentina by my father's ploy and who eventually settled in New Jersey. With great humility, I think of my father's acts of bravery whenever I hear the quotation from the Talmud: "Whoever destroys a soul, it is considered as if he destroyed an entire world. And whoever saves a life, it is considered as if he saved an entire world."

Love, Ruth

The Nazi downstairs

Dear Lauren,

Our downstairs neighbor was a newly minted Nazi by the name of Mr. Agricola, who drove his motorcycle in parades and loved dressing up in his new black uniform. He owned a hardware store, which had been abandoned by a Jew as he fled from Germany and had been handed to this Nazi as a reward for being an obedient party man. This Nazi seemed to us children a grotesque, laughable figure, strutting in parades, wearing an ill-fitting black leather outfit in adulation of his masters, and looking pompous on his newly acquired motorcycle. In his tall shiny boots, he was especially ridiculous. Nature had provided Mr. Agricola with O-shaped legs, probably from rickets in his childhood; the boots stood away from his body and impeded his walk. Even tripping over his own legs could not make him give up those boots. It made Zev and me snicker, but only when he was out of sight.

He took his new status as superman seriously and proceeded to make my brother's life and mine miserable. To us children, he was a menace. If, as children do, we would race up the stairs or move a chair, he would bang on the ceiling to show his disapproval. If a chair were to be moved even slightly, he would hear the noise. His embedded radar announced when we walked into a room too often or trod a little too heavily for his delicate nerves. On such occasions, he would poke the ceiling with a broomstick to remind us that he was a member of the master race and that we were mere nothings, or to warn us that a denouncement to the Gestapo was not forthcoming only because of his generosity.

But then came a time when my parents put over on him such a deceit, it made all the harassment worthwhile.

In March of 1938, the Nazis annexed Austria in an act known as the *Anschluss*. Jews fled to whichever country would accept them. Very often they crossed borders illegally, hoping to make it to safety in Holland or even England (which kept Jewish immigration to a minimum) and from there to some overseas country.

With the Anschluss, my parents became involved in rescue work, which was not too easy a task considering the Nazi who lived downstairs.

Our apartment became a stopover for groups of young men, five or six at a time. In all, my parents hosted several dozen men fleeing Austria on their way to safer destinations. My parents fed them, cleaned their clothes when necessary, and provided money. Often enough, my father made sure that their papers were in some semblance of legitimacy, looking plausible even if the papers were forged.

Cleanliness and the status of their clothes were supervised by my mother. Some of the young men had left their homes in a hurry and arrived in work clothes often torn to tatters from travel on their escape routes. This problem left my mother to scrounge for suitable things, a difficult task because Jews were not entitled to receive the wartime clothing coupons available to the non-Jewish population.

I have one memory in particular of these events that stands out in its absurdity. A man had arrived in a muddy, torn work suit, entirely unfit to meet civilized society. It fell to my mother to find something presentable. A woman in our building offered to sell a perfectly good secondhand suit. Just when my mother started to gloat over her good fortune, the hapless new owner tried it on, and it was discovered that the vest and suit were equipped to accommodate and minimize a woman's breasts. It suddenly dawned on us: the daughter of the house, a radio singer, was a cross-dresser. In those days, any hint of aberrant sexual direction was punishable by a long jail term, concentration camp sentence, or even death. The mother could have dumped the incriminating suit, but good frugal Hausfrau that she was, passed the bargain on to her Jewish neighbor, knowing full well we could not complain or even talk about this. I am sure this odd piece of clothing did not put any obstacles in the path of the young man's escape. Yet, how absurd that this mother would sell the evidence!

The young men slept in whatever beds were free, and often made do with a blanket in our hallway. They stayed a night or two, received identification and money, and left. Many mornings, Zev and I would wake up and find unmade beds and cots in the hallways of our apartment – the only sign they had been there.

There must have been an underground network that referred these young men to us. How else would they have known where to find us? Since this was a most secretive operation, we were never told about it. Neither my brother nor I were ever told the real reason so many young men stayed with us. We Jews were isolated, but a million eyes spied on us.

The process to aid escapees seemed to become more and more difficult all the time. I hope that the men on the run found refuge in free lands. Perhaps some may have found hiding places, but I never knew of anyone going into hiding in Germany.

What puzzles me to this day is how that Nazi, conscious of every one of our moves, was kept in the dark about the activities going on a level above his head. But my parents pulled it off and were never caught. I will never know how old Agricola did not hear the movement of people, but I am grateful he never did.

Eventually the flow of young men in and out stopped. I never heard from these young men later in my life. Their first stop was usually Holland, but I hope that they went further, before that country was occupied by the Nazi army.

Love, Ruth

Eduard Lederer – A man on the run

Dear Lauren,

It is amazing how the knowledge of underground activities spread surreptitiously and how the desperate gravitated to every bit of hope my father could possibly give. With my father established as a conduit of rescue, a very desperate man appeared at our door around the end of 1941.

This man, Eduard Lederer, was from Czechoslovakia. He was a member of a well-known literary family and had known Uncle Julius. I was told that he was a very important person. It seemed that he was recommended by both my uncle and the underground organization that smuggled Jews.

Eduard Lederer, it would soon become apparent, had escaped from Pilsen. Under threatening conditions, he made his way west and was on the run, with the Nazis just steps behind him. So precarious was his circumstance that he did not want to meet my father at our house a second time. They arranged to meet at dusk on Saturday evening at the edge of the park. Meanwhile, my father explored the possibilities of escape from the ever-tightening clamp on Germany.

They met on several Saturday afternoons for a casual walk at the edge of the park. The park was forbidden to Jews, and the men would not chance being seen inside. I did not know the real reason for their meetings. Was it for Mr. Lederer's own rescue, or were they coordinating the rescue network? I'll never know.

One Saturday, my father returned early, devastated, with agitation and anger and fear overwhelming him. Mr. Lederer had not shown up. Perhaps Mr. Lederer was forced to flee, but I think that he was arrested. He must have been caught and either jailed or sent to a concentration camp, only my father did not know it at the time or would not tell us. Instead, my father told me that Mr. Lederer had left for Palestine. He tried to reassure us by saying that it had only made him sad that we could not leave, too.

After the war, when reading some literature on the Holocaust, I came across information on Mr. Lederer. There was documentary evidence of his role in rescue work. I was reminded of him and of my parents' involvement in rescue work with him. I had not thought about it in many years. I had such limited information as a child. Unfortunately, I did not ask my mother about it before she died in 1985. Since then, it has become a continuous source of questions for me.

Love, Ruth

Dear Ruth,

The stories of your parents' involvement in the rescue network are incredibly admirable. I also wish we knew more.

I've researched the fate of Eduard Lederer. Information about him can be found in the Shoah Victims Database and Theresienstadt records:

Name: Eduard Lederer

Born: May 16, 1876

Place of Residence before Deportation: Pilsen

Deportation: Deported from Pilsen to Theresienstadt on January 18, 1942

Deportation: Deported from Theresienstadt to Zamosc[1] on April 28, 1942

Status: Murdered

Love, Lauren

The jewelry box

Dear Lauren,

When my parents became engaged in 1926, my father made my mother an ebony-colored leather jewelry and manicure box. On the

---

1. Town in Poland where Jews were ghettoized and, in the main, deported to death camps.

cover was a design in pink suede, embossed and stylized, while inside, on the yellow silk lining of the lid, was painted a sensuous Pan tootling his pipes and enchanting a nearby bird.

As a child, I was awed by my mother's jewelry box. I inspected it and admired it. Most intriguing was the front panel of the box, which unfolded forward when a hidden button was pushed, thus revealing a secret chamber just large enough to hold special pieces of jewelry, probably more valued ones than those in the top compartment. As I was growing up, I took great pleasure in rummaging through her baubles. Later she forbade me to open the secret panel. By the time I was a little older, I had long ago given up playing with my mother's jewelry box. I had determined that there really were no interesting new treasures to be found in it.

One day, after our school had closed, and several weeks after Mr. Lederer had disappeared, two infamous Gestapo men came to our house, unannounced, as was their wont. These two Gestapo men were active in the city. The boss, by the name of Mr. Hollander, was a fierce, cruel person, whom we avoided if we saw him far away in the street. His assistant, Mr. Raab, possessed similar traits.

When they showed up, my brother and I were busy playing on our violins the barcarolle from *The Tales of Hoffmann*, by the Jewish composer Jacques Offenbach. Playing Offenbach, Mendelssohn, and all the other Jewish composers, or even any composers remotely related to Jewish composers, was prohibited. They heard us scratch away, and they asked us what we were playing. We were afraid to say what it was. We explained, falsely, that the music was permitted for playing. I guess they figured we couldn't do much harm with our playing, so they didn't say anything more about it.

Our father was at work at the time. Our mother left us alone with them while we did our artistic command performance. To my great consternation she disappeared from the room; I could not understand why she would leave us alone with these two monsters. What seemed like hours later, the menaces walked out without finding what they came for, and to this day I do not know what they wanted.

Only much later did Mother return to our room. My surprise that she left us exposed to those two diminished when I went into the bedroom and noticed that the jewelry box, with its hidden compartment, had been moved to a far less prominent place than before and looked as though it had been rummaged through in a hurry.

I never learned what it contained: it was too dangerous for children to know such things. Was there information on illegal travel? Fake passports? Names of helpers? Again, I shall never know. Everything was so controlled, and the last thing our parents wanted was to have us in on something that would pose a danger to us.

After the war, we got back the jewelry box, the secret compartment empty, with its hidden secret irretrievably gone.

Love, Ruth

Quotas prohibiting immigration

Dear Lauren,

The world was indifferent to the plight of Jews. We tried to leave Germany, to leave Europe, but there were no countries willing to take us in. The doors to Palestine were closed. The United States of America was off limits due to a quota system that severely limited the entry of any refugees or other immigrants.

If the Nazis had gone out of their way to create a more avid collaborator in the killing of Jews, they could not have had a better choice than the United States Department of State, and in particular the American consul in Stuttgart, a mean-spirited, evil man.

The procedure to try to leave for the United States was to request from relatives in the United States an affidavit assuring that at no time would the applicant become a burden to the government. At that point, the infamous quota system became the overriding factor. Each country from which emigration was expected was allotted a certain number of openings to be handed to its hopeful.

Since my father had declared as a Czech citizen, we were in the Czech quota figure. The allotment for that country was seven applicants a year. Our number was 77. From the time this rule went into effect, probably in 1937, it would have been 11 years until we were called. Obviously, we were never called.

The quota for Jews from Poland was higher but so was the number of applicants. It was almost better to be registered with the German quota. I understand that even with the small number dealt to German Jews, many slots remained unfilled at the end of each year – a result of the very capricious methods of admission practiced by consular officials.

Finally, if the lucky day came when a given family was called to Stuttgart and passed the rigorous two-part test, they were enviously congratulated. But if one member in the family failed, the whole family was doomed.

It happened that way with Irma's family. Her father, 36 years old at that time, had been a lawyer who thought it best to step out of a career of brainy pursuits and become a chef so that his family would not be a burden once settled in their new country. They passed their mental evaluations easily, but then they were trapped by Mr. Stern's physical assessment. It seemed that when he was in his late teens, Mr. Stern had had one kidney removed. He went on to graduate from the university, marry, have a family, pursue a career, switch to heavy manual work, and lead a normal life. Yet, to the powers over life and death in Stuttgart, he was a great risk to the economy of America, and because of this cavalier attitude, their application for visas to the United States was denied. The whole family was killed.

Those who failed the mental test were similarly discarded. One particularly sad case comes to mind. A hapless woman, whose husband had managed to leave for the United States earlier, was called together with their seven-year-old son before the consul. Granted this was not a sophisticated woman, but considering the fear invoked and the stakes involved, who could have done better... The inquisitor asked her, among other questions, what it was that her husband had in his pants. The poor woman tried to stutter her way out of this embarrassing question, and when the examiner had enjoyed his fill of fun, told her that it must be a set of keys, a wallet, and a handkerchief. Both mother and child were forced to remain behind and most likely perished in the cauldron.

Tales such as this abounded and only served to increase the terror. We were indeed caught between the murderous intentions of the German regime and the callous indifference of our so-called friends.

Love, Ruth

Father's business expropriated

Dear Lauren,

My father's leather business specialized in manufacturing such items as belts and women's purses. The business had been in Offenbach, across the river from Frankfurt, but when it became unsafe to conduct business in an outlying town, he and his partner moved to the city. They set up the business in a loft in a large warehouse on a commercial street behind the main railroad depot. His partner was fortunate to leave for the United States sometime thereafter.

In 1939, the Nazis made it illegal for a Jew to own a business. Soon after this came to pass, my father's leather business was expropriated. It was given to an SS man, a dentist with questionable dentistry ability. His name was Dr. Holtzmann. We believed he was an SS executioner, because every time we heard through the grapevine about a shooting of German dissidents, he had been away from the business. It was amazing how accurate those grapevine sources were in wartime. We could easily imagine that he was the assassin and, as a reward, had been given a Jew's business.

Dr. Holtzmann walked around with a gun, and he kept his gun in what had been my father's desk. When he needed to discuss designs or other business, of which he understood very little, he opened the drawer, put the gun on the desk, and consulted with my father over the gun. Dr. Holtzmann wanted to keep my father around, because Holtzmann himself knew absolutely nothing about running a business. Because of this man's need for my father's expertise, our family of four was among the last full-blooded Jews to remain in the city.

Eventually we were called for resettlement in 1943. Only my father, who was needed to run the incompetent Dr. Holtzmann's business, would be allowed to stay. So important to the business was my father that his "boss" offered to have him exempted from deportation.

My father was faced with the choiceless choice of staying behind and letting his wife and children go, or coming with us. Because the dentist would not exempt the family, too, my father did not accept this offer. He went with us on the transport to Auschwitz. Perhaps he thought he could protect us, or at least he had to try. Ironically and most tragically, he was the only one in our immediate family who did not survive. My brother, mother, and I managed to scratch out of it alive.

Love, Ruth

No chance of hiding

Dear Lauren,

You may wonder whether we ever tried to hide. The short answer is: we could not hide, because there was no one in Frankfurt willing to help us or hide us.

My father had a friend, a devout German Catholic, a seemingly pious man, a devoted father of five, a rational man who often ridiculed the Chaplinesque look and moves and the wild diatribes of the little dictator. This man had a spacious home and an orchard with a garage that could fit up to ten cars and must have been horse stables at one time. He owned a prosperous business as a builder of churches. His name was Jakob Marz.

If the thought "let's hide a family here" had ever crossed his mind, it would probably have been very easy for him to do it. Mr. Marz could have made room for us in a small corner of this place. He could have hidden us, but he did not. I do not know if my father asked him about the possibility of hiding us. If he did, Mr. Marz must have refused. He certainly did not offer. There was no help to be expected from anyone.

Most often, Mr. Marz brought us a pound of cheese, a commodity we were forbidden to buy. Our ration cards, exempt from discrimination for a short time due to our Slovak citizenship, now had a "J" for *Jude* stamped on it, which meant that we could not buy anything at the grocer's store until the late afternoon, when few vegetables and other foods were left. We were glad to find potatoes on a good day, but mostly we had to make do with those heavy yellow turnips that had been reserved for hogs in normal times. Cheese was something even the Christian ration cards could not buy very often.

In return for the cheese, though, Mr. Marz chose some of the best leather goods my father had salvaged from his business before that demented dentist had taken over. It seemed to me, perpetually starved as I was, that this was a good deal for us, even though the trade was less than even.

Only one kindly woman grocer, living in a musty alley protected by a ragged German shepherd, saved for us some of those vegetables that were forbidden. With a knowing wink she ordered me, an unobtrusive child of 12 years, to come late in the day and then generously filled my shopping bags with the much-appreciated stuff, to the howls of that mangy beast. Some of those groceries I toted to the *Home for the Chronically Ill*.

My mother had an association with the Home. Years before, in the good times, my mother and her friends had played bridge, and the winnings were donated to the Home, which was located on a hilltop surrounded by trees and open land within the city of Frankfurt. The staff and some of the residents had escaped as best they could, but a skeleton crew and many disabled were left behind. At a time when the Nazis killed their own birth-defected children to preserve the image of the strong Aryan, the fate of those left behind in a Jewish home for the chronically ill is easily understood. It is possible that their deportation was delayed so that the Nazi doctors could use them for their own nefarious experiments.

At least some – no more than 12 – were still in the home during the last few months we were in Frankfurt. Their food rations had been cruelly cut back. My mother, having once had her pity recruited in favor of these unhappy beings, now continued to channel as much as we could find to these poor ones and their wretched caregivers. Late afternoons found me slinking along the walls, up the steep incline, to the almost empty kitchen. One of my mother's favorite sayings was that one cannot become poor from giving to charity. Sure enough, like a biblical miracle, our larder was refilled with something or other after every trip to the home; the old greengrocer lady had some extra potatoes, or Mr. Marz came through with another pound of cheese.

When the Gestapo ordered us out of our home, my parents packed up a steamer trunk with what was deemed most important to our family. We gave the items to Mr. Marz for safekeeping until our return. Our worldly possessions he was willing to hide for us.

Among the items were two sets of Sabbath candlesticks, a set of silver wineglasses, a few small antique paintings, my mother's blue felt hat, some photographs, and other things. The trunk with the items we had left for safekeeping with his family would sit in a garage facing his lavish home.

It was Mr. Marz, though, who proved to be the greatest disappointment to us when we returned to Frankfurt after the end of the war. In hindsight, we should have known he was a devoted Nazi party member all along.

Love, Ruth

No Escaping Nazi Germany

Dear Lauren,

Not only was hiding not an option for us, but there was no way to escape from Nazi Germany. There was no way out and no way in to any other country. We tried twice to leave but did not succeed.

Why, if my father was able to arrange a number of escapes, were we, his family, caught without any hope of leaving? I have searched my mind and my soul, but the answer after all these years is as elusive to me now as it was then.

My parents, after much deliberation and after helping others to escape, finally decided to escape Germany themselves. My father had kept his Czechoslovakian passport. During the time between the wars, that country was recognized as the only true republic in Europe – a fact my father always reminded me of with a great deal of pride.

His passport had enabled my father to transverse the tightly controlled borders in almost every European country, especially to France, where he occasionally traveled on business. Now we relied on that passport, hoping to get into France. In normal times, my father's Czechoslovakian citizenship would have permitted him access to almost all European countries, but when we really needed it to cross the French and Swiss borders, we were refused entry.

At one point we sold our household goods – everything – and made our way to the French border. At the border we were stopped. No amount of pleading or pecuniary inducement permitted us entry. Many Jews in the same predicament swam across a nearby river under the cover of darkness. Some succeeded. How long they were able to avoid the Nazis who swept Europe with an iron broom, can only be guessed. My parents did not want to chance a swim in the dark river with two children.

My parents, my brother, and I were forced to spend the night in a farmhouse at the border. The farmhouse, contrary to the legendary cleanliness of the Germans, was as filthy as the pigsties that surrounded it. We were devoured by bedbugs, which added to our miserable mood. Years later, when I read of the travels of Michel de Montaigne, I found a part where he described a German farmhouse on his travels near the French border. It had clean rooms, yet very filthy bedding. Could this possibly have been the same farm, with the same linen, 400 years later?

In the morning, my father tried one more time to appeal to the officials – in vain! We were not admitted, but it really did not matter. The Vichy government dealt with Jews, especially the foreign born, in the same familiar fashion as did the Germans. Later that day, we returned to Frankfurt on the morning train. We made our way back, dejected and upset, full of despair and fear. Not long after, in an almost identical trek, we went to the Swiss border, only to be rebuffed again. There was no way to escape, nowhere to go. All borders were closed to us. The countries of the world were unwilling to take us in.

Love, Ruth

Temporary protection from deportation

Dear Lauren,

Jews were rounded up and transported out of Germany starting in late 1941. They told the deportees that they would be resettled in the East. These ostensible "resettlements" were actually deportations transporting them to almost certain death in a concentration camp or death camp after a week of starvation in cattle cars. We thought they would resettle us in the vast open lands that the Germans had occupied out east but where currently no populations lived.

The caprices of war were in our favor at least once. My parents, brother, and I had been temporarily exempted from the transports. We owed this postponement to the fact that we held Czechoslovakian citizenship. The Czechoslovakian Jews living outside of Czechoslovakia were temporarily protected.

The Catholic priest Father Tiso was the head of the Slovak government. He was among the first foreign leaders to hand over the Jews in his territory to the Nazis for extermination. Yet, at the same time, there was some sort of arrangement giving tenuous protection of sorts to those Czechoslovakian Jews living outside the country. We were among them.

When German Jews were ordered to wear the yellow star, we were exempt for about the first six months. In the beginning our food ration card did not yet even carry the letter "J" as did those of other

Jews. Moreover, while my friends were rounded up and sent to their death, we were ghettoized – but we remained in Frankfurt.

By late 1942, Frankfurt had become almost completely empty of Jews. Irma was gone, and so were all the friends with whom I had grown up.

In the end, Father Tiso was either forced to – or wanted to – please the Nazis: he handed us over to the German government to do with us as it pleased.

Love, Ruth

Eviction from our home

Dear Lauren,

Happy second birthday! Today is March 25, 1988. You are now a precious toddler, full of energy and life. So smart and so beautiful! By now you have a nice pile of letters about my childhood to read. I am saving them to give to you once you are older. These have been difficult for me to write. I will resume the rest of my story when you are a bit older.

Sometime in early 1942, about a year before we were sent to Auschwitz, we were ordered out of our apartment. We were forced to move into a group house. The group home was in a building that had been an orphanage. It was an old house in the East End, the Jewish area near the former medieval ghetto, where the poor of our people had lived. The place was chosen for us because it was largely empty, since so few Jews were left in the city. The house was a dilapidated old place in a ghetto-like area. We were imprisoned there.

The group home had a communal setting. The four of us lived in one small room. We ate in a common dining room. Only my father, who had permission to leave for his place of work, was able to escape six days a week. Zev and I played chess and checkers to pass the time. There was no more school, and we were not permitted to leave.

For a year and a half or so, we lived with the constant fear of being deported on the transports that had taken away Irma, my friends, our teachers, and all the community of Jews from Frankfurt. However, my family was left behind, hoping the war would end before Hitler realized his evil intentions. Living in this ghetto-like community building made me wish that I were with Uncle Abba in what seemed like the most marvelous freedom of all: our own nation-to-be – Palestine! I never had any doubt that an independent Jewish nation would come about very soon.

Despite the conditions, we Jews never gave up on religion, on belief, and especially not on hope. Sabbath services went on almost as usual. Rosh Hashanah and Yom Kippur, dismal as the surroundings were, were still celebrated. During Chanukah of 1942, we lit candles in our room in the saddest of moods. I remember bursting into tears as we lit the candles. Maybe it was a premonition of what was to come four months later. But we hoped. Maybe somewhere there would be remonstrations to save us. Maybe if our plight became known, we would easily be rescued.

Inhumane as I found this forced move to be, it was minuscule in comparison to what would follow. We did not know the horrors the near future held for us, or we might have found it more bearable. We were called for resettlement in the East. Not knowing what it meant at the time, we would soon follow our relatives and friends to Auschwitz. Our deportation from Frankfurt in April 1943 marked the end of my childhood.

Love, Ruth

PHOTOS

Ruth holding baby Lauren with big brother Jeff and daughter-in-law Nancy, New Jersey, 1986.

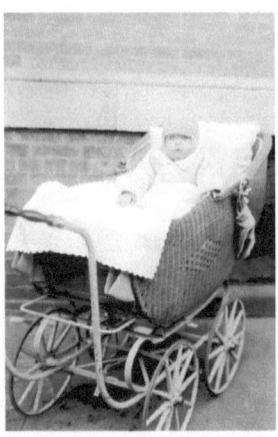

Ruth as a baby in her stroller, Frankfurt, 1929.

Ruth's parents, Chana and Yitzhak Krautwirth, in Frankfurt around 1928.

Ruth's uncle, Julius Krautwirth, in Frankfurt around 1923.

Ruth's uncle, Abraham Krautwirth, in Frankfurt, around 1935.

Chana's family (the Grossmans) including her parents (seated) in Poland, around 1920.

Ruth's father Yitzhak (center), uncle Julius (right) and possibly their father, Jacob, Frankfurt, 1915.

Ruth's brother, Zev Krautwirth, with the yellow Star of David. Photo taken by the Gestapo in Frankfurt, on April 1, 1943.

Ruth and Zev Krautwirth in Frankfurt around 1938.

A plague with the name, date of birth, and unknown date or place of death of Ruth's best friend Irma Stern at the Holocaust Memorial in Frankfurt, 2017.

SURVIVING THE SHOAH

Deportation, April 1943
Auschwitz-Birkenau, April 1943 to November 1944
Ravensbrück, November 1944 to May 1945
Liberation, May 1945
Frankfurt am Main, Late 1945 to February 1947

As told through letters to Lauren, 1999
With letters from Lauren to Ruth, 2017

ARRIVAL AT AUSCHWITZ BIRKENAU

Deportation and separation from my father

April 10, 1999

Dear Lauren,

Mazel tov, Lauren. Today, April 10, 1999, you became a Bat Mitzvah. This signifies that you have reached adulthood according to Jewish law. It was such a special day for you and for us. How proud I was to see our rich Jewish traditions pass on to you as you read beautifully from the Torah. I was honored with giving an *Aliyah*[1] blessing, as were your other grandparents and aunts and uncles.

As a gift for reaching this milestone, along with this letter, I am enclosing all the letters about my childhood that I wrote to you when you were just a baby. Please read them and ask me any questions you have. Now I must make good on my promise to continue telling you my story.

---

1. "Ascent" refers to ascending (moving) to Israel or being called up to the Torah to give a blessing before the Torah reading (Hebrew).

Passover concluded just two days ago. It was on Erev Pesach, April 19, 1943, that we were rounded up and my childhood came to an end. I was 13 years old, just two months shy of my 14th birthday, the same age as you are now. My brother Zev was nine, a month away from turning ten years old.

Hitler was in a foul mood just before his birthday on April 20, 1943. Already by 1942, the German armies were losing on about every front. They had already lost in El Alamein and in Stalingrad and Leningrad. England did not show any signs of falling into the hands of the bloody tyrant. The Japanese were beginning to lose. Resistance in every occupied European country was becoming better organized. Meanwhile, among the most vulnerable of Hitler's so-called enemies, a few unfortunate Jews of Frankfurt still existed in the city, trying to be as invisible and inconspicuous as possible.

For Hitler's birthday, the Nazi High Command decided to give him a present – to make Germany *Judenrein* [free of Jews]. They were probably trying to cheer him up.

We were deported one day before Hitler's birthday. The SS could now boast to him that Frankfurt was Judenrein. The murder of families wrapped as a birthday gift. Destroying the helpless remnants of children and grownups was the great salvation for these "heroes." It is hard even for me, who has seen and been witness to all of this, to believe that there were people who thought the wanton destruction of human beings could be a gift to other humans. Until this day I fail to understand the motivation, the curious satisfaction, they received from this. Keep in mind that the exploration of this insanity is only just beginning and will perhaps never fully be discovered. I have resolved that I will never understand the reasoning of such sick minds, the insanity, the pure hatred, of those who handed us in for extermination as a birthday present to Hitler. Those were the times of madness.

Coincidentally, April 19, 1943, was also the onset of the uprising in the Warsaw Ghetto. The destruction of the remnants of the Ghetto was also intended to serve as a birthday gift to the great Führer. This date was later chosen for *Yom HaShoah* because the Warsaw Ghetto uprising was the first clearly documented act of resistance, putting to rest the tale that Jews went to the slaughter like sheep. My mother overheard one of the guards say something about an uprising there. We were part of a small transport of 37 Jews. The Nazis had a racial hierarchy, and our group was the last of those they considered "full-blooded" Jews, not those from mixed marriages, converts, or other *Mischlinge* [mixed-blooded Aryan and Jew]. From this city that had once held 30,000 Jews, where I was born and where my family had spent so many productive years, our small family of four was among the last 37 to be deported.

We were deported to Auschwitz on a sunny day. If God thought to atone to us by sending us such a day, He fell much short of his goal.

The Nazis rounded us up and walked us from the group home to the south station of the local train depot system. At the train station, the Nazis separated the men from the women and children.

My father was separated from us right there on the platform in Frankfurt. The last thing he said to me was a promise that I would live, since we were the descendants of a very important rabbi. Once separated on the platform, I saw my father from far away.

That was the last time I ever saw him. I never had the chance to say goodbye.

We were chased onto the train by SS men in meticulous uniforms with polished boots and clean white gloves. These "heroes" were accompanied by fierce, giant dogs. I was loaded onto one train with my mother and brother, while my father was loaded onto a different train with other men. We were relatively comfortable on a passenger train, unlike so many who had traveled this path before us in cattle cars.

My mother, when she realized we were really headed for an extermination camp, suffered a panic attack, crying and finally becoming mute. Until that moment of embarkation, we had hoped, bolstered by the news of German defeats broadcast on Radio Luxembourg, and Mr. Marz's assurances that the war was swiftly coming to an end, that we might be forgotten amidst the bad news from the war fronts.

We traveled those few hundred miles for seven days. The journey from Frankfurt to Auschwitz should have taken only several hours. We rode only during the daytime. The train stopped at night, and we were taken off. Moving at night would have made the train a good target for British Royal Air Force bombs. The RAF was retaliating for the bombing of English cities but would only fly at night. Allied planes had no way of knowing who was in the train. If they had thought the train carried ammunition, they would have bombed us.

At night, the Nazi train guards made us stay in different places along the way, such as prisons. One time, we spent the night in the basement of a jail, peeling potatoes for I don't know whom. There were no knives; they gave us sharpened shoehorns probably taken away from some mutinous prisoners.

On the way to Auschwitz, wherever we stopped, we were joined by Polish prisoners. They were non-Jews, forced laborers, women who had been taken into Germany when the Germans occupied Poland. They were probably being sent to the concentration camp for being dissidents, together with the last 37 of us Jews from Frankfurt.

Our descent into the abyss was complete.

Love, Ruth

Ineffable horror

Dear Lauren,

Nothing had ever prepared us for Auschwitz-Birkenau. There is no place on earth to this day that equals that place. There cannot be any place in outer space or on other worlds that will ever come close to this hell. And to this day I cannot think of words that would describe what I saw. Perhaps by retelling some of the events in as plain a language as possible I can convey this horror.

I will keep my words simple, my sentences easy to grasp. How often can I use words such as "terrible," "horrible," "brutal"? How do we honor the dead, tell six million tales, explain their deaths, when our words are poor and the sound becomes trite?

Can I describe the smell of prussic acid when I know that was their last gasp? Do you know what splinters of bones feel like crushing under your feet after they have just been spewed out from a chimney? Are not the bullets the same bullets that find their way over and over again into human flesh? Can I throw the club which broke so many skulls? Can I throw this club into the fires and end once and for all its dreadful mission?

I know these words do not tell the agony. I am of this earth. The language of the other, and even a name for it, eludes me. That language has not been found. It clogs our brains. It chokes our throats. It begs for release, but its sounds are inadequate.

I pray to find them, these words of hell, to relate, to articulate before it is too late.

ARBEIT MACHT FREI [work shall set you free] is the cynical sign atop the entrance gate to Auschwitz. This was not true, because you went into Auschwitz and the adjacent camp Birkenau through these gates, and working hard only made you weaker until you finally died. There was no setting free. Yet, this is the sign that greeted the people and deluded them into thinking they would be in a camp just working and nothing would happen to them.

A better logo would have been: ABANDON ALL HOPE YE WHO ENTER HERE, but even Dante's *Inferno* did not hold the horrors of Auschwitz-Birkenau.

The Nazis did everything in their power to dehumanize us. They called us *Schweinhunde*.[2] But I knew who the real *Schweinhunde* were. Over and over I told myself that I was in the right, verifying my own humanity and keeping my sanity.

My mother and I remained together the entire length of our imprisonment. My brother was allowed to be with us only temporarily. My mother and I were in Auschwitz-Birkenau for the next one year, six months, and one week, from April 25, 1943, to November 3, 1944.[3]

I will describe for you as best I can the details of our daily existence during that time, using the words of this universe.

Love, Ruth

Arrival

Dear Lauren,

The day we arrived, April 25, 1943, was bright with sunshine and soft breezes. It was a beautiful spring day. It seems almost impossible

---

2. "Pig dog"; dogs that watch pigs on a farm, used as a degrading insult comparable to the word *bastard* (German).
3. This is remarkable because the typical life expectancy for prisoners admitted into Auschwitz-Birkenau was a few weeks or a few months.

that something this horrible could go on in the world on such a beautiful day.

Konzentrationslager Auschwitz was the name of the vast concentration camp complex. We were in the part of the Auschwitz camp called Birkenau or Auschwitz II.[4] This was separate from the Auschwitz I main camp, the Auschwitz III camp, called Buna or Monowitz, and the other subcamps. The word Birkenau translates into a beautiful image of birch-treed lanes. There were no birch trees in Birkenau.

There were many transports to Birkenau, before and after ours, where 100 percent of the people who arrived were immediately sent to the gas chambers. Other transports faced a selection upon arrival, whereby some people would be admitted into the camp to work, while the others were sent immediately to the gas chambers.

Our transport did not face a selection upon arrival. We were all admitted directly into the camp. Since we were a small group consisting of us original 37 full-blooded Jews, plus the other prisoners picked up along the way, it would not have paid for them to run the gas for so few people. Instead, they admitted us into the camp, where they knew the starvation, the diseases, the selections to the gas chambers, the beatings, and the vermin would surely eliminate us. My brother, mother, and I were admitted into the women's camp.

As far as I know, of the people in our group who left from Frankfurt, I believe there were four survivors: only my mother, brother, me, and one other young boy, Ziggy, who had been a friend of my brother. Our survival rate was high considering the total annihilation of other transports that were gassed upon arrival.

When we were unloaded from the trains, we were met by elegantly

---

4. The names Auschwitz, Birkenau, and Auschwitz-Birkenau are used interchangeably in this book. While Ruth mostly referred to the camp as Auschwitz, she was in imprisoned specifically in the Birkenau camp within Auschwitz.

uniformed SS men in perfectly tailored and creased clothing, spotless white gloves, and polished boots. Well-tended dogs were on short leashes. It was just like the pictures you can see today of the SS men and dogs.

Shortly, we were ordered to remove our clothes and put aside any possessions we had managed to hold onto. Our clothes were taken away.

Prisoners recruited for the task shaved our heads. When my hair was shaved and we were standing completely in the nude, I was frightened. We stood in line naked, waiting for clothes to be given. I called out for my mother, and she answered me. I turned around to look for her, but I didn't recognize her, because she had no hair. I had never seen her like that, totally in the nude with all her hair cut and totally shaved off.

Other prisoners then tattooed us with an instrument that can best be compared to a fat ballpoint pen. It was painful. There wasn't any disinfectant put on the needle or anything, so everyone's tattoo became slightly infected for the first few days, but then the infection went away.

I have a number on my left arm, on the outer part of the arm close to the elbow. Below the number is a triangle, half of the Star of David – the Magen David – that identified people as Jews. I was given number 42716. Mutti was given 42715. Zev was given 117492. The tattoo is blue, very thick and deep – too thick to remove later in life with skin grafting. Nowadays I usually do not show my tattoo to students in classes when I speak about my experience. I do not like it, but I show it if they ask to see it.

We were given clothing only after our heads were shaved and our arms tattooed. Contrary to what you may think, inmates did not necessarily receive prison uniforms. When we arrived, I was given what must have been, a long time before, a beautiful hand-knitted skirt, only now it was dirty, loose, wide, and stretched. It fell right off me. The prisoner in charge of clothing distribution took pity on me and handed me a belt with instructions on how to use it to keep the skirt in place. In addition to the tattered skirt, I was also given a wool sweater and wooden clogs.

We were also given an enamel dish, chipped and rusty, which served as a soup bowl, a wash basin – when we found water – and a night pot on those nights when we were not permitted to use the latrines. Near the rim of the bowl was a hole. We were ordered to pull a string through the hole and tie it around ourselves like a belt. This way we let the bowl hang from our clothes so that our hands would be free to work.

We were met by a woman by the name of Edita. She was the *Blockälteste*, the block leader or block elder, whom we called the *Blockova*. Edita was a Czechoslovakian Jew, just a few years older than me. At age 19, Edita had been taken with her mother and with several thousand other young Jewish women to the newly opened Auschwitz. She took us to brick barracks in the "A" *Lager* [camp] amid shouting and barking and beating by the SS. Barracks number 20 in the women's compound of Birkenau was the same as other barracks that can be seen in some of the horrific photographs taken of the camp. The cots were doubled in height. Four prisoners shared a layer, which would increase to six or eight as the population of the barracks increased. It would decrease again as typhus, spotted fever, and those dreaded selections took their toll. We were first in barracks in the "A" camp, and later in the "B" camp.

The block leaders, I learned later, were people who had been in the camp for a while. Some were Czechoslovakian Jews like Edita. The Jews of Czechoslovakia had been transported out of their country around 1941–1942, and were among the first prisoners in Auschwitz-Birkenau. Most of them died right away or within a year. The Jews who had arrived in Auschwitz so early and managed to survive through this point became the "upper echelon" of the camp.

We also learned later about the plight of those original prisoners who were in Auschwitz-Birkenau from the time when it first opened. The first winter they slept on the ground outdoors because there were no barracks. They had neither the hastily built brick barracks nor the wooden horse stable barracks that awaited later prisoners. They didn't even have the crude facilities that we had by 1943. For toilets they used the ground. They were put to work sawing planks for the barracks and pushing the road grader to make some sort of road. The drinking water was yellow, and some sort of oily film formed as soon as it came out of the hose. It was still the same when we were there. For sustenance they were given 200 calories a day. Vermin and rats were their constant bane from the beginning. Their population was decimated.

As the Nazi leaders planned for the expansion of Auschwitz-Birkenau as an integral part of implementing the Final Solution, the original prisoners were called before the SS guards and told to prepare for the arrival of great masses of prisoners. Because they knew the camp by then, they were rewarded with jobs as block elders. The block elders took their orders from the SS.

The block leaders became the bosses over the people who came in. They were responsible for quartering the new arrivals, distributing the "food," emptying the barracks at *Zahlappell* [roll call], and keeping the barracks clean by emptying the barrels that served as toilet bowls for the night. They had other menial tasks as well. In addition, they had to chase out any prisoners who were too sick to go to work but who risked beatings to stay behind. In all, their task was not easy. They had to navigate between the foul mood of the SS women and the curses of the prisoners. Even though they were the bosses over other prisoners, their lives were very far from good, but this is what happened by the time they were there for a while.

The SS prison guard or *Aufseherin* who presided over us throughout our time in the camp was a woman by the name of Margot Elisabeth

Drechsler. We called her Frau Drechsler. She was more of a beast than a woman. Edita reported to her. We would soon learn that Frau Drechsler was the most feared, and the most brutal of all the women guards in Auschwitz. Prisoners tried to hide whenever they saw her, even from a far distance. She was tall and lanky, her bony face matching the death-head insignia of the SS. She could work herself into a frenzy without any provocation. Beating or shooting a prisoner was as casual to her as flipping a speck of dust off one's sleeve.

Led by Edita, our group of new arrivals came to a halt to regroup after being taken to the barracks. I saw a corpse being carried on a primitive stretcher a few feet away. Her arms wobbled along the sides. Her head was barely covered. Her legs were dangling almost to the ground. I had never seen a corpse before.

Bettina, a nurse in our transport and a Romanian citizen who had received the same temporary protection from her country as we had from ours, tried to avert my head. Her efforts were an empty attempt. She told me that this person must have fainted and probably would be taken to a hospital. Little did we know at that moment that nothing in Auschwitz was made to preserve life, but only to promote death.

This was the first of the thousands of dead I would see in the following years. During my imprisonment in Birkenau, there were times when I walked in narrow aisles between the bodies, skeletal from malnutrition, with sores along the legs and lips parched with bloody gums protruding, piled at least six feet high, waiting to be removed to the infamous crematoria. Soon I learned to rationalize. I could walk between the bodies of the dead without fear; it was the living who menaced us and threatened destruction at every turn.

It was on that first day that we learned the not-so-subtle nuances of daily life in camp. We heard of the "selections." An SS man would stand there and point his finger to the left or to the right and so determine who would die in the gas chambers. I would go on to survive ten or so selections over the next year and a half in Birkenau.

We went into the camp that day, and the next day we had to start working.

Love, Ruth

INHUMANE CONDITIONS

Roll call and work

Dear Lauren,

Each day began with Zahlappell, the counting of the prisoners. Then we did torturous physical labor, the purpose of which was to demoralize us, destroy our spirit, sap our strength, take away our energy, and weaken our bodies. The second daily roll call was held upon our arrival back from work in the evening.

The morning roll call began at dawn. First, we were chased out of our barracks by Edita. Everyone, even those within a few hours of death, had to appear for roll call. The block leader and her helpers screamed and beat and shoved those near-skeletons and propped them up close to the healthier prisoners. There the sick prisoners stood, rags hanging from their emaciated bodies, lips parched so that their teeth protruded, blood running from the gums, pus oozing from open sores, their eyes unseeing and dull – a picture of Hell as Dante never foresaw it. Many people who were already within the grasp of death died because Edita needed to enforce the rules or be killed herself.

Second, we were counted. Those of us who lived through the night lined up, standing five-deep in line outside. The SS had us stand in rows of five because it was easy for them to multiply by five to count us. Most of the time we waited for about an hour before the SS women in charge had received the numbers from the Blockälteste.

The block leader forced the prisoners to move the night's corpses to the front of the building. The dead were added up together with the skeletal living. The numbers had to match the previous night's tally. They did this to ensure no one had escaped from the camp. When someone had been too ill to get up but had somehow escaped Edita's search, the count was thrown off and we had to wait until the culprit was brought out and beaten, more often than not to death, or at least close to death.

We had to stand at total attention during the morning call, when SS Frau Drechsler inspected the rows. If a prisoner even so much as dared to follow the walk of the beast Drechsler with her eyes, she was called out of line and severely beaten. Often prisoners were made to kneel in the muck or to stand for extended periods for any imagined infraction.

The weather conditions did not matter, for they wanted us to get ill and die – the sooner the better. Auschwitz was wet and cold and swampy, so when the morning roll was taken, we shivered from the cold and from the fear.

After the morning roll call, we were taken to our work assignments. The work assignment was the same for several days, weeks, or even months in a row. We worked every day of the year except Christmas Day. Starting the very first morning in camp, we were made to work.

At first my mother and I were assigned just to dig. We were put to work digging a moat that would connect the latrines with sewer pipes leading past the electrical wires outside. Often the moat did not connect properly, and we had to fill in a hole and dig another. They would make us lift a heap of soil and move it to make another pile out of it. When the first pile was leveled and nothing was left, we had to do it all over again with the new pile. We did not have shovels but used the red enamel soup bowls we had been given upon arrival as scoops. After that, we dug ditches outside the barracks and then filled them in again. When the ditch was sufficiently empty, we were told to fill it in with the soil we had just removed.

Over and over again we would dig. The area was marshy and undredged. The soil was clay-like and heavy. Trying to move even a small scoop became torture. Digging was an exercise especially designed to break our spirits and weaken us.

One of our next work assignments was to flatten the roads. The roads in Auschwitz were terrible and muddy. When the mud dried, the road was full of ruts. To flatten the road, there was a big steamroller, only it wasn't propelled by steam – it was pushed by prisoners. We had to fill it up with sand to make it heavy enough to flatten the roads. This made it tremendously heavy and almost impossible for us to push. I do not think it was very effective at flattening the roads.

Part of this task to even out the roads involved digging out spots wherever the road was higher, and filling in spots wherever the road was lower. It really did not make any sense, because we dug parts of the road out to fill in another hole.

After we dug ditches and filled them in and dug them out again in an endless exercise of debasement, we graduated to better work: digging up potatoes in a nearby field. We were marched to a potato field outside the camp.

The potatoes were covered with heavy, slimy mud. Often we could not tell if it was a rock or a potato we had dug up. We were to dig for potatoes with our tiny spoons, throw the potatoes into a wagon, and push the wagon into the camp at the end of the day.

One of the work assignments we had toward the end of our time in Auschwitz-Birkenau was to sort through material possessions in

"Kanada."[1] All luggage, packages, personal belongings, and bedding stolen from the arriving transports were taken away from their owners and collected in Kanada. Officially named the *Effektenlager*, it was called Kanada because of the wealth of goods that passed through its sad barracks. Canada and the Americas represented all that was lush and plentiful.

The confiscated goods were brought into the 30 or so barracks that made up the Kanada section to be sorted by prisoners. The loot was then packaged to be shipped to material-hungry Germans. Almost as soon as the Nazis came to power, they shifted to war production and cut back on manufacture for civilians. Ten years later the shortages were critical, and the German population would have been restive had the Nazis not eliminated dissent.

My mother and I worked in Kanada, mostly sorting blankets and comforters that people had brought expecting to use. Most of the owners of these items did not even live to see what was happening with their possessions. In the camp they had these tattered old rags for blankets. They were full of lice, and every so often the blankets and the straw mattresses were cleaned.

One time, while at work sorting the possessions, I found a book, Gotthold Lessing's *Nathan the Wise*. The SS woman, that beast Drechsler, was on her lunch hour. I took advantage and began to read. There was a tremendously high pile of comforters. I crawled up on top of the pile, hiding, and hoping no one would see me. I read the book up there. I read with the hunger born of scholarly starvation.

Drechsler returned early and could see me from a distance up there on the pile of comforters. I was caught. She called me down, took the book, threw it away, and really boxed my ears until I was dizzy. I got the worst beating of my life.

---

1. The German spelling of Canada, the country, is with the letter *k*.

That was my punishment for reading. This small attempt at culture or education was put to an immediate stop. I don't know if you realize, but *Nathan the Wise* was written by a German in praise of a Jew. I didn't know this at the time, and she probably wasn't aware of it either. It's just that she didn't want any reading at all or any leisurely activity like this to be available to us.

Several times, as we sorted items among the bedding, we found suffocated infants. Maybe in the rush and turmoil of an arriving transport, the babies had been taken away from the mothers and pushed in with blankets until the babies were just mangled and smothered in the blankets. Or maybe the mothers had hoped to save the babies' lives by separating them before going to be gassed. Maybe the mothers tried to save the babies by putting them in with the belongings, hoping someone would pick up the babies like in the story of Moses.

But nothing like that happened. No miracles saved them. They were rolled in blankets and other things until they suffocated to death. The infants were later found dead by us prisoners.

The lives of children were very cheap and expendable during those times. It was a terrible thing. One million of the six million who were murdered in the Holocaust were children. We will never know all the potential that was killed.

To this day, it sickens me to my stomach when I think of what happened to the infants in Birkenau.

Love, Ruth

Prisoner clothing

Dear Lauren,

There were two types of clothing in Auschwitz-Birkenau: prisoner uniforms and civilian rags. The prisoners arriving in Auschwitz, whether they were taken to the gas chambers or brought into the camp, were forced to undress and to fold their clothing into neat piles. No one received their own clothing back. The clothes were sorted in the Kanada barracks and sent to Germany. Only damaged or odd things found their way into the camp and became attire for the prisoners – the "civilian rags." The prisoner uniforms were the striped outfits that the camp is known for.

We originally had been given civilian rags to wear upon our arrival. Several weeks later, when we were made to work in the potato field outside the camp, we were given the scratchy, striped prison uniforms. Later, when we were working inside the camp in Kanada, we were still not allowed to wear what would be considered civilian clothes. In Kanada we were not supposed to wear anything that was still usable and could be shipped to the Reich. We were supposed to wear the prisoner uniforms.

Not a single item of civilian clothes, no matter how ragged, was permitted outside the barbed wire. The striped prisoner uniforms would make us immediately identifiable if we attempted to escape. However, even when wearing civilian clothes inside the camp, an armband was required because it identified you as a prisoner. If you wanted to escape, you had to undo the band that was sewn on, and it was a job to take it off. Since the SS never needed much of an excuse to beat us, wearing anything civilian only meant tempting danger. Whether we wore the civilian rags or the striped clothes, both identified us as prisoners. We simply could not run away.

Quite frequently the clothing assigned to new arrivals had been taken off corpses without the benefit of even a perfunctory cleaning. After the SS ordered other prisoners to remove the clothing from the dead prisoners, they sent the clothes through the gas chamber to delouse them. The clothes were then handed unwashed to the next arrivals. Size, style, and seasonally appropriate textiles were obviously of no importance.

Lice lived in the seams of our clothing, especially in the sleeves and upper sections, where they deposited their nits. They thrived in the dark, warm, moist human joints and crevices. Mites lived in the clothing, too. When the louse infestation became too great, the worn prisoner uniforms or raggedy dresses were taken away from us and put in the gas chamber to kill the lice. The SS used the same Zyklon B gas to kill the bugs on the clothes as they used to kill the people. We received the clothes back with dead nits still sticking to the seams.

I can still visualize it in my mind: our skeletal bodies were covered with those horrible striped dresses, and our shaved heads were given rags that passed for scarves.

Prisoners were also given shoes or wooden clogs when they arrived. My mother and I received the wooden clogs. They were just wooden soles with little canvas strips to put the feet in. There was only one size.

The earth in Auschwitz was very muddy. The soil was yellow, heavy and viscous. We were told that the Polish government had used the area for fish hatcheries between the wars, because the area was very wet and humid. The countryside was a swamp. When it rained, it was impossible to build anything. The soil turned to clay.

In the rain, our shoes would get stuck in the mud, and we had to force our feet to pull up out of the mud. Walking in the sticky mud then became impossible. Most of the time, our shoes could only be extracted with great strength, which we scarcely possessed. It must have used up most of the calories we were allotted for the day. Just walking a few yards was enough to drop our strength for the next few days. It was awful. If the shoes were stuck and we tried to pick them up but weren't fast enough, we got a beating.

I can picture it in my mind. There we were, skeletal beings, our feet mired in muck, trying to wrest loose. It required superhuman effort. We felt so weak.

After the rain, the ground dried very unevenly, with footprints and everything. When the weather was dry, it was difficult to walk in the ruts. We would slide off the sides of the ruts and twisted many an ankle while trying to stay in line. Only after a long dry spell, when the ruts were tramped down, was it possible to walk a little more easily. The road was the furthest thing from a paved road. It was terrible to walk on.

The prisoner uniform dresses were very long. The bottom of our dresses always caught the soil along their hemlines, and the bottoms were always covered with yellow mud that we could only scrape off after it dried. The dress was heavy and very difficult to remove. It dragged us down. We didn't have much strength to drag ourselves, let alone drag a muddy dress and shoes. The fact that I had lost so much weight and had been sick made this process even more difficult.

Those clogs were the least desirable shoes we could get. When we were able to find an old pair of shoes, we tried to exchange the clogs for them and to adapt the shoes as best we could to our use. It must have been in Kanada that I found a different pair of shoes: boots that had long pointed toes and buckles. They must once have been very fancy. The elegant ladies wore them at the turn of the century when these boots were very fashionable. They were one of the things that would not have been sent to Germany, since no one would wear those shoes – they had long been out of style. The fact that they could be tied to the foot so they would not get stuck in the mud was their greatest advantage.

The problem with the shoes was they were at least three sizes too small for me, and so they were very, very uncomfortable. The boots had a sole where the foot would go, leather on both sides, and a two-inch heel. Rather than wear them the proper way with my foot on the sole, I put my foot on the leather side of the shoe. I wore them with my heels pushing out of the soft leather part. The heel of the boot wobbled uselessly on the side of my foot. If I put my foot further towards the toe area, the heel part would stick up into the air in an absurd configuration, bobbing up and down with every step I took. The boots were still preferable to those wooden clogs, but not much preferable. They killed my feet and back.

Eventually the SS guards permitted us to use some strings to hike up our uniforms and to blouse our dresses over the strings. The prisoners ripped up pieces of rags as belts of sorts, tied pieces together, and pulled up our dresses.

We still were not allowed to wear any civilian clothes that would be considered an adornment. Despite this prohibition, I wore a belt that I had found in Kanada under the fold of my dress, over the string that was attached to the bowl. Because I bloused my dress over it, my belt was hidden from enemy eyes.

The belt was made of midnight blue felt with yellow and red felt flowers sewn along the length. The Greek girls who came to Auschwitz had brought in a lot of knitted dresses with beautiful rose designs sewn into the hems and tops, so when I saw the belt, I thought it was Greek handiwork. Since I was so fond of the Greek girls, I felt very sentimental about the belt. Years later, when I showed it to someone, it turned out that the belt was not Greek handiwork. Regardless, I had my beautiful belt. It was for me the only cheerful reminder of a normal world that once existed outside this place.

As I used my belt in Birkenau, it became a measure of my decreasing state of well-being. From the increasing looseness of the belt, my mother lamented my loss of weight. She kept saying, "Oh Ruth, look at how thin you're getting, my poor child. Look, this starvation is terrible for you." She would keep saying, "Oh my God... my child... she's getting thin... she's losing weight... look at her..." In response I kept telling her, "But no, I'm not getting any thinner; the belt is getting longer; the belt is stretching." That was how I tried to appease her. I do not know how I kept my sense of equilibrium. The belt kept getting looser and looser on me all the time as I lost a significant amount of weight.

After a while, the buttonhole frayed and the button was lost. I used an old, rusty safety pin that I found to hold it together. The belt went with me even when we were taken to a forced labor camp. There I had a different kind of skirt, so I was able to use the belt just as an adornment, but no one paid any attention to that anymore. I had the belt with me all the time.

At the end of the war, just after the death march from Malchow, I finally found a pair of shoes somewhere in a German farmhouse. Those terrible boots were the first things that I threw away. After liberation, I would not part with my belt. I could not wait to shed every last thread of the boots, but I kept my beautiful belt.

It is in this state, with the rusty pin still attached, that I gave my beautiful belt to the U.S. Holocaust Memorial Museum in Washington, D.C., where it is occasionally displayed. I regret that I didn't save the degrading boots, but I hated them so much. They did terrible things to my feet, but they would have been a poignant memento to donate to the Holocaust Museum, had I saved them.

I am very happy that the Holocaust Museum could make use of my belt, because if you were to go through my belongings and see it you might think, "Why is my crazy grandma saving this raggedy, dirty, old faded belt?" Now that the museum has the belt, visitors can see there is a whole story behind it. The belt was my cheerful companion at the most cheerless time of my life.

I never met the original owner of the belt. No one ever walked up to me to say that it had been hers in a different time, in a different world. The simple cheerfulness of its design and the bright colors are now a memorial to this unknown one, the one we think of on Yom HaShoah, the one who wanted to live but was robbed of life.

I have been told that wearing the belt was my way of proving my resistance. While it does not have the same quality of bravery as the fighters in the Warsaw Ghetto, it was, for me, a stubborn assertion of my need for something, anything, of beauty – a defiant preservation of my own humanity.

Love, Ruth

Zev is separated from us

Dear Lauren,

My brother Zev, who had initially been let into the women's camp with us, was taken to the children's barracks in the men's Lager in early spring 1944.

The cynical reason given to separate Zev from his mother was that it was immoral to let a young boy stay with all those women, because they were sometimes in the nude. The SS men did not consider how immoral it was for them to have us get undressed and parade naked in front of them anytime they wished. At the slightest whim, the SS conducted nude inspections of us. We had to appear that way in front of all the SS men, who did all kinds of terrible things to us. Women were beaten in the nude.

We did not know my father's whereabouts, but we thought, if he was still alive, that he was in the men's section of Birkenau. I had wanted to look for my father in the nearby men's section as best I could, but it was impossible. The SS were all over the place. The men's camp and women's camp were separated by barbed wire, with armed guards overlooking, ready to shoot, from high guard towers. The SS did not let anyone look, let alone run over to the men's camp for a visit.

After Zev was removed from the women's camp, we did not know his whereabouts either. We did not know if we would ever see him again. After he was taken away, I hoped to catch a glance of him, too, but I did not. You can imagine the anxiety this separation caused us.

As a child, Zev was mostly exempt from work and roll call in the children's barracks. Somehow, Zev managed to live through it, and he survived.

A decade would pass from the time when we were separated in Birkenau in 1944 to the time when we were reunited after the war in the United States in 1954.

Love, Ruth

Starvation and disease

Dear Lauren,

We hardly had any food in Birkenau. The little food we had was horrible. I do not know the exact number of calories. At the very most it was 400 calories, but probably closer to 200. We used up an awful lot of calories doing the work that we were doing, but there was practically nothing to eat. Considering this miniscule amount of food, by the time I was liberated I weighed a skeletal 66 pounds.

We got little pieces of bread daily, something called "tea" that came out of rusty barrels, and sometimes what was called turnip soup. In addition, we got a small piece of salami or liverwurst once, twice, or three times a week.

The bread tasted horrible. But to us it was good bread. We were starving. Occasionally we got a pat of margarine, which was enough for one slice of bread.

Some of the prisoners worked in a kitchen. They made soup out of turnips. The turnips weren't peeled. Sometimes in the soup there were potatoes that didn't have the sand or mud washed off. When people were put on a transport, they sometimes brought food. These bags of food managed to get into the camp and went in a pile to go to the kitchen. But nobody sorted this food; the prisoners in the kitchen just emptied everything into the pot of soup they were cooking. We found combs, compacts, soap, razors, and things like that in the soup, and it was disgusting. But we were so hungry that we ate anything.

The salami or liverwurst they gave us was probably about an inch thick or a little bit less. One time the salami had a terrible odor. They said it was made of horsemeat. It had the flavor of urine. One evening I had just been given a piece of this salami, when I looked out the window and saw the crematorium going at full force. It was at night, so I could see the fire. I was thinking of the people who were destroyed there, and I thought, *Oh my God, I hope the salami doesn't contain human flesh.* I threw up. This was toward the end of my time in Auschwitz.

After that I was never able to eat a piece of the salami. Whenever it was given to me, I traded it for the slice of bread. Some people didn't have the same experience and were eager to trade with me and give up the little piece of bread. I could never eat a piece of salami like that again, even though I did not really know...

With only a few hundred calories a day, everybody was getting sick, and lost weight rapidly. One result of such weight loss is that the body cannot menstruate. None of the women ever had their periods in Auschwitz.

Many women died of starvation. And many women also died of malnutrition, the lack of nutrients that resulted from this hunger. A sign of malnutrition and vitamin deficiency is sores, and people had terrible sores that festered on their legs. It was just awful. Having the sores of malnutrition or the scratches from scabies was sufficient reason to be taken to the gas chambers.

Diseases of all kinds were rampant in Auschwitz-Birkenau and were deliberately left untreated. Typhus, scabies, and malaria were endemic, in addition to all the conditions brought on by malnutrition and filth: diarrhea, bleeding gums, open sores, and infestations of lice, fleas, and rats. Sanitation was not only nonexistent but also intentionally worsened by our captors.

Auschwitz was full of rats, mosquitos, and bedbugs. We killed what we could. The rats ate from the corpses. Whenever we saw corpses, which were all over the place, usually part of their flesh, whatever little meat was left on their bones, had been eaten away by the rats. There was also an abundance of fleas jumping at our feet and crawling up to our thighs. These parasites brought diseases. It was filthy.

In medieval times, fleas living on rats caused bubonic plague. First the smaller black sea rats brought the plague to port cities, and then the larger gray land rats spread the plague inside the countries. Jews were blamed for every outbreak. Had there been such an outbreak of the bubonic plague in Auschwitz, I am sure the Nazis would have simply gassed the whole camp at once or bombed it. They might have introduced such a powerful bacterial killer themselves, but they could not have controlled it.

Almost every one of the prisoners suffered from scabies most of the time. It is a highly contagious disease, like a skin rash, transmitted by mites. It spread in the camps through the untreated clothes, the filthy straw used for sleeping in the bunks, and just by the crowding of at least eight women into the space of one bunk about the size of a regular double bed. There were times when spontaneous healing occurred, though the victims became infected again and again. It took only a few days after our clothes went through the gas chambers to kill the parasites for new infections to appear, brought on by the same conditions as had prevailed.

Scabies can be cured with a few cents' worth of sulfur cream. No one had this medicine, and the SS were not interested in saving anyone. They were interested in having people get sick and die.

Even more so than the mites that caused scabies, body lice were the true scourge, since they carried the one disease responsible for most deaths in the camp: typhus. The lice of Auschwitz, and the resulting spread of this dreadful disease, deserve a unique place in the recitation of our terror.

There are three types of lice: head lice, body lice, and a type that invades pubic areas. Head lice proliferated in those conditions despite head shaving every few weeks. Genital lice, which are spread by sexual contact, did not exist in that barren place. Body lice were the culprits behind the spread of typhus.

Typhus spread throughout the women's camp of Birkenau, and the men's camp across the way, and the Roma camp at the end of the long road along the electrically charged wires. Typhus was endemic, not just in the Auschwitz-Birkenau camp complex but also in all the other concentration camps, wherever the Nazis plied their evil deeds.

We could always tell when a prisoner began the arduous trek toward her death. First came the open sores along the shins due to malnutrition. Then came the fever and diarrhea running along the legs. These unfortunate ones never made it to the barrels that stood at the edge of the barracks as toilets, and they certainly could not use the latrines several barracks away. Almost immediately, fever and diarrhea were followed by extreme dehydration, which made palates recede from teeth, made gums bleed and lips crack open. It was then only the matter of a few days before the victim's emaciated body would join the pile of corpses in front of the barracks, piled up nice and neat, one on top of the other, to be slung into the primitive hearse of the burial squads and taken away for cremation.

Love, Ruth

THE SELECTIONS

Being chosen to die

Dear Lauren,

Medical doctors today take the Hippocratic oath to do no harm. The Nazi medical doctors took no such oath. In fact, the entire medical profession in Nazi Germany believed in the theory of racial hygiene and was instrumental in the implementation of the Final Solution. The Chief Camp Physician, Dr Josef Mengele, performed inhumane medical experiments, particularly on twins, in his capacity as camp doctor. The doctors in Birkenau did the opposite of protecting life. They saw to it that people would be killed.

When we first came to Auschwitz my mother needed some medication that she had at home. The doctor in charge was standing there. I simply went up to him and very naively told him that my mother needed this medication. He just laughed at me and walked away. There was irony in his laughter. Why was I bothering him with this nonsense about medication?

Nothing in Auschwitz was made to preserve life – not even the hospital. The so-called hospital barracks was located in the Auschwitz main camp not far from Birkenau. It was called an infirmary, but that didn't mean anything. That hospital was a hoax. They had no medication. They had no doctors – at least no doctors who were dedicated to healing or preserving life.

Auschwitz-Birkenau was notorious for the selections presided over by the infamous Dr. Mengele. What, exactly, were we selected for, you ask? The doctors selected the weakest of the prisoners to become part of the next group to be killed in the gas chambers. After the Nazis gassed a large group of victims, they forced the prisoners working in the *Sonderkommando* to cremate the bodies in the crematoria.

We were told that when the Auschwitz main camp first opened, there had been a gas chamber, but soon the facility was too small and too inefficient. That is when the SS decided to build the big twin gas chambers with their five chimneys in Birkenau.

Every few weeks a selection took place but not on a regular schedule. I was in ten of them in the *Frauenlager* B [women's camp] section of Birkenau. Others took place in the *Männerlager* [men's camp] section of Birkenau and directly in Auschwitz. They also took place in *Frauenlager* A, which held the hospital and the holding barracks for those destined for the gas and a few barracks for regular prisoners, as well as in the *Zigeunerlager* [Roma camp].

When the Nazis needed extra people to fill up the gas chambers, they would go into the infirmary and clean it out, so the hospital barrack was nothing more than an antechamber to the gas chambers. Sometimes, between selections, some sick people were sent there. The unfortunate prisoners were kept there overnight, in overcrowded conditions and without food. The Nazi mentality was that they were, quite literally, "useless eaters."[1] There was no use wasting food and

---

1. "Useless eaters" and "life unworthy of life" were Nazi terms given to the people

water on people who would be dead in a day or two. The prisoners in the hospital were isolated, without any of the comforts that we other prisoners, who were ourselves doomed, could have given them in their final days. Then the SS would fill up the hospital again for the next time. Only very few ever came out of the hospital. Almost all were included in the next shipment to destruction.

For the selection, the chief doctor and his associates would round up all the prisoners. The whistle blew, and everyone had to line up. Most of those dreaded selections for the gas chambers were conducted in the nude. We stood five in a row. When we knew someone was extremely ill and would be singled out for the gas chambers, we would put her into the third row, in the middle, and prop her up as best we could. This way, we could try to preserve her life for another day. We hoped that perhaps her health would somehow improve by tomorrow. That tomorrow rarely came for those dying of typhus, malaria, malnutrition, and the many other diseases that plagued us in the camp.

The doctors stood there in their Aryan superiority with beautifully pressed uniforms and impeccably polished boots, with well-fed, properly cared for German shepherds at their sides, choosing from among the skeletal, abused, sore-infected bodies that once were women, those who seemed least able to perform the unnecessary labor that the Nazis designed only to weaken and hasten death.

I can still picture it in my mind to this day. Dr. Mengele stood at the selection and hummed Mozart, with one flick of the finger pointing to the side, picking women from among those who passed in line in front of him, deciding who was destined for the gas chamber and who was destined to stay in the camp a bit longer. He went *this way* and

---

that the Nazi regime considered a burden on society, the "unfit" who required help from society but did not contribute to it. Early on in the Nazi regime, people in this category, such as the disabled, were sterilized and systematically killed, notably in the *Aktion T4* euthanasia program.

that way with his finger. Left or right. This way or that way, he pointed us to one side or to the other. We often did not know which direction was the one he meant to go to the gas chamber and which one he meant not to go to the gas chamber. Since we were all emaciated, it was hard to guess which side was selected to die. The "healthy" ones among us would live for another few days or weeks.

Sometimes today, when I sing Mozart, I catch myself thinking, *Look, you're doing the same thing that Mengele did.* Once, when I introduced this detail while speaking about my experiences, one woman was shocked that Mengele was able to sing Mozart as he performed the selections. She said she wondered how much of Mengele is in every person. I do not believe this is necessarily so. I don't know. I don't want to philosophize. I don't know if or how these people were bred or conditioned to do this sort of thing. Yet, I wonder what could lead someone, especially someone who might have known the story of Mozart – a person who really wanted to see equality for all people – to abuse the music. Perhaps Mengele wasn't even thinking.

I consider it the supreme manifestation of my humanity that I can still retain my love for the music of Mozart.

Although they did not need any excuse for their selections, sometimes Dr. Mengele or one of his malevolent cohorts went through the motions of checking for scabies and sending those with the infestation to the gas chamber. Scabies, though ordinarily not fatal, proved to be deadly during the times when conducted a selection for the gas chambers. This nonlethal disease became the handmaiden of death. One time, I was very fortunate. I had scabies, but it somehow didn't spread into my face or hands. It stayed on my neck and on the core of my body. There was a selection, but that day they did not make us take off our clothes. As a result, they did not see I had scabies. That saved my life.

The group who was selected for death was taken to the gas chambers, led by other prisoners who were assigned to do the dirty work. The Nazis were standing back and snickering at the humiliations with which they could douse us before they delivered the final humiliation: naked death in a shower of gas.

The final affront came after the victims' lives were taken: cremation, the denial of proper Jewish burials.[2]

The chimneys would run all day and all night. The SS gassed and burned the arriving transports, in addition to those selected for death from among the camp inmates. We could see the chimneys from wherever we were in the camp. In the daytime we could see the smoke coming out. At nighttime we could see not just smoke but also the flames and the red of the fire. It turned the sky fairly red.

We could smell the burning of the bodies – the human flesh burning.

We could smell the gas when it was let out from the gas chambers.

We could hear the grates of the crematoria being cleared. It was similar to the sound that your own oven makes when you move the grates around, except it was much noisier. We could hear it all the way in the barracks. To this day when I clean my own oven, I am reminded of that noise of the crematoria grates being cleared.

Spewing out of the chimneys were the ashes. The wind blew the ash all over the ground of the camp. The bodies had been turned to ash, but not entirely into fine, delicate ash. Rather, the ash often contained whole segments of bones that were not entirely ground down to ash. We felt the splinters of bones crushing under our feet when we walked. Because the bones and the ash of the Jews were

---

2. Judaism requires the dead to be buried intact, partly due to the belief in a future resurrection during the Messianic era. Modern interpretations say that the law requiring burial does not apply to Holocaust victims, who were cremated against their will, and that these victims will also be among the Jews to return during the Messianic redemption.

spread over all the camp, today the entire earth of Birkenau should be considered consecrated ground.

One time when I was off working somewhere, before my brother had been separate from us, my mother and brother were taken to a selection. My brother was just a child of ten years. An SS doctor told my brother to go to the side with the group that was being sent to the gas chambers.

Somehow, my mother and brother were suddenly taken by a German guard, pulled away, and hidden behind a pile of coal in different barracks for the rest of the day. In this way, they survived the selection. My mother asked him why he had done this.

The guard said that while he was in Poland, he had witnessed the mass shooting of people from a certain village, where they were taken to a pit and everyone was shot and then thrown into the pit. Sometimes they weren't even shot. Sometimes they were still alive when they were thrown into the pit. I do not know if this guard had been part of the *Einsatzgruppen*, the mobile killing squads, or had played a more active role in such massacres.

One of the Nazi officers in that village had said to a woman who was walking up towards the pit with two children, one in each hand, that if she picked one of the children to be shot, she and the other child could live. This woman saw no hope, so she firmly grabbed both of her children and jumped into the pit.

The German guard said he witnessed this and was so touched by what the woman had done that he swore to himself, at that time, that if he ever could save a mother and child, he would make it his mission to do so. He did that by saving my mother and brother from the selection and hiding them for the day behind a pile of coal.

I never knew who the man was, and my mother did not know him either. It was just a very humane gesture in a sea of inhumanity. It was touching that something like that could happen even there. It was very unusual.

There had been other Chief Camp Physicians presiding over Birkenau before and after Dr. Mengele. After we had been in camp for a little while, the selections temporarily stopped. We heard through rumors that this had happened because apparently a new camp doctor had declared a moratorium on selections. The other prisoners told us that since his arrival the selections had stopped; he had ordered this. Rumor had it that he had objected to Berlin and was awaiting new instructions. He did this consciously with the assurance of personal danger to himself and probably his family. Was he outraged that this slaughter was happening?

The Nazis did not want a humanitarian camp doctor. He was transferred out – destination unknown. One day he was gone. If they did not shoot him outright, he probably ended up on the Eastern Front with the same result. The Nazis disposed of those who did not agree with them by the simplest method of murder: send the merciful ones to the Russian Front, and surely they will die defending their fatherland. I can only assume this became the doctor's fate.

The fate of this doctor has caused me a dilemma of conscience. Should I rehabilitate his name, since he temporarily stopped the selections and was punished for it? Perhaps out there in the world are descendants who would welcome having the stigma of Nazi cruelty removed or reduced from this man. Maybe somewhere there is a family who is ashamed of this man's past, and they should be consoled. Yet, I hesitate because he wore the same hated uniform as the others. He was an SS doctor. He, too, was tainted. Perhaps writing will give me the impetus to have him revealed for his decency.

I have tried to research his fate or find information on his history, but I cannot find any information on a person by the name I remember, Dr. Wolpe. The researchers I have been in touch with have not come upon this name among SS doctors in Auschwitz. They have no confirmation of a case in which an SS doctor stopped selections even temporarily. There is no documented case of a doctor being sent from Auschwitz to the Russian Front because of refusing to do selections.

Was it all just hearsay? This is a problem that has bothered me now for years, and I am not sure how to approach it or what to do about it.

I heard once that Himmler came to the camp. This was long before I got there. They say that when he saw what went on in the camp, he went off somewhere and vomited. Maybe it was from the odor or from what he saw. However, this did not stop him. The killing went on, and he was the most notorious of all the killers. After the war, Himmler went on to evade punishment by committing suicide.

As for Dr. Mengele, he escaped to South America after the war and later died without ever having faced justice.

Love, Ruth

I survive typhus and a selection

Dear Lauren,

Almost everyone became very sick within a few months of arriving in the camp. By summer 1943, I came down with typhus. I have very little memory of what went on while I had it. My mother contracted malaria at one point, but she never contracted typhus. What I know is that during my illness my mother dressed me every morning, took me out to the *Appell* [roll call], and dragged me to work so that I wouldn't be beaten. She did this so that the beast Drechsler wouldn't send me to the "hospital," which as I described previously was a death-barracks holding cell where prisoners destined for the gas chamber were kept only until there were enough skeletal prisoners to be gassed.

I was lucky that during this time our block leader Edita didn't denounce me for being sick, and she didn't have me handed over to the gas chamber. In our barrack, Edita had become known as a cruel enforcer of Nazi rules. If she had not enforced the rules, she would have been killed herself. The prisoners despised her for this, but she did what was needed for her own survival. We cannot pass judgment on the morality of the situation. The concept of morality can only apply to life under normal circumstances. We cannot speak of morality or ethics as it pertained to life in Auschwitz-Birkenau. That place was void of any such notion. Life had been harsh to Edita. Like me, she was in the camp with her mother, and perhaps that was why she was relatively nice to me.

In time I lost consciousness and all awareness of time and place. But I do remember that my mother sat by my side and held my hand – the only remedy she had against this dreaded disease. I remember thinking vaguely through my hallucinations that I must make an effort to live, if only for my mother's sake, since she had lost so much already. Somehow, I did recover – weak and decrepit but alive. My mother saved my life. She managed to get me through typhus by taking care of me in whatever way she could.

After I survived the bout of typhus, I looked like a *Muselmann*. This is the term used to describe the camp inmates whose death was imminent. The Nazis delighted in ridiculing us with such names. We were the shunted, the unwanted, those who had given up already, those who were destined for death within the next few days, the ones who were just "wasting food" – the 200 or 400 calories worth of food they gave us every day.

During the next selection, we stood outside naked while the SS doctor surveyed us and nonchalantly pointed a finger to the right or left, and I was pointed into the crowd of *Muselmänner* to be taken to the gas chambers. And so, this *Muselmann* was selected by the SS doctor, polished boots and all, with the deadest eyes I have ever seen in a living creature, to make my way to the gas chambers.

My mother was sent in the other direction. My mother began to plead with the SS doctor, saying that I was her child, and couldn't I come with her? But nothing helped. "If you are so concerned about your daughter, then go with her." His curt answer meant that if she loved her daughter, she could accompany me to the gas chamber.

My mother was about to do this when Edita materialized out of nowhere. I never knew how, but she just appeared and pulled me away from the scene. She grabbed one arm, and together with my mother, dragged me back into the barracks. I can still feel the tug on my arm.

By some kind of miracle, we were not stopped; the SS man did not notice or pretended not to notice us. We just kept going. I was very sick, so I cannot recall the precise emotions of the moment. I don't know how it possibly happened, but I do know that my life was saved that day. I do not know why she did it. Maybe she felt some kinship watching my mother and me, because her mother, too, was with her in the camp.

I found out much later that when the surviving camp prisoners were forced to go on the death march,[3] Edita's mother was shot and killed. The last I heard of Edita was that she survived and was living in Connecticut. She had been recognized by one of the former prisoners. Her life was threatened, so she rarely left her home after that.

All I know is that during one selection, she grabbed my arm and walked me away from the line that was destined for the gas chamber. Without even a glance behind her, the block leader prevented my death that day. Despite her cruelty, Edita saved my life.

Love, Ruth

---

3. The death march from Auschwitz, beginning January 18, 1945, was when the camp was evacuated and prisoners were forced by the Nazis to march westward pending the arrival of the liberating Soviet Army.

No possibility of escape

Dear Lauren,

You may wonder if my mother and I ever tried to escape. The short answer is no. There was no escaping from that place. We wore prisoner clothes and had shaved heads. The local population on the outside would not have helped us. There was no way to get past the guards and the barbed wire fence to get outside in the first place. It was pointless and impossible to try to escape. They said that the only escape from Auschwitz Birken was through the chimney.

My mother witnessed a very young man get shot. The young man was working in the camp shoveling mud while being supervised by a group of Nazi officers. He started whistling "The Internationale," which is the communist anthem. The Nazis were very much opposed to communism. That is how they came to power, after all. Hearing "The Internationale" was the ultimate thing they would hate. Upon hearing it, the Nazi officer shot this young man to death immediately on the spot. I do not know if the man was truly a communist and that was why he was in the camp, or if he hummed the song deliberately, knowing it would mean instant death and thereby bring about an end to his suffering. His murder was his escape from this place. My mother was very agitated about seeing it happen, and she was still upset and agitated when she told me about it later.

The punishment for trying to escape, if they didn't murder you on the spot, was to be hung on the public gallows at the Auschwitz compound. I remember one public hanging of a woman who had tried to escape. They made gallows in the camp for all to see, and they hung her in front of us. They made the prisoners watch the execution. The woman was dangling there in the wind for days, and we saw her.

This was a warning: "Don't try to escape," because this is what would happen to you. I remember seeing her and feeling sad that she had not been successful in her attempt.

There was another woman, Mala Zimetbaum, who tried to escape once. She was some sort of privileged prisoner. She and another privileged prisoner had connections, so they managed to get Nazi uniforms and escaped from the camp. A few days later, Mala was caught and brought back to the women's camp. She was sentenced to public hanging for escaping.

First the Nazis tortured her. For a few days after they brought her back into the camp, they dragged her around with broken legs for all to see. One of the things that everyone was saying was astonishing. It was that, according to the Geneva Conventions, you're supposed to cure prisoners before you execute them. My mother and I were amazed by this. What attention did Nazis pay to the Geneva Conventions? They dragged this poor woman around with broken legs, and then they murdered her.

Around the time of Mala's execution, the Nazis wanted to make sure we were all accounted for and that no one had escaped. They held an extra roll call every hour, every single hour of the day. It was very strict: we weren't allowed to move at all – not one bit.

Drechsler came to take the Zahlappell, and my mother stood perfectly still, but she followed Drechsler with her eyes. Drechsler saw my mother's eyes moving, so she pulled my mother out of the ranks and slapped her. My mother fell to the ground. Drechsler then beat my mother very badly, damaging her ear. Luckily, Drechsler didn't shoot her right then and there.

My mother's ear never healed completely. This beating impacted my mother for the rest of her life. She had an ear ailment until her death in 1985.

Love, Ruth

A TRIBUTE TO LOVED ONES

Mutti as camp mother

Dear Lauren,

My mother became a dispenser of hope, a maternal figure for the women in the camp. She was really the heroine of the camp as much as anyone could be under those conditions.

Many of the women were lost. Most were in their early twenties and were all alone without their mothers. Young women torn from their homes, severed from every anchor to family, sick and desperate, confided in my mother. They sort of adopted my mother as their own. Everybody came crying on her shoulders. She was affectionately known as Mutti. I called her Mutti, and so soon the others called her Mutti, too, although her name was Chana. She became all the mothers that our fellow prisoners knew by now they would never see again.

Mutti cheered up the women as much as she could. "Things will get better; we'll get out of here," she told them. The big pastime in Auschwitz was to talk about food. Even though we were starving, we talked about all these wonderful dishes to cook: chicken soup, gefilte fish, stuffed cabbage. We talked about the recipes we would use and the menus we would create. My mother spoke of gourmet cuisine at a time when we were dealt barely any food at all. I remember her sitting at the edge of the bunk exchanging recipes for fancy banquets with the other women, as if each were the grand hostess of her own home, entertaining a crowd of elegant guests, and not a flea-bitten, lice-infested *Muselmann* barely keeping her soul within her body and with hardly any prospect of survival. When my mother wanted to give the women hope that they would survive, she talked about the good food they would be able to cook once they were liberated.

She could not give the girls and women anything except a picture of the future in normal surroundings among new friends, but she knew that for most of them it was an empty hope. She promised they would see their own mothers again when the war was over. Almost all the women would be dead within a few weeks. Yet, she brought them comfort while she could. She gave so many of them strength.

One time, my mother saved a woman's life. I am not entirely sure of all the details of the story. What I know is what my mother told me. There were two sisters who were brought into Birkenau. I think they were from the area of Katowice, Poland. One of the women supposedly had given poison to her children. There was not enough poison left for her. She wanted to commit suicide at the first chance. She was very despondent.

This woman ran toward the moat that was out by the barbed-wire fence. Whenever the guards saw someone running to that ditch, they would start shooting immediately. The soldiers in the guard houses on top started shooting at her. My mother saw her starting to run to the ditch and ran after her. Amidst all the bullets, my mother was able to pull the woman back. My mother saved her life.

Both the woman and her sister survived. They came to visit us after the war, but since then I have lost touch with them. We never mentioned this occurrence to the woman after the war. We did not want the retelling of what happened to cause unnecessary pain.

Love, Ruth

Remembering the Roma

Dear Lauren,

I fondly remember the warmth of the Roma people.

The story goes that the Roma people crisscrossed the borders of European countries in their caravans for centuries. Roma lived everywhere in Europe, and yet they were despised wherever they appeared. In no country were they ever welcome. It was said that they led a nomadic life and that national borders had little significance for them. They supposedly could be seen in their caravans of wagons drawn by scrawny horses and filled with exotic people. Stories of thefts and abductions preceded them and then followed them after they broke camp. Local people would hide their children and animals for fear they would be abducted.

The Nazis, in their zeal to make the world ethnically pure, blond, and Aryan, decreed the same dismal fate for the Roma as they did for the Jews. In the hierarchy of "supermen" that the Nazis created, the Roma were also considered *Untermenschen*.[1] The Nazis considered them about one level higher up than the Jews. The Nazi mentality was that they still had to be eradicated.

A special camp, the *Zigeunerlager,* was set aside for them in Birkenau in 1943. The Roma were collected from wherever in Europe the Nazi was lord. The Nazis then shipped them to Auschwitz. Into the

---

1. "Less than people" or "subhuman"; Nazi term referring to anyone considered racially or socially inferior according to Nazi racial theory (German).

Zigeunerlager poured the Roma population of the conquered countries. The camp was systemically emptied when the prisoners were sent to the gas chambers and crematoria, while new arrivals filled in at a rapid pace. The Nazis killed them by the family. On August 2, 1944, they liquidated the *Zigeunerlager,* sending some of the Roma out to another concentration camp and killing the remaining 3,000 prisoners in the gas chambers.

I speak about the Holocaust very often with schools, churches, and colleges, and I always want to mention the Roma. Until recently, there were no memorials for them. No one did anything for them. The poor people – so many died unnamed. Someone should remember that they are a people, a kind and gentle people. Throughout the history of Europe, they were denounced and feared, but I remember those I met as very nice, gentle, and helpful.

Their memory should be honored for their decency and their humanity and because they died only for being members of the Roma race.

Love, Ruth

Mimi Benmayor

Dear Lauren,

I met a girl who would leave me with the memory of one of the finest persons, the most courageous, the truest to herself, the "friend I cannot find again" to quote Michel de Montaigne. Her name was Mimi Benmayor.

We had arrived in Birkenau around the same time and met shortly after. Mimi was 16 years old. She was in Auschwitz with her sister, who was a year or two younger. The girls were from Salonika (Thessaloniki), Greece. When Mimi and her sister were taken away from their home, their mother was not taken with them on the transport to Auschwitz. The girls were under the impression that their mother remained safe at home.

Until I was in Birkenau, I had not even realized that the Nazis were trying to eliminate Jews as far south as Greece. Most of the Greek Jews in the camp were from Salonika. The girls from Greece danced beautifully; many had glorious voices, spoke several languages and had an all-around excellent education. They had been reared in the schools of the *Alliance Israélite universelle*. The Alliance was a self-help group of Jews based in France who saw to the education of Jewish youngsters in the Near East and Eastern European countries. When the need arose (and, oh, how often it did), the Alliance interceded politically.

I was fascinated by the Benmayor sisters' ancestry, which they told me could be traced back to King David. I had studied Jewish history during my days at school. Living in the city of Frankfurt, which had been home to Jews since the 11th century, we were plied with wonderful doses of Jewish history, a subject of which I never tire. We studied the 15th-century expulsion of Sephardic Jews from the Iberian Peninsula, and the havens they found in other parts of Europe. After the 1492 expulsion from Spain, and somewhat later from Portugal, Jews fled into Holland and Greece. The Benmayor family had lived in Salonika ever since then.

The Nazis did not prevent prisoners from communicating with one another. Each person would speak in the language she knew. In Auschwitz, there were Jews from all over Continental Europe. The Nazis, aware that Jews brought with us our own languages, could not stop us from speaking in our native tongues. Every European language was spoken in the camp except for English. The Nazis didn't get as far as the British Jews. Without English-speaking people, that language was prohibited.

Mimi and I communicated in English. We had both studied English and French, but my elementary French was laughable, so English was the only language we had in common. Communication between us was easy in English. Because it was forbidden, we spoke in English as our way to show our resistance and tweak the noses of the oppressors. What greater form of resistance could two rebellious teens offer than to break this prohibition? I was 14 years old, and I thought I was very brave!

Mimi dreamed of becoming an opera singer. She had a beautiful voice. To us at the time, when Mimi sang, it was the most beautiful sound you could ever hear. To me it sounded like an angel singing. Whenever there was the chance, Mimi would sing for the prisoners. We had so few mental escapes. We had so little of anything that it was nice when she sang. We begged her all the time, and whenever she was halfway in the mood, she sang for us. One of the things Mimi sang, which had been part of her training, was "Ave Maria," the Catholic prayer put to music by Franz Schubert. We always begged her to sing that.

Then came the day when her sister died of typhus. Every spark of life left Mimi. She became numb, indifferent to her surroundings, indifferent to all who tried to console her. How could she have been otherwise? A child torn from her roots, brought into the filth and depravation of hell, with her last link to family torn away. After her sister's death that summer day, all the spirit went out of Mimi; she just lost hope. After that, she did not sing anymore.

One day, I returned from work a little later than my mother. I was greeted into the barracks with the whispered news that something terrible had happened. In a place where no good news ever penetrated, it still threw us into the depths of despair.

Two SS people oversaw our area in the camp. One was the bestial Frau Drechsler that I have spoken of. The other was Adolf Taube, an equally murderous and ferocious monster. Taube had heard of the

Jewish young woman with the heavenly voice and ordered the *Blockälteste* to have Mimi report to him. Taube was determined to enjoy her gift all to himself. Though the Nazis prohibited sexual liaisons with prisoners, especially Jewish ones, soldiers rarely heeded that ban. His command went out. He ordered her to his quarters to be, ostensibly, his housekeeper. He proposed that she live in his house and sing for him.

Mimi feared what this meant: rape, abuse, ongoing subjugation at the hands of this SS monster. She refused without even a moment's doubt or hesitation.

Lauren, you must appreciate the sacrifice she made. This "offer" meant getting presentable clothes, an adequate amount of decent food, clean living quarters, clean sheets, a bath, and a chance to muddle through and await the end of the war. You must realize that she would have been alive, and she could be hopeful every day for some kind of release. The sacrifice she made was tremendous.

Taube was a swain scorned, and he did what every Nazi killer would do: he recorded her number and made sure that with the next shipment to the gas chambers, she was included. When the time came for the next selections, her number was prominently mentioned, and there was no way that anyone could have erased that number. He made sure that she went to the gas chambers. Her life was cut short at just 16 years of age. She would never become an opera singer.

To this day, whenever I am invited to a Catholic wedding and I hear "Ave Maria," I begin to cry. Everyone must be thinking: *Look at this Jewish woman – how touched by 'Ave Maria'!* They do not know the memories I have of Mimi. Her friendship was the most unforgettable one that I formed in Auschwitz. Her murder brought an end to one of the most valuable friendships of my life.

Telling you about her is my tribute to all the women of all European countries who did not return from Auschwitz. I have told my sons about my friend Mimi. All their lives they have heard about her and the heroic stand she took. What bravery! Mimi will always be known in my family as the girl with the voice of a heavenly bird and the courage of a lion. In 1966, we traveled as a family to Greece. I did not want to look for Mrs. Benmayor, for how could I meet a woman, if she were even still alive, whose daughters I had seen die, unable to help them even with the smallest comforts?

When I was in Jerusalem in 1981 for the World Gathering of Holocaust Survivors, I looked for people from Salonika. At the gathering I met many Jewish men and women from Greece and had a great rapport with them. Recalling the past and hearing beautiful Ladino[2] melodies brought back so many memories of Mimi.

On the last evening, when Prime Minister Begin was speaking at the Wall, I heard a man behind me say he was from Salonika. My ears stood up, and I asked him if he knew anyone from the Benmayor family. I mentioned that my friend had been Mimi Benmayor from Salonika, but she had been killed in the camp.

He told me there was still a Mr. Leon Benmayor in Salonika. He was the head of the Jewish Community, and I should get in touch with him. The only thing I knew about how to go about getting a foreign address was to get in touch with the Jewish Agency. Within half an hour, I had the address of the Jewish community in Athens. I wrote a letter, and they forwarded it to Mr. Benmayor.

Leon Benmayor was a cousin of Mimi and a survivor. I found out that although the girls believed their mother was safe at home, their mother and father had been deported shortly thereafter. Both parents perished in the Holocaust.

After the war, Leon had married his cousin, also a Benmayor, who had found haven in Istanbul during the war. Today their descendants

---

2. Judeo-Spanish language spoken by Sephardic Jews.

live in Greece, Israel, and the United States. Mr. Benmayor came to visit New York, so we met, and we corresponded for a while. It was very gratifying to be able to reminisce with him about all things Mimi.

Love, Ruth

Christmas 1943

Dear Lauren,

The 25th of December 1943 is one of the few days that I remember very, very clearly. It is still very much ingrained in my memory. This is the account of Christmas Day in Auschwitz-Birkenau.

Ms. Wandzai was a Polish-Catholic prisoner at Auschwitz. She had been a member of the Polish aristocracy. She was tall. Her appearance and manners were regal. Not long after the subjugation of Poland, a German officer was found dead outside the gate to her garden. She was happy with the knowledge that she had helped the war effort. Luckily for her, the German army surgeon botched the autopsy and never detected the poison. Her life was saved because they could not prove their suspicions, but just to make sure, they sent her to Auschwitz anyway. There she became a privileged prisoner.

Ms. Wandzai shared her primitive lodgings, an almost bare set of planks covered with a thin layer of flea-infested straw, with three other Catholics. These three other women had been friends since childhood. Together they had been slave laborers in Germany. When they complained of a 16-hour workday, they were called idlers and together were sent to Auschwitz.

These women were among the non-Jewish laborers in our barracks. The Polish prisoners, I think, were allowed to have two-times-a-year packages mailed from home. Ms. Wandzai received one at Christmas time. I don't think the other three women got any Christmas gifts.

The three Polish slave laborers worked outside the camp but stayed in the barracks. They were treated almost as badly as Jewish prisoners. They got the same food, the same everything. The only exception was that non-Jewish prisoners were never taken to selection. If they died, they died; nothing was really done by the German authorities to help them. Of course, not having to be in the selections made a large difference, but otherwise they were treated similarly.

This Christmas story also involves Miriam, a Jewish prisoner. Miriam and Jacob had married in September 1939, the same week that the German Army invaded Poland. When they learned of the intended fate of the Jews, they fled into the woods and joined the partisans. One day early in the spring of 1943, Miriam left her hiding place after overhearing much shooting and crying in the area. She wanted to seek out survivors from what they were sure had been a massacre of Jews. Head on, she met a patrol of the SS and was captured. The very next day, she was on a train that took her and several hundred non-Jewish prisoners to Auschwitz. A few weeks later, she realized she was pregnant.

Even as her pregnancy went along, she was losing weight. She became emaciated. She wore the ill-fitting striped prison clothing. Between those baggy prisoner clothes and her emaciated body, her condition remained a secret.

The other prisoners now became solicitous of Miriam. They knew they would be beaten, but still they tried to make her as little visible as their poor means afforded.

The rows of the ritual roll call every morning and evening were always five-deep. No one was permitted to move. The prisoners always put Miriam in between themselves, where her pregnancy wouldn't be as noticeable. It was like an unwritten order. As the pregnancy progressed, Miriam found herself always in the middle of the row.

Christmas Eve and Christmas Day were free days, the only exceptions in the year. The guards and the SS staff were off, and no roll call was taken that evening or the next morning. The 25th was different from any day I had seen at the camp. The guards in their towers were not at their posts. Every other time, they would shout their acknowledgements across the empty space, keeping each other alert and us aware that we were watched.

I was incredulous. Were we witnesses to some upside-down theater of the absurd? The murderers were praying to the God of Mercy. This hell was a madhouse. My mother did not have an answer. There would never be an answer, and she knew that. From long ago, she remembered a quotation from Heinrich Heine's book *The History of Religion and Philosophy in Germany*:

"*The old stone gods will rise from their long-forgotten ruin and rub the dust of a thousand years from their eyes; and Thor leaping to life with a giant hammer will crush the gothic cathedrals.*"[3]

She still needed to say more to me. Perhaps if she explained she might herself come closer to understanding. "No, this is not a prelude to redemption," Mutti said. "This is an immutable evil. It will last and never leave. Maybe if we live, we can heal the hurt. Maybe…"

On Christmas Day, the whole camp seemed to be enveloped in a pink mist. There was a certain sense of awe about it. A strange light radiated. Strangely quiet, every sound was muted. In this stillness, we

---

3. Heinrich Heine, a German-Jewish poet, wrote in 1834 that Christianity had subdued German brutality. He predicted that if Christianity ever lost its hold over Germany, German aggression would be unleashed, and the world would be filled with terror. This line is about old pagan gods, including Thor, the god of thunder and war, destroying Christianity (along with its 1,000-year rule and its cathedrals) and thereby putting an end to the force which had tamed German brutality. Many viewed this prediction as having come true 100 years later, as evidenced by Hitler's regime.

felt as though we had been lifted off our earthly site and were now afloat somewhere removed from the deaths and the filth and the horror.

There was a feeling of otherworldliness. We were suspended over hell but not quite on earth.

With no roll call, it was the only free time I remember while I was in Auschwitz. Most prisoners took advantage of the day and slept to preserve their energies. On that day, my mother and I walked outside. We were anxiously looking across to the men's camp for even a glimpse of my father.

Meanwhile, the four Catholic women never explained how or where they found a sprig from a pine tree, not longer than a finger. But on Christmas 1943, one of them carried it into the camp, hidden in the folds of a sleeve.

They crossed the ditch in front of the barracks. This ditch had been dug by the first prisoners. It connected the pipes that flowed from the latrines with the crude sewer pipes that ran under the electric wires to outside the camp and probably joined up with the general sewer system of the nearby city. Every few days some male prisoners came into the camp and poured some white powder into the ditch. The powder took away the smell and disintegrated everything in its path. In contact with liquid, its efficacy became tenfold.

The Catholic women carried the twig into the barracks. One of them chewed a small piece of bread to make a base and planted the twig in it. They began to celebrate their most holy day.

Miriam had gone into labor that morning and delivered a boy in the afternoon. She had tried to suckle the child, but her breasts were barren. Exhausted, she fell asleep. The hungry baby had cried for most of the afternoon, but finally he, too, fell asleep.

The Catholic women, however, were convinced that a miracle had just begun. The otherworldly fog and the birth of a boy, a life in this place of death, could only be a heavenly sign. They spoke with hushed voices, awed by the signs they had witnessed. They could not contain their joy. They told the good news to all who were awake enough to hear.

We wanted to believe. Oh, how we wanted to feel the outstretched arm of justice leading us to freedom!

It was such a strange feeling. Between a little Jewish boy being born on Christmas, and the strange pink light around us, these Polish women kept saying that a miracle was happening. This must be the miracle that would free us. Today would be the day.

We were desperate for salvation. "Well, maybe there is some truth to the story... Maybe you just have to hang onto it..." This went on almost all day. I mean, we really did not believe it entirely. We were too realistic, and too many things had happened to believe in a miracle. Yet somehow, we felt that maybe, just maybe, something good could happen.

Even though I was not brought up to believe in the story of Christmas, I somehow decided to believe what they said. I still had not lost the hope to be free. They thought it was their Second Coming. We all hoped for redemption. Would Messianic redemption come today? Would we be liberated from Birkenau by a divine miracle?

No. By nightfall on Christmas Day, the spell was broken. We were all brought back to the reality of the camp by hearing the familiar rattle of trucks driving up the gravel road, making their way to the gas chamber, carrying the prisoners to their deaths. Four trucks in all, crowded with Jewish men.

The trucks drove between the men's and the women's camp, which were separated by high, electrically charged wires, and then the trucks drove around the bend to the gas chambers. From the women's camp we didn't see the actual compound, but we could see the tall chimneys.

The trucks were preceded by the command car with several German officers. The trucks were followed by a little jeep-like wagon with the Red Cross painted on the sides and roof. To the pilots of the Royal Air Force, it would look like a mission of mercy, some charitable or humanitarian project. Instead, the little wagon held the canisters of sky-blue pellets, which became the powerful gas that killed millions.

The trucks approached the crematoria compound. When the first truck came within sight of the chimneys, the men began to sing "Hatikvah."[4] The anthem was picked up by the group of men on the second truck, then by the next group of men on the third, and finally by the men on the fourth truck, until all the men were singing.

Kol ode balevav P'nimah – Nefesh Yehudi homiyah – Ulfa'atey mizrach kadimah – Ayin l'Tzion tzofiyah. Ode lo avdah tikvatenu – Hatikvah bat shnot alpayim: L'hiyot am chofshi b'artzenu – Eretz Tzion v'Yerushalayim... [As long as the Jewish spirit is yearning deep in the heart, with eyes turned toward the East, looking toward Zion, then our hope – the 2,000-year-old hope – will not be lost: To be a free people in our land, the land of Zion and Jerusalem...]

Soon the trucks disappeared into the compound. As they were driven in, the voices stopped singing. The first truck stopped first, then the second, and then the third. Finally, the last truck, and all the voices stopped. Instead of singing, we heard the familiar noises of the steam going. We heard the noises of the grates of the ovens as they moved.

We smelled the cyanide as the chambers were aired out so that the *Sonderkommando* could process the bodies for the ovens.

---

4. "The Hope," poem expressing the Jewish longing to return to Zion (Jerusalem). It has since become the national anthem of the State of Israel (Hebrew).

Then the camp became covered with ashes and small chips of bones as the chimneys spewed their products into the night sky.

Later that evening, one of the women in the barracks awoke with a start. She nudged her neighbor and whispered something. Together they woke the third and then yet another. Stealthily, they made their way to Miriam's bunk. Without words, they took a striped prison dress from nearby. Eight hands each held a corner of the dress. Still in silence, they placed the dress over the infant boy and pressed down as hard as they could.

For the rest of their lives, they each would remember the exact thoughts they had at this exact moment:

Each of us would be killed if it were known that we harbored a pregnant woman, one thought.

And then the other, *They would take Miriam and the baby to be killed, but maybe this way she will have a chance at life.*

The third thought: *Miriam is young yet; perhaps in a normal world she'll have strong, healthy boys.*

And the fourth: *No redeemer was born here today, but I am sure, as sure as I am still alive, that he died here today.*

Just as they had come, they receded back into the dark of the barracks.

Ms. Wandzai, who had not been one of the four women involved, woke and sensed at once what had happened. She lowered her head into the folds of the dress. "Forgive me," she cried. "Forgive us."

She wrapped the body in the striped dress, filled a tin cup with muddy water, and made her way to the ditch that connected the latrine pipes with the sewer system. Carefully, as though not to disturb this child at rest, she placed the body on the excrement and the white powder in the ditch. She poured the water all around the corpse. The white powder began to bubble, and the body began to melt into its surroundings. By the time the flow carried it to the end where the drainpipe met the ditch, only the outline could still be seen. The shape kaleidoscoped as it entered the pipe and disappeared into the sewer. As though he had never been.

The next morning, December 26, there was roll call again. As we were standing for roll call, the powder that remained of the disintegrated body of the baby washed out into the ditches. There had been no miracle.

After this happened, my mother dreamt that my father told her it was now time to say Mourner's Kaddish[5] in his memory. I do not know how much of my mother's conscious mind went into this dream. We believe that he was one of the men on the four trucks who was gassed on Christmas Day 1943. We have kept that day, a memorial to my father, because it is the only day that is tangible, and it is as valid as any other day. We use that day as my father's *yahrzeit*.[6]

Love, Ruth

Dear Ruth,

Your father died in Auschwitz on November 19, 1943. It was less than a month before the horrific events you just conveyed to me.

The records kept by the Nazis in Auschwitz were hidden in Soviet archives until 1989 and only made available thereafter. According to the Auschwitz Office of Former Prisoners, where Nazi records are now kept, here is the information as I received it by e-mail:

In response to your request for information about Ignatz Krautwirth I

---

5. Prayer praising God that is recited during times of mourning (Hebrew).
6. Date commemorating the anniversary of a death (Yiddish).

would like to inform you that we have searched through our archives and found the following information:

Krautwirth, Ignatz Isak

Frankfurt am Main

b. 1897–05–24 (Bardejov),

denomination: mosaisch [Jewish].

date of death: 1943–11–19 w Auschwitz

Krautwirth Ignatz Isak; born May 24, 1897, in Bardejov; son of Jakob Krautwirth and Rosa Wertheim; husband of Hana Grossman; place of residence Frankfurt a. Main, Ostenstrasse 18; was imprisoned in KL Auschwitz. Date of his deportation and his prisoners' number is unknown.

He died in the camp on November 19, 1943. The official cause of his death was listed as heart muscle insufficiency.

Source of information: Death Books from Auschwitz

They had even created a death certificate for him.

I asked for clarification. What is heart insufficiency? A heart attack? Being gassed? Was there any public hanging or execution that day? The reply:

Most of the postmortem documentation was falsified and was intended mainly to cover the traces of crimes. [The] act of death of Ignatz Krautwirth is [based on] one record including his name [contained in] partially saved documentation. In this situation [it] is difficult to say how he really died. There is no information about an execution in the camp on this day.

While our family will continue to use December 25 to remember your father, I will also think of him each November 19.

Love, Lauren

The order to leave Auschwitz

Dear Lauren,

We spent most of the year 1944 in Auschwitz Birkenau. I recall nothing of the two birthdays I had there, turning 14 on June 23, 1943, and turning 15 on June 23, 1944. We did not have a calendar or newspaper or anything of the sort to even know the date.

By the end of 1944, we were told that within a day we would be leaving Auschwitz to go do other work. We heard, and it turned out to be true, that the German war machine was suffering. They apparently no longer had enough workers or material.

To what we owed this fortuitous relocation, I'll never know. It might have been strictly by chance, or perhaps because Edita had taken pity on us and submitted our names to leave as laborers.

My mother and I left Auschwitz the same way we arrived: by train. [7] We were loaded onto the same cattle car train that brought people into the camp. On one side of us was the crematorium, and on the other side was the route to the western part of Germany; death if we headed east, maybe a chance at life if we headed west.

We were sitting on this train for a while, and we didn't know which way it would go. We were hoping that it was true, that we were really being taken to Germany for labor, but it could just as easily be the other way: we could be going to the gas chambers.

The first time at this station, I had desperately tried to make some contact with my father. I never saw him again, not at the station or any other place ever again. I had not noticed the chimneys then.

---

7. This is in comparison to other prisoners who were later evacuated from Auschwitz on the death march.

Now, aware of their purpose, we waited to be taken there. We could just as easily have left Auschwitz by being blown from the crematoria into the night sky.

Instead, the train lurched forward, and we headed westbound. As the train finally moved out, we were indeed taken to Germany. They took us to Ravensbrück, a concentration camp inside Germany. I did not know the exact date then, but I know now that we left Auschwitz on November 3, 1944.

Love, Ruth

A visit to Barrack 20

Dear Ruth,

I am writing you this letter in the year 2017, but you are no longer here. I am writing to express the things I wish I could tell you but cannot.

After leaving Auschwitz in November 1944, you never returned to it. I have visited it twice.

I remember asking you why you had never made a return visit to Auschwitz. I wanted to visit it one day and wanted to know what your thoughts on it would be. "Do you think I should have gone back? Would you have gone if you were me?" you asked in response to my question. I replied that you were absolutely justified never to set foot in that place again, and I probably would have done the same in your shoes. My question was not to criticize you. I could never know what it was like to have the experiences that you had, and so I was in no place to judge. I think you were inclined to tell me not to go because I think you were trying to protect me.

Why would anyone go there willingly? you must have wondered. When I told you that I wanted to go out of respect to see what it was like, to see the setting of my one-day-to-be-written-book, you changed your mind: "Bring a stone from home to place there for my father."

I did just that, placing a stone at the steps leading into the ruins of the gas chambers and crematoria in Birkenau as the rabbi in charge led us in the Mourner's Kaddish.

My first visit was a trip with the Jewish Enrichment Center in 2013. Walking through the Auschwitz and Birkenau camps, the tour guide explained what we were seeing. I kept talking about you and telling your stories to the other people on the program. Later that evening, the sunset over Oświęcim[8] was radiantly pink, just like in your story of Christmas Day 1943. Were you there with me, comforting me?

The second time I went to Poland was this year with my parents. We did a six-hour guided study tour. I was overwhelmed with the enormity of it all. In Auschwitz main camp, we saw the blocks with exhibit of prisoner life, blocks with the prisoner clothing and wooden clogs, blocks with maps and statistics showing trains across Europe leading to Auschwitz, and blocks with striking drawings by children of corpses and hangings.

There was a replica model of the entire complex with a display of empty canisters of Zyklon B, and the Zyklon B pellets that were poured into the gas chambers. We walked in and out of the first gas chamber to be built, which was scary. Still intact, the walls were stained blue from the gas even so many decades later. We saw the so-called hospital barracks, the torture cells, the execution wall, and the house where Commandant Rudolf Hess lived with his family next to it all.

I contemplated the enormity of Birkenau, and how impersonal that

---

8. The town of Auschwitz (Polish).

enormity felt. We traveled to see this camp which once held so much horror, to see the remnants of the infrastructure that was used to murder over a million people, but we must try to personalize it.

I remembered you said the fragments of bone and ash would blow out into the night sky. Now green grass replaces the mud that you described so poignantly. For a second time, I left a small stone on the ruins of the gas chambers where the stairs descend for my great-grandfather.

When our tour concluded, we left the group and found Barrack Number 20 in the women's compound of Birkenau. The brick building still stood. Everything was in its original condition, surely somewhat deteriorated in the decades that have passed, but not replaced with replicas or upgraded. The door was locked, so we could not enter, but we peered inside through the windows. I could make out some names scratched onto the walls. Standing at the back window, I knew that it was right here where Mimi Benmayor sang her last song before her life was taken.

This was where so many of your stories took place. Where we stood was where you stood for roll call and where bodies were dumped. The overgrown grass blew in the wind. By knowing and remembering your stories, by seeing your specific barracks, I accepted the overwhelming enormity of Auschwitz. In this terrible place, which is a graveyard for those who were forced to come here before us and which now serves as a memorial to the victims, I found meaning and a personal sense of connection.

Yet I still found it unsettling. What could be learned from visiting Auschwitz-Birkenau? It is my obligation to remember, but how can I remember an experience that was not my own? How can I relate and understand what you went through? I thought visiting the camp would bring me closer to understanding, but I changed my mind.

I realized I felt the closest to understanding when I was closest to you, hearing your stories directly from you as I asked you questions over dinner. So, what does that mean for the future when there are no survivors left? How can I teach others so they learn something from this too? My heart aches for you. My mind contemplates these thoughts, and I am more dedicated than ever to making sure your words transcend your lifetime.

Love, Lauren

RAVENSBRÜCK AND MALCHOW

Sabotaging the Nazi war effort

Dear Lauren,

After several days on the train we arrived at Ravensbrück, a camp in northern Germany, very close to the North Sea. By then the two slices of bread and the barrel of fetid liquid that passed for tea had long been used up. The same sign, *ARBEIT MACHT FREI*, hung over the gate.

When it was built, Ravensbrück was a prison camp for non-Jewish women: German prostitutes, Polish women who had displeased the regime, and communists and other dissidents from throughout occupied Europe. In 1944, when the Nazis needed labor, they consented to use some Jewish workers. Ravensbrück became a way station for Jewish prisoners on their way to other labor camps.

I later learned that my aunt Bella, too, had passed through Ravensbrück. She did not know the date. We would not have been able to recognize her and would never have been able to make contact if we had been there at the same time.

At first, we were kept in a very large tent, similar to a circus tent, for several days with neither food nor water. Picture this: 1,000 women in a circus tent during a northern European winter, without cots or food or drink, barrels dispersed along the periphery for toilet use.

We were beyond feeling the cold or the damp. We were sort of used to starvation, but being without water is awful. The need for drink is more acute than for food. Water is what we craved. Being without water was the worst of all.

When I think back on those times in Ravensbrück, my first memories are of the continuous rains and the huge drops that rolled off the canvas into little puddles. But there was no water for us. Desperate, we stuck our rusty spoons out under the tent and tried to collect this valuable substance, only we did not have the patience to wait for the spoon to fill up. Every few moments, when a few drops had fallen onto the spoon, we sopped them up eagerly, never accumulating enough to satisfy our thirst.

Finally, after about five days, we were given a cot and a ration of food. A few days later we were taken to actual barracks in Ravensbrück. By miniscule degrees, the cots in Ravensbrück were cleaner and the food better than in Auschwitz.

After a few days in the main camp, we were loaded onto a train and rode to Malchow, a subcamp of Ravensbrück. Malchow had originally been designed as a labor camp equipped to imprison about 1,000 people, primarily foreign slave laborers. When we got there, the camp was nearly empty. We heard that 700 prisoners had been there before, but they had been sent to who-knows-where. That was late 1944. Throughout the time we were there, into the first few months of 1945, the number of people grew from just our group to several thousand.

Malchow had unheard-of luxuries, such as furniture and everything. Actual tables and benches! There was a round water fountain with some 20 spigots that had long ago given up their ostensible duty.

There were bunk beds that slept two to a bed instead of six with actual blankets. Our cots were relatively clean, and crude closets for clothes storage were attached to each bed set.

Instead of trenches for toilets, there were holes cut into planks, making it possible for the first time in many years to sit. The best of all luxuries was that there were none of the rats, fleas, or lice that had been our daily torture in Auschwitz.

We had no clothes other than what we wore to put in the cupboard, but the closets, together with the non-working water fountain, were reminders of a civilization we had forgotten existed. It is remarkable how much we had grown unaccustomed to these things even though we had lived with the equipment of civilization before the war. We saw these crude closets, and we were astonished by this evidence of civilization. We were really amazed – there was something other than Auschwitz out there.

The next day we began our work. Although it was a labor camp, it was, in effect, a concentration camp, because the SS guards were still there. Some of them came from Auschwitz with us, while others came from different camps.

We were marched daily through miles of forest to arrive at the factory to work. Birds sang, squirrels chased each other, ferns grew, and the trees gave off a spicy smell of pine. Such delightful serenity! Of course, an excursion into the wild was not our captors' motivation.

We only had to look to the top of the trees to see that this was no ordinary forest. Where the foliage was sparse, tree limbs and leaves were placed overhead on a net. To the pilots of the RAF or the American Army Air Corps, it looked like an innocuous, bucolic forest. It was a masterpiece of camouflage. There were nets with leaves overhead to cover up the things that were going on beneath the treetops. The whole camp, with all sorts of different factories, was hidden underneath the netting. The forest was honeycombed with little hills and secret workshops. Into several of the hills, little doors had been constructed. Moss covered the tops. The doors were recessed by about three feet, and when we passed through, we found ourselves in a sparkling clean, white workroom. There was also a sand hill with some trees coming out of it, and on the side was a door. Once we passed through this door, we were in a very clean, modern-looking laboratory. The factory was like a combination of advanced technology and the workshop of the Seven Dwarfs.

One type of work we did was in the *Weberei*, a weaving mill. We were given strips of cellophane plastic and told to braid them. Radar was coming into prominence at that time and was probably not too sophisticated. The British forces used it in their efforts against the Nazi air force. The Nazis tried to stop this activity by causing static and interfering with the radar. I am not entirely sure it was true, but through the grapevine we learned this woven plastic was supposed to be thrown in front of a British RAF airplane, and it would supposedly interfere with the radar transmission. I thought, *How is this possible? A little thing like that is going to confuse a big airplane?* We tried to sabotage this as much as we could.

Another work assignment for our group was to make bullets in an ammunition factory. Prisoners in other sections worked on hand grenades and different small missiles. There was danger working in a Nazi munitions factory, because it could have been a target of Allied bombings. However, on a personal level, even though there was still danger, it was less so compared to what we had been through. I felt less threatened at Malchow than I had at Auschwitz. As a matter of fact, our working conditions were clean, and we received a decent amount of food.

We worked at a long table with about 30 other prisoners. An SS woman stood on each end watching our every movement. For being such a modern factory and so cleverly designed and hidden, the way we made the bullets and the equipment we used, were very primitive. The SS handed us a tool very similar to a waffle iron containing a board with hollowed-out small holes. The two halves were attached to each other at one end with hinges. We were given one half of a cylindrical little metal thing, one for each hole, so we put half a bullet capsule in each hole. Once each hole was occupied, we filled the bottom half of the cartridges very carefully with a grayish powder. After we filled up the holes with a certain amount of gunpowder, we closed the top half of the board over it. The other half of the capsule was in the top board, so when pushed down, it closed the two parts and made the bullet. The boards were calibrated to mesh into each other with precision. With some strong pressure applied, a bullet from each hole had been produced. A fraction of a millimeter off and the bullet would be a dud. That is why we were so thoroughly watched.

Carefully, under the eagle eyes of the guards, we lifted the upper board and set it down on the lower one. It was difficult, but I tried not to line up the top part of the board with the bottom part of the board, as much as I could without being detected. I did not want to be beaten or killed. Yet, even with their constant vigilance, I was at times able to shift each side just a millimeter. I tried to sort of squeeze it in a crooked way, so it would close but not quite. Every mismatch was accompanied by my prayers. I was hoping that these bullets would misfire, and I was hoping that in this way it would be part of my war effort against the Nazis. Whether it worked or not I never found out. This was my proud contribution to the Allied war effort. This was my way of protesting, of sabotaging what the Germans were doing.

Love, Ruth

The generosity of the Roma

Dear Lauren,

When we left Auschwitz in November 1944, the other prisoners had remained behind.

In the beginning of January 1945, the Nazis emptied Auschwitz as the Russian army neared the camp. Before they evacuated, the Nazis quickly tried to destroy all evidence of their atrocities. They hurriedly blew up the crematoria. When the order came to evacuate Auschwitz ahead of the Russian army, the prisoners were ordered to march. The SS did not have time to gas them. They sent these remaining prisoners on a long journey west. These are now known as death marches. With practically no clothes or food, in the harsh winter weather of Eastern Europe, the captives died en masse; stragglers were shot. Only the hardiest survived.

By the end of January, the Russian army had arrived at Auschwitz and liberated the few remaining prisoners.

The Auschwitz prisoners were marched to other concentration camps farther west. A lot of prisoners were brought from Auschwitz to Malchow. As the number of prisoners in Malchow swelled, the concentration camp system was starting to break down.

Many Roma arrived at Malchow with the evacuees from Auschwitz. Their people had been almost entirely wiped out. In the few months prior, the Roma camp at Auschwitz had received the last remnants of their people from around Europe. The survivors had been dragged on the death march as the camp was emptied.

Being somewhat used to finding food in the countryside, the Roma managed to supply themselves with the necessities of sustenance. Carcasses littered the roads from Poland to Germany along the escape routes of the German army. The Roma salvaged meat from the officers' horses that died along the way. They brought the horsemeat into the camp, where they barbecued it.

The comical aspect is that they had to look for wood to use to make a fire. They saw no reason to respect Nazi property. For their bonfires, they dismantled doors and frames. When they ran out of doors, they simply took the boards off the toilets. As a result, there was no more bathroom, so we were back to squatting over a hole instead of the little wooden frame that served as a toilet. These were the same toilets that I was so impressed by in the beginning.

The Roma generously offered to share their food with everyone who came along. These wonderful people shared their treasured meat and other rare morsels with us, who in the last weeks of the camp did not even receive the usual scant rations. It was exceedingly rare, exceedingly nice, and extraordinarily hospitable. For this, I have wonderful memories of the Roma people. I will never forget their generosity.

In addition to food, the Roma and Sinti people brought a large measure of cheer. Despite what they had been through, they still seemed to have a zest for life. During the evenings, I remember that they produced a harmonica and began to sing and dance, much to their own enjoyment and to our entertainment. They lit bonfires, played their harmonicas, and generally tried to cheer the cheerless.

Maybe they were cheerful at this time because, it just so happened, they could tell that the end of the Nazi era was coming. Having been in Malchow for months, we were not as aware of the approaching end as they were, since they had marched from Auschwitz to Malchow. Perhaps they had seen what was going on as they went hundreds of miles from one camp to the next. Perhaps they had seen the German army retreating. Several families of Roma even brought news of the fighting.

I remember the Roma people sang and celebrated long into the nights. Their optimism should have rubbed off on us, but a strange mood began to overtake us. We enjoyed the entertainment, only we could not permit ourselves *huzzahs*, not with the memory of death enveloping us and choking off every gladness. We were so aware of the atrocious past. What celebration could there possibly be with the picture of death constantly before us?

Love, Ruth

The end is near

Dear Lauren,

On April 12, 1945, less than four weeks before the war officially ended, President Roosevelt died. I was able to overhear some of the guards' conversations. Most of them were aware that the war was lost, yet some saw the president's death as a sign of a turnaround, and they did not hide their glee. Only relying on rumors and being unfamiliar with politics, we settled into gloom. Had the war come so far only to be lost by some terrible quirk? What would become of us? Who was Harry Truman? But the war was truly coming to an end.

More and more people kept coming into Malchow. The roads were so congested with people on the move that we could not get to the factory anymore, so we just stayed in the camp. Sometime in April, we stopped working. The whole system completely stopped functioning. Nothing was happening anymore. But what did happen in the last few weeks at the camp before the war ended is that, with all this chaos, the SS did not give us any food. Fear was rampant. We were sure the camp, sitting on top of a gunpowder reserve, would be bombed.

Since we prisoners did not get any food, we were starving. We rioted to get into the warehouse to access the food. The warehouses had bread, and we were sure there would be additional supplies of food inside. Encouraged by the pending defeat of the German Army, we raided the food silo. The ruckus made one Nazi guard fire a gunshot into the air. When he could not dislodge the starving prisoners, he fired into the crowd. We still managed to break into the food storehouse and the adjacent kitchen and dining room. Food was left on plates, uneaten on the table. Chairs were turned upside down and sideways. It looked like the SS guards left in a rush. They must have heard that a liberating army was on its way, and their escape was more important than guarding a few bedraggled Jews.

When we stormed the food storage barracks at Malchow, I found what I thought would surely be a rare treat: noodles! I saved them for later.

We were called by the SS guards to the gate where we were told we were going to march out of the camp to the west, away from the Russian Army which was approaching from the east. This was to be a forced evacuation on foot.

The death march lasted about a week. These were the final few days before liberation. We were marching out of Malchow, and did not know it yet, but we were beginning our walk to freedom. By April 30, 1945, the Soviet Army would liberate Ravensbrück, its subcamps, and the prisoners who had been marched out.

We heard rumors of a pending German surrender but had no newspaper or radio to confirm it.

We could barely march anywhere because the roads were so crowded. Eastern Europeans were trying to get back to their homes. German soldiers from disorganized units were trying to run away from the approaching Russian army by going west. The *Volksdeutsche,* ethnic Germans having lived in western Poland, who had welcomed the occupying German army and had become very enthusiastic Germans, who had sheltered the infamous "Fifth Columnists," were trying to escape the wrath of the Russian Army. Now that the Russians were coming, they were afraid of what would happen to them if they stayed behind, so they were walking all the way back into Germany. Vehicles and armaments and an occasional rider on a horse brought movement almost to a standstill.

Slowly it occurred to us that we would not be bombed after all. Any escape route would have been destroyed if this road, so close to the camp, had been blown up.

We found ourselves on a mountain peak a few hundred feet above a peacefully meandering river. On our side of the mountain an enterprising restaurateur had built an inn long ago when civility and good living still were in vogue. A bombed-out bridge lay at the bottom. Some inventive citizens had taken tables out of the inn, turned them upside down, and tied the legs with wire to make a long chain spanning the river. It was a most precarious arrangement. Only the desperate would venture across such a makeshift bridge. We crossed the bridge one at a time. Again, we knew the German guards would not spill us into the river, for they too needed the bridge for escape.

Many prisoners disappeared, and eventually so did the guards. Some guards were still hanging on. A few diehards insisted on staying with us to the last. We considered running and hiding, but they were such fanatics. Shooting a few more Jews in the back would have been a justifiable joy to them. We were too close to freedom to risk it.

After crossing the bridge, we walked for several hours to an unused sugar factory, where we would spend the night. We settled in to whatever accommodations there were. The corridors were empty.

That night I met with the horror of the SS for the last time. I saw her again – the beast Drechsler. Drechsler had risen from her netherworld. I thought that we had left her behind in Auschwitz and would never have to see her again.

I had gone alone down what I thought was an empty hallway. She was in a small office on a chair in front of a table cleaning her gun. A she-devil from hell, she ordered me into the room: "You." To my surprise, her fear was palpable. I never thought she could muster any human emotion. "I suppose you will do to us the same as we did to you." She told me that soon we would be free (and other hopeful things) and would take revenge.

Could I answer her that there was not enough punishment on Earth or in Hell for her?

She was still the one holding the gun, so I just mumbled something about things not being as bad as they looked to her right now and I was sad she would be leaving us. She motioned me to leave. Years of putting up with her had taught me not to reveal my emotions. I remained calm and stoic. What else could I have said or done when she was holding that gun and looking through its lenses?

Love, Ruth

Dear Ruth,

Sometime shortly after your last encounter with her, around May or June 1945, the Soviets captured SS woman Margot Drechsler, condemned her to death, and executed her by hanging.

Love, Lauren

LIBERATION AND RETURN TO FRANKFURT AM MAIN

The noodles

Dear Lauren,

The entire time we had been marching, I held onto the food that I had found in Malchow when we raided the food storage area: a rare treat, noodles. If it looks like noodles and feels like noodles, that is what it had to be, I determined.

When I saw the noodles, I looked for a suitable container. There was none. I was the bedraggled owner of two pairs of underpants: one gray flannel pair held up by a frayed string, a standard issue for prisoners in Auschwitz; and a pink, silky pair that I had found in Kanada. Such a luxury was not permitted to prisoners, so I wore the pink ones close to my body, the gray ones on top doing a fair job of hiding my infraction. Not seeing anything of use to hold the noodles, I stepped out of my gray underwear, pulled out the string, tied the legs together, and filled this bag with noodles.

I carried the underpants as a bag filled with noodles – out of the camp, into the woods, and along the shoreline of the sea. I carried them all that distance. When we were made to walk for the seven or eight days out of the camp, I held onto my noodles for dear life.

During the march, we had to forage for our own food. When we were walking, we walked past potato fields. Some of the farmers had left some potatoes in the ground. We took the few potatoes we found at the edge of the estates we passed. There was no way to wash them. We roasted them in the bonfires we hastily constructed. Since we were starved, we did not give the broiled potatoes the chance to be fully cooked. The taste of half-raw, gritty potatoes will never win a Michelin star.

We walked with very little food. The Swedish Red Cross had sent food packages to be used specifically for prisoners. The fortunes of war had indeed changed. At the height of their triumphs, the Nazis would never have let us have these rare delicacies. Luxuries had not been available in Germany since the Nazi agenda had begun calling for the production of war material instead of consumer goods. Now they were afraid to steal such treats, lest this too would be a war crime.

At first it was two people to a food package, then three, and then four. By the time we got a box, it was five prisoners to one box. This fact of having to share was for us a lifesaver. The boxes held sardines and butter and other fatty things, rare foods, which we eagerly gulped down. But our systems were unaccustomed to such delicacies. The body needed to readjust to consuming this type of food. Many prisoners who had a larger portion came down with dysentery. (After we were liberated, some prisoners were treated in British army hospitals, including my mother, and quite a few died. Even this belated gesture of help worked against some prisoners.)

Cherishing my bag of noodles, I finally said to my mother, "Okay, now let's cook the noodles." At last, my mother found a rusty tin can and some water to make a meal out of this treasure. At the edge of the fire, we began to cook. We anticipated a fine treat. She put water in and started to prepare the meal over this bonfire.

We put the noodles in, and they grew and grew and grew. Something was wrong. The things grew, my mother added water, and they grew some more, reaching the top of the tin and finally spilling over. At that point we became suspicious.

One taste confirmed my disappointment. They turned out to be nothing more than dehydrated potatoes. I was so sick and tired of potatoes. I had sworn off all potatoes after days of eating those other disgusting potatoes. Plus, I had schlepped this bag along the whole way... But, then again, we were starving, so we ate.

Lauren, whenever you or your cousins asked for a story from my past, I always tell you the "noodle story." It is one of the less atrocious tales that you and my other grandchildren never tire of hearing!

Sometimes one of you asks me, "How can you still eat potatoes?" "Well," I reply, "I have forgiven the potatoes for what they did!"

Love, Ruth

Liberation

Dear Lauren,

One day in the late in the afternoon, sometime in early May, after days of marching, we saw army tanks. There were some unfamiliar markings on the tanks: five-cornered white stars. Then we saw Allied soldiers milling around who spoke another language, and for once we were not cursed at. Americans! This was not far from the Elbe River, where the American, British and Russian armies met.

We realized that the long-hoped-for liberation had arrived. We were free at last! Freedom! A mix of emotions came over me. I try to recall my exact thoughts at that moment, but I cannot.

Our Nazi guards took off. It was our first time without supervision since imprisonment. We were free to go, but where to?

Soldiers were everywhere, and some were not kindly inclined toward our raggedy crew.

Soon we saw a long, wide line of men and women in German army uniforms being inspected in their armpits by those very same Allied soldiers. Everyone was examined, including us.

For identification purposes, the SS had sometimes tattooed some insignia under one of the armpits of each of its members, never imagining it would backfire. Those cowardly Nazis tried to hide among the prisoners and tried to remove the small tattoo under the armpit, which had identified them as members of the master race in times more propitious to them. This made them now identifiable to the Allied armies. We recognized the SS, and so did the Allies.

The Nazi suspects were rounded up and led away. We could see the Nazis squirm, as they feared repayment for the myriad tortures they had inflicted. How afraid they were of the Russian soldiers, who remembered their butchery, their savage acts in Stalingrad, Leningrad, and in the outskirts of Moscow!

Much later, when the atrocities were glossed over for political reasons – despite the good intentions of these front soldiers – civilian courts and accommodating military officials set many of these unrepentant criminals free. Unfortunately, because of world politics, they never got what they deserved. The Americans wanted the rocket builders and took the rocket scientists to Huntsville, Alabama. The Russians, not wanting to be outdone, began to coddle those Nazis they found useful. Time went by, and many of the Nazi guards lived out their lives as if they had been the nicest folk in the world.

As for where to go, an English officer patiently explained to us that there was a building with space for the night for all of us. In the morning, we would be taken to a collection place.

We spent the night in a coffin factory. The owner of the factory had his home in a house by the road. In the back was a beautifully kept orchard with unripe fruit on the trees. It was springtime; the blossoms were gone but small fruit had begun to grow. The grass was well-manicured. On one side was a wide building holding the coffin factory, where we settled in for the night.

For a short time, I just stood there, leaning on a wall as if to find refuge within its shadow, not knowing what to do next. Soon that feeling left. We were free. I try to recall the exact feeling I had, but again it escapes me.

In a nearby castle, liberated prisoners of war held a dance. Someone asked us to join. How could we? We former prisoners, now survivors, could not really enjoy our freedom. Our families had been destroyed, our homes torn apart, our synagogues burned. All our points of reference had been taken from us. This reality was not easy or comforting. We had the smell of the cyanide from the gas chambers fresh in our nostrils and the memories of family lost in the upheaval. Our own bodies still reeled from malnutrition and filth. We opted for the quiet of the coffin factory.

It seems that in this town the Russian contingent also began to celebrate the end of the war in their own way. That is, they liberally partook in the fruit of the vine and found themselves safely ensconced in the arms of Bacchus.

Around midnight the drunken Russian soldiers discovered the stairs to the coffin factory. In their eagerness for adventure, they were racing one another, although two were on motorcycles and one was on horseback. We heard them trying to mount the steps. Being thrown back by us was part of the glee, liberally spiced with curses and interspersed with off-key songs of drunken splendor. They never made it up those stairs.

In the morning we evaluated the situation. Two women had crawled into coffins. Several women had painted their faces black, hoping the darkness would hide them. Out on the manicured lawn, a horse was tethered to a tree, churning up the grass and freely chomping off the leaves.

That day the mayor of the town came looking for an interpreter. A Russian officer had something to ask him. The closest the mayor could find was my mother, whose repertoire included 17 Russian words. But one did not need to speak the language to get the Russian officer's meaning; simply: he wanted sex with the mayor's daughter. Why he went through the formalities of a request is one of the enigmas of war.

We were hungry. Early in the morning, my mother went out trying to scrounge up some victuals. A Russian officer, a gentleman of the old school, asked her purpose for such an early foray. She explained that she was looking for food. "No problem. See that chicken crossing the road?" He grabbed the chicken by the legs, spun it around, hit it against the wall, ripped off its head, and gave it to her to cook. It was the first chicken dinner in years. He promised to bring us fresh fish after the planned fishing expedition for the day, and he kept his word.

Soon after, we were taken to the collection place and ended up in a British Displaced Persons (DP) camp. We were in the DP camp for several months.

I barely remember any details from the time I was in the DP camp. I became sick with typhus and was treated in the hospital for a very long time. One thing I do remember was the barter system. There was coffee, soap, cigarettes – all being traded without currency. I do not recall my 16th birthday, June 23, 1945.

Eventually, as the summer of 1945 came to an end, the British army knew they could not keep us outdoors in the winter. The British made travel arrangements for the displaced persons to go to various destinations by truck, or cart, or rail, or whatever was available. They asked us where we wanted to go.

Frankfurt, we told them.

Love, Ruth

Looking for my father and brother

Dear Lauren,

Before the deportation to Auschwitz, my mother, father, brother, and I had agreed that, if we were to become separated, would try to go back to Frankfurt when it was all over to be reunited as a family. There was no question of staying there. We would never do that. Together we would decide where to go. Then we would leave Frankfurt as a family.

My mother and I arrived in Frankfurt sometime in the fall of 1945. The time had come to reunite with my father and brother as planned. My mother was sure there was no one left to meet. I could not endure the idea of such a loss and wanted to forge a return to the way things had been.

When we returned to the city of my birth, it was in ruins. The city was practically destroyed in Allied bombings. Almost everything was gone. Where houses once stood lay large mounds of stones. Roads and their signs had been erased. Gates and fences made a surreal image on the skyline. We saw rubble and mountains of rubble. Very few houses were still standing. It was rare to see an intact wall.

Even my mother – who had no great love for anything German after what had happened – was shocked and saddened when she saw this horrible destruction. When she saw the city in ruins, my mother admitted she was frightened.

I looked at the ruins and gloated that now there was not one stone attached to the next one. To me this was wonderful. I said, "Oh good, I'm glad the Allies made a whole mess out of the city. The Germans deserve it..." At the time I thought, they followed their Führer and deserved what they got. I was sure there were corpses under those piles, but I would not have wanted to be present when they were found. I would not trust my feelings. I began to grope with my return to normal responses in a civilized world. I can probably trace my own tentative healing process to those times.

The German people did not deserve what happened to them; the people of Frankfurt fared very well during and after the war! Frankfurt and all of Germany became prosperous and rich. No one spoke of revenge or anything like that. The Allies had learned from World War I not to "punish" Germany for its transgressions. My American tax dollars would later go to rebuild Germany. Nothing ever happened to punish them for what they did. No justice was done. They deserved worse retribution than the destruction of their cities, but they were never dealt it.

In the days immediately after our arrival, we were housed in a hotel near the railroad station. That area became a meetup location for all kinds of people. Everybody shared their experiences, and there was no place else to go. The United Nations Relief and Rehabilitation Administration (UNRRA) and the United Hebrew Immigrant Aid Society (HIAS) collected as much information as they could about the survivors – name, place of birth, origin, and so on – and printed lists to help people look for their relatives.

An American soldier came in and looked at the lists of survivors. He was looking for family in Frankfurt. He had left Germany before the war and served in the American army. He was now looking for his relatives who had stayed behind and was hoping that someone could tell him what had happened. Seeing that we were from Frankfurt, he asked us if we had any information. We did not know what had happened to his relatives, but in our conversation he mentioned that while he was stationed in Italy and other places he had been asking about his relatives to anyone he met who was from Frankfurt.

In Italy, he had spoken with a young boy from Frankfurt. This young boy fit the description of my brother! We fit the description of the young boy's relatives! It was my brother! That was how we found out that Zev was alive, and we learned of his whereabouts. He was in Bari, Italy, at the time, about to embark on a journey to Palestine. We asked this soldier anxiously how we could write to him. How could we get in touch with him? The soldier gave us an army post number, and we wrote to Zev.

Shortly after our return to Frankfurt, our former downstairs neighbor, Mr. Agricola, went on trial for being a Nazi. My mother and I testified against him. The court found nothing wrong in harassing us, and even with many complaints from other witnesses, he was found not guilty. He must have lived out his remaining years at peace with himself.

At one point, my mother and I traveled briefly to my mother's hometown of Radom, Poland, to see if anyone there had survived. We did not find any of our relatives there.

The living situation for us in Frankfurt was terrible. For a while, we were put up in the Jewish Hospital, the Gagernstrauser Hospital. Later we were in the same apartment building as many "former" Nazis.

For several months, while we stayed in the apartment, I was hoping – even though I knew better – that somehow my father would make his way back. I kept saying: "My father will come back... I can't leave until he comes back."

I wrote to the Jewish organizations in Czechoslovakia, his birthplace, thinking maybe, somehow, he had ended up there. Maybe he was sick. Perhaps he was somewhere in a hospital. I waited for him on the train station platform where I had last seen him. We looked for his name on the lists and in the newspapers of the Jewish agencies that were working to reunite people. However, my father did not return to the city. My hope was gradually fading.

I wanted to stay in Frankfurt only until I knew with absolute certainty that my father was not coming back. It was just impossible for me to accept. How could I be so naive to think that he *would* return? Yet, despite all I had been through I could not fathom that my father would *not* return.

Love, Ruth

The betrayal of Mr. Marz

Dear Lauren,

After we returned to the occupied and rubbled city in the fall of 1945, we ran into Mr. Marz in the street. He was the man who had helped provide us with some extra cheese before the war, who was willing to safeguard some of our possessions but never offered to hide us on his extensive property.

He now told us that his wife was ill. His sole daughter, Marie, had been killed in an air raid, and his son was suspended from his teaching job pending denazification. He said that their situation was exacerbated by the loss of their home to the occupying American Armed Forces. He pleaded with us to try to intercede with the American authorities to restore the house to his family; he had, after all, been such a good friend.

My mother and I traipsed from one US Army office to another until we finally found the right one. The officer in charge searched his records and produced a file several inches thick.

It seemed that our good friend and devout Catholic Mr. Marz had been a member of the Nazi Party since 1932, a time when such membership was purely voluntary and was not needed to further his business, as many excuses for such memberships were later couched.

Needless to say, my mother and I slunk out of that office, shocked by our naiveté and defeated by our misjudgment. An allied officer accompanied us to Mr. Marz's home to help us get our possessions back.

When we entered his home, now possessed by the Allies, two of my parents' paintings were on his living room wall. He surely thought we would never be back to claim them. Without a title document, the soldier took our word that the paintings were ours. He took down the two paintings and returned them to us. The rest of our expensive items were gone.

Mr. Marz must have known that we found him out, for he never attempted to contact us after this. He was one of our greatest disappointments, for we believed he was our friend, and we were humiliated by how he had fooled us.

We had hidden some precious items with the old greengrocer woman before the war. She was the one who lived in the alley near our former home and spared some rationed vegetables for me when she could.

We retrieved our items from her: my grandmother's tablecloth, my mother's jewelry box, a silver candelabrum, the necklace my father bought for my mother when my brother was born, and a few photographs.

We had hidden some leather goods from my father's business with her. We had thought we could use them to rebuild life after the war.

We recovered these articles, too. Now it was the time to rebuild, but my father was still missing.

Love, Ruth

Germany is no place for Jews

Dear Lauren,

Realizing that my father would never return, my mother and I decided to leave Germany forever.

Stubbornly I did not cede to leave easily. Jews had been in Germany since the Middle Ages. We had every right to stay in Germany. The Enlightenment and Emancipation had finally made us equals. I was as dutiful a citizen as the next. A thousand years' residence gave us the right to live as Jews and continue to be Germans, contributing to the country with the best we had to offer. But the memories were too overpowering. Although the Thousand Year Reich[1] lasted only a short 12 years, to us every minute was too much. The German people were still deeply antisemitic. Germany was no place for Jews. We had to decide where to go.

Our preference was to go to Palestine. I agreed with those who sought a national home. We Jews were a nation unto ourselves. I felt Palestine was our country. Despite Palestine then being primitive, socialist, and underdeveloped by comparison to the United States, I wanted to go there. I firmly believe if Israel had been a country in the 1940s, there would not have been an Auschwitz, at least not to the same extent as it was. My Uncle Abba and his wife lived there, and

---

1. Reference to the Third Reich (1933–1945), which Hitler anticipated would last for 1,000 years.

my heart was always there. My mother wanted to reunite with Zev. But to go there was impossible; we were not allowed in.

My mother preferred the United States as the next best option. Had I known then what I know now about some of the American indifference to the plight of European Jewry, perhaps I would have insisted more on settling in Palestine. Unlike before the war, it was now very easy to leave Germany to go to the United States. HIAS and UNRAA provided help. We heard from someone with one of the Jewish organizations that we could just sign up to leave. We could just go to the American Embassy or Consulate and get our papers.

My mother and I went to the embassy and got visas which were good for a certain date range. We waited to leave, because I thought of my father, and I still wanted to wait as long as we could for him to return. On the very last possible day that we could leave while our visas were still valid, my mother had to drag me out of Frankfurt.

We set sail on February 21, 1947. We embarked on the ship and essentially had to give up dreaming that my father was alive. But I did not give up hope entirely. Even throughout the voyage, I kept thinking, *Oh well, maybe somewhere, somehow, I will hear that he is someplace...* But that never happened.

I do not remember the voyage very well because I was seasick. Mutti was seasick, too, practically before the boat even started moving. The trip was uneventful. We were en route to Ellis Island, New York.

Love, Ruth

PHOTOS

Ruth and Lauren at Lauren's Bat Mitzvah in West Orange, New Jersey, on April 10, 1999.

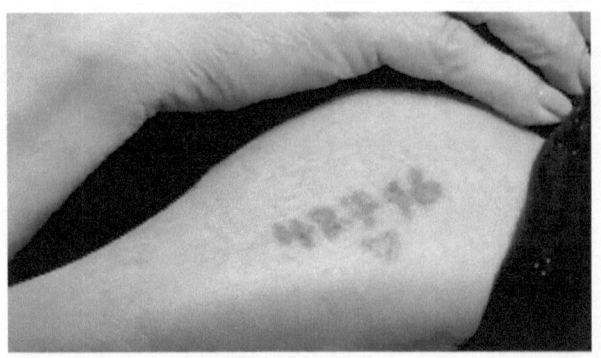

Ruth's left arm with her Auschwitz-Birkenau prisoner number. She was given number 42716 and a triangle (half Star of David) to indicate she was Jewish.

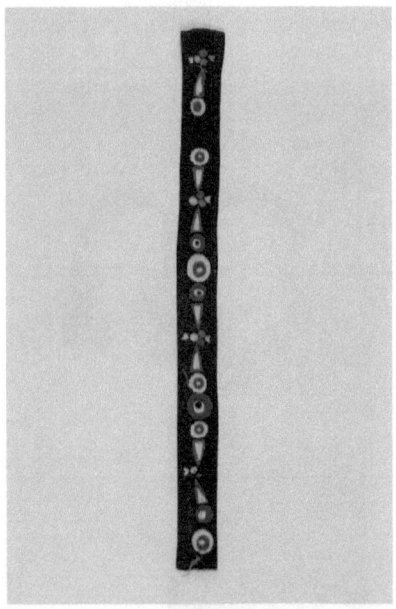

The belt that Ruth found in the Kanada section of Birkenau, wore throughout the war, and donated to the United States Holocaust Memorial Museum. Museum collection item 1988.99.1_001.

The death certificate of Yitzhak Krautwirth issued by the camp registry office in Auschwitz-Birkenau on December 31, 1943. It is now part of the archive collection of the Auschwitz-Birkenau Memorial and Museum, Oświęcim, Poland. According to this document, Ruth's father died in the camp on November 19, 1943, at 5:15pm, from "heart muscle insufficiency."

Ruth's father Ignatz (Yitzhak) Krautwirth, Frankfurt, 1935.

Ruth and Chana's photograph for their visas to go to the United States, Frankfurt 1946.

Ruth shortly after her return to Frankfurt, December 1946.

Lauren with her parents Nancy and Mark finding Barrack 20 at the Auschwitz-Birkenau Memorial and Museum, Poland, 2017.

Lauren at the Holocaust Memorial in Frankfurt pointing to the plagues for her great-grandfather Yitzhak and great-granduncle Julius, 2017.

LIFE AS A HOLOCAUST SURVIVOR

New Jersey, United States
1947–2006

As Told Through Letters to Lauren, 2006
With Letters from Lauren to Ruth, 2006, 2017

NEW BEGINNINGS

A story to preserve

2006

Dear Ruth,

I am writing to you from Israel. It is my first time here. I am on a Birthright trip with other Jewish students from the University of Michigan. We've been traveling all over the country, seeing different sights, learning the history, and going out late. I'm exhausted from all the activities, but I'm having a great time!

Yesterday, though, we visited Yad Vashem. There are 30 people in my Birthright group, but only a few of us are grandchildren of survivors. To some of the other students on this trip, the Holocaust is something that is learned in school or museums as an important historic event in Jewish history. To me, it is so much more personal than that. It is surreal to realize that you, someone I am so close with, survived such a tragic event in Jewish history and that it didn't take place all that long ago.

I walked through the main exhibition and then exited outside to a spot with a view overseeing the beautiful, lush rolling hills. I stood there contemplating what I had just seen. One of the Israelis who was accompanying our group on the trip came up beside me. I mentioned how powerful and moving the museum was and that even though my grandma is a Holocaust survivor and I know a lot about the Holocaust already, I still learned new information.

I began telling him about your experience and what you had gone through during the war. In that moment, I needed to talk about it. Then it dawned on me: I need to write it down. I need to put all the stories you've told me over the years onto paper so that they can be preserved.

I would like to write your biography. What do you think?

Love, Lauren

Dear Lauren,

I received your letter from Israel in the mail. By now you are back at the university to resume your studies. I am glad that you had a fun time in Israel and felt inspired.

You've asked for my thoughts on writing my biography, so I shall share them. Sometimes I am filled with self-doubt and think there would be no audience interested in my story. People were not really interested in hearing about it after the war, but these days I suppose there is more interest. If you think it is a good idea, then please, go ahead.

Writing my story is something I have always wanted to do, but I always found it to be too challenging. I've written many stories and articles over the years. At one point I attempted an autobiography but could not bear to complete it. The next time you come home, take everything I have written. The papers are upstairs by the computer, in the study, near my collection of books about Judaism and the Holocaust. You can keep them.

If you can manage it, then I encourage you. Preserve my story for your children. Ask me more questions. I'll tell you what I can. What else can I answer for you?

Love, Ruth

The postwar years

Dear Ruth,

I am so grateful that you have shared your stories with me about your childhood before the war and your experiences in the concentration camps. But your story does not end with the uneventful boat ride to New York. I'd like to hear about your life after the war. Let's continue to write while I am at college so I can gather more details.

You were just 17 years old when you began life anew in the United States. I am 20 years old now and embarking on my adult life. It's incredible how different life is for us, just two generations apart.

Tell me about the thoughts and ideas that occupied your mind while you rebuilt your life. What issues continued to plague you? Were you able to live a happy, meaningful, and fulfilling life after all you had been through? What was your motivation to become such a vocal educator on the Holocaust?

Tell me about your life experience with this new status called "survivor."

Love, Lauren

Dear Lauren,

Wonderful questions. I'll start by giving you a summary of my life after the war and what the following few decades were like. After that, I'll discuss the topics you've proposed so that you can have a glimpse into what life was like for me as a Holocaust survivor. I'm happy to continue our exchanges while you are away at college.

My mother and I arrived in the United States in 1947. In 1948, I met and married your grandpa, Harry Meyerowitz.

Harry and I started a family. Our oldest son, your Uncle Allan, was born on May 3, 1952. His Hebrew name is Yitzhak. I named him after my father. It had been seven years since the war had ended without any word from my father, so I was sure by this point that he had died. As you know, our middle son, Mark, your father, was born on April 11, 1955. His Jewish name is Joseph Lieser, after my grandfather, Mutti's father. Our youngest son, your Uncle Norman, was born on September 2, 1958. His Jewish name is Benjamin, after Harry's father.

All three boys were born in Paterson, New Jersey. We lived in Fair Lawn, New Jersey. You once asked me if I ever wanted a daughter. I was happy with the three boys. It didn't matter to me if my children were boys or girls as long as they were happy and healthy.

I earned a bachelor's degree in history and then a master's degree in English literature by taking classes in the evening on a part-time basis over many years. I remained a lifelong student. By the time you were in middle school or so, I had completed all my coursework for a PhD in history. I wrote my dissertation on "Minority Rights in the League of Nations." I retired and did not defend my thesis, so I did not earn the PhD.

Harry and I set up a family business, Meyerowitz Furs, in 1950. Do you remember the fur store? We did retail and custom manufacturing of fur and leather goods. My career was working in the fur store from the time we established it until the time I retired. The store was originally located on Tenth Ave in Paterson, New Jersey, and we lived in an apartment nearby. In 1954, we bought a new home on Fourth Street in Fair Lawn. By 1971, Paterson had deteriorated so much that we could no longer run our business there, so we moved the business closer to our home in Fair Lawn. Around that time, we had a new home built with a nice deck and swimming pool in a new development in Fair Lawn. In 1982, we built a new building for our business, again in Fair Lawn.

My life was made up of the normal things of life in the 1950s to 1980s: being a wife, mother, business owner, and student. Your grandpa and I ran the fur store every day and raised the boys. We were members of a Conservative synagogue and kept kosher at home. It was important for us that the boys be active in Jewish life. They participated in Jewish summer programs, and each had a bar mitzvah. The boys also played baseball and football, had toy train sets, and had binoculars and astronomy sets to see the stars at night. Mark and Norman joined the family fur business once they completed college. Allan became a Conservative rabbi.

I did not often raise the topic of my experiences with the boys, but it was never off-limits. We never forced any discussion of it on them. Yet, without ever telling our sons very much about my past life and the time in Auschwitz, my sons just knew from school and reading and other sources what it was all about. I answered any questions they raised matter-of-factly and tried to stress to them that we cannot allow such things to happen again. I always wanted to emphasize the positive side of Jewish life in Europe. Despite persecutions and threats, there was a very rich life in the ghettos and shtetls. I would rather talk of the synagogues and the seats of learning. We can be so proud of our community organizations, which only recently have been copied by the leaders of the general population. I did, however, make sure to tell them about Irma and Mimi. I told them how protective my mother was of me in the camps and about conditions in the camps. I am sure your Uncle Allan's decision to become a rabbi was influenced by our family history.

All three of my sons got married in 1979. Your father was the first. Your parents were married on June 24, 1979. My first grandchild, your brother, Jeffrey, was born on my 54th birthday, June 23, 1983. When he was born, I was so excited that I jumped up in the air and, upon landing, broke my toe! You came along later, on March 25, 1986.

On the last night of Chanukah, December 23, 1979, your Uncle Allan married Robin Sack. Your cousins are: Yael, born March 12, 1984; Ayelet, born April 9, 1987; and the twins, Shai and Chana, born June 27, 1990.

On July 11, 1979, your Uncle Norman married Joyce Setty. Your cousin Shira was born on December 25, 1984. God works in mysterious ways, giving me a newborn granddaughter 41 years to the day after my father was gassed in Birkenau, on the same day that our fellow prisoner Miriam's newborn boy was born and killed.

After losing my husband and mother, I decided to move from Fair Lawn to West Orange, New Jersey, to be nearer to Mark, Nancy, Jeffrey, and you.

Love, Ruth

Starting a new life

Dear Lauren,

Back to the past. Mutti and I arrived in New York on March 3, 1947. We were met by ladies from HIAS and UNRAA. HIAS put us up for a few nights in a hotel.

My mother found a job at a nursing home, the Daughters of Miriam, in Clifton, New Jersey, where she worked in the kitchen. The job included room and board, so we lived in the nursing home and stayed in our own rooms. I was 17 years old when we arrived, so I was enrolled in high school. I had studied English as a child, so the language was not too difficult for me to pick up. Although my secondary education in Germany had been cut short, I was able to enter the same grade level as others my age.

A few people became interested in what had happened to me. A woman from the local newspaper interviewed me. An article by Gladys Francis, with the title "Auschwitz Prisoner No. 42716 Now Clifton High School Girl" was published in 1947. The caption under my photograph read:

"Death Camp Survivors – 17-year-old Ruth Krautwirth and her mother, Mrs. Hanna Krautwirth, who survived Nazi atrocities and murder at Auschwitz, have found shelter at the Daughters of Miriam Home on Hazel Road. Her father is missing, but her brother, she learned recently, is in Palestine. Ruth will resume her study of music, which was interrupted by the Nazis."

The article reads:

"While some of the terrifying experiences of Ruth Krautwirth may fade into unreality at times, she has only to look at her forearm where the number 42716 is tattooed to bring back to mind some two years of mental and physical anguish which she suffered in her native Germany under Hitler's rule.

Ruth, who is now a 17-year-old student at Clifton High School, is disinclined to make capital of her story, but she feels strongly that Americans who have accepted the Nazi brutality stories in their stride because of their repetition or who are half-disposed not to believe them, should be impressed with the truth of the criminal treatment accorded all who failed to accept Nazi doctrine."

The article briefly describes my experiences at Auschwitz and Malchow, and then concludes:

"While Ruth gives full credit to the Germans for their native abilities in the fields of music and science, they are helpless, she said, without a leader. Unless Americans give full credence to the stories of their brutality and maintain constant vigilance of their affairs, the process of the two world wars will be repeated, she believes."

"She and Mrs. Krautwirth are living at the Daughters of Miriam home on Hazel Road. Ruth's ambition is to become an X-ray technician and to earn enough money so that the family may start life over again. The one note of cheer in their situation is their having learned that Ruth's brother is now safe in Palestine, and they hope for a reunion with him when matters can be arranged."

In general, life was very difficult for survivors arriving from Europe after the war. Most of us were without family, with our whole background destroyed, and without any means of support. I did not want to be a burden on HIAS; I considered it a charity, and I wanted to get away from it as quickly as possible. However, to do that we really had to struggle.

Although the woman from the newspaper showed interest in my story, I am not happy to talk about the way that other people reacted to us survivors once we got to the United States. It seemed like we were not treated as having gone through the experiences that we had gone through. Somehow, we were not treated as equal human beings. We were told to take work as laborers, as domestics, and that sort of thing. In general, I found that a lot of people had the reaction that everything and everyone European was inferior.

I remember overhearing one of the American women, who happened to be not so good-looking, loudly complaining at the gym that the European women were stealing all the men. I retorted back, "Just look at me, then look at you, and you'll know why!" I recall that she acquiesced after that.

One of my first jobs after high school was working in a science lab at Barnard College. One day we did an experiment with cyanide. I remarked that the experiment smelled like Auschwitz. The others were taken aback by my comment and started to discuss the effect of smell on memory and experience. They were interested in my experience from that angle.

I became active in a local committee of survivors attempting to organize a Holocaust commemoration. The men who worked on it before me told me they had faced a lot of resistance to having a memorial ceremony or even speaking about their experiences. No one wanted to listen. The people just did not want to hear about it. Maybe they did not believe it really happened. These survivors had difficulty getting a stage to conduct a memorial service. It would only become fashionable much later – in the 1970s – to speak about the Holocaust and not to consider it a badge of shame, which it was not.

Many of us survivors tried to forget the past and start life anew. We did not want to dwell on the atrocities. We did not want to speak about what had happened or to relive the pain. Instead, we tried to look forward, to move on. We were told to get over it, and for the most part, we all wanted to get on with our lives. We could not bring our loved ones back. What good did it do to dwell on it every day? As prisoners of the Nazis, we survivors had been told that we were *Untermenschen*, that we were not up to par. I think it had been so drilled into us that some of us kept believing it was true. What we really should have had was a lot of counseling.

The charitable organizations were focused on more immediate needs: clothing us, feeding us, and finding shelter for us. What was not known at the time was that post-traumatic stress is awful, and people need as much help psychologically as they need physically. It should have been considered just as important as our other needs. It is very important to get help immediately. The importance of counseling is one of the things that has been learned since then. Now most people receive mental health help after hostage, war, or other traumatizing situations. This is one of the things that cannot be stressed enough. There would not have been any resources for the mass of survivors to go to therapy. Many survivors floundered or have had terrible, traumatic lives, even after the war, due to their experiences. The suicide rate among survivors demonstrates this. How could we be expected to live with the pain while trying to rebuild our lives? The burden was almost too great.

I never went to any therapy. I was numb from the experiences in Auschwitz. I felt as though I was sort of drifting through life without really having a real purpose and without realizing my potential, like an animal just following an instinct. There were great opportunities for me, but I did not take them. It was a real mistake I made. I did not take them because, well, depressed was probably the best word to describe how I felt.

Love, Ruth

Harry – my husband, your grandpa

Dear Lauren,

Harry and I married on December 5, 1948. I was 19 years old. Harry was 27. We were young, but it was a normal age at which to marry at the time.

As a teenager in the United States, I often moped around and stayed home. I graduated from high school. I did a lot of reading while my mother was working. All I wanted to do was read, and I was very anxious to improve my English. My mother didn't like the idea of my being home by myself all the time reading. She told a young woman she knew to take me out with her whenever she went out. There was a dance at the Y in Paterson, New Jersey. This friend of my mother and I went to it together, but she somehow disappeared, and I was left there alone.

It was at this dance when I found myself alone that I met Harry Meyerowitz. A woman named Mrs. Kraus introduced us. Harry asked me to dance, but I did not really want to. I was not thinking of dating, and I did not really want to go out, so I just said to him I would dance for that evening and then go home. He offered to walk me home afterward, but I did not let him. But he was persistent! A few days later, I saw Harry again near the City Hall. I was walking along on one side of the street. He was walking along the other side of the street and then crossed the street and tried to catch up. He met me at the bus stop. After that, he convinced me to give it a try, and so we started dating. That's how it began.

We called your Grandpa Harry by his nickname, Hershel. His Hebrew name was Tzvi. He died when you were just a baby in 1986. You may not remember him, but he loved you, your brother, and your cousins very much. He thought you were a real beauty.

Harry was born June 24, 1921. Since my birthday is June 23, we would celebrate our birthdays together. Harry was born and raised in Paterson, New Jersey. He was the youngest of four siblings. Al and Abe were his older brothers. Cele was his older sister.

His father, Benjamin, was born in 1880 in Russia and emigrated to the United States through Ellis Island in 1892. Harry's father died on January 21, 1936, at age 56, when Harry was just 14 years old. This was during the Great Depression. It was a difficult time for the Meyerowitz family.

His mother, Esther, was born in Grodno, Russia, and had also emigrated to the United States sometime before 1910. After Benjamin died, Esther remarried a farmer, Mr. Goldman, who owned Fair Lawn Dairies. They were relatively well off. His mother sent Harry to live with his older sister, Cele, for a while because her new husband was not tolerant of having him around.

After high school, Harry went for some college and military training in Oregon. After the war, he went to Rutgers University in New Jersey, where he earned an undergraduate degree in accounting.

Harry was an American soldier during the war. He served in the 89th Infantry Division. This division was one of the first American divisions to advance into Germany and liberate concentration camps. In April 1945, he and his troops liberated Ohrdruf, a subcamp of Buchenwald. Ohrdruf was later visited and documented by General Eisenhower, so the liberation of Ohrdruf became rather well known.

To Harry, I was brave enough to survive the camp. He understood what incredible strength, luck, and perseverance this required. To him, I was certainly to be treated as an equal human being. Unfortunately, his mother Esther did not go along with this. Even though she was born in Eastern Europe, to her, everything that was European was lowly, despised, and despicable. She wanted to stay away from everything European and not have anything to do with it, so she thought I was not good enough for her son. I had no money and I was an immigrant – these were not easy selling points for Esther. She even called me a German! I had a lot of problems with her.

But my life with Harry was good. We started our family fur business together. We used to joke that if we had to do it all over again, we would marry each other again... but, since December is the busiest month for us in fur retail, that we would opt for July!

Love, Ruth

Our three sons

Dear Lauren,

There was always a deep sense of responsibility and empathy for the Jewish people in our household. Let me tell you a bit about the adventures of your father and uncles when they were young. My three sons have made me very proud.

When World War II ended in 1945, the Jewish world was stunned by its losses. We never supposed that any sizable group of Jews was left alive anywhere in Eastern Europe. But then the famous writer of the Holocaust Elie Wiesel visited Russia and came back with terrible tales of spiritual and ethnic genocide against the three million Jews still living in the Soviet Union. He even wrote a book: *The Jews of Silence*. Many young people, including my three sons, took this threat very seriously. They saw a repetition of the events of the 1930s and 1940s, and they were determined to speak up, to call the fate of Soviet Jews to the attention of the world, and not to stand by idly while people were tortured and worse. To be sure, persecutions in Russia were not the same as they had been in Nazi Germany, but one tyranny is not much different from another.

The boys became active on United Synagogue Youth (USY) trips, including some to Russia in 1973. At just 18 years of age, your dad was over there meeting with the dissidents, talking and walking in forbidden areas, encouraging them, and giving them hope. It must have been a revelation to these Jews, who were deprived of any real news, to meet with Jewish youths who were free and able to do as they wished in their country. All who were involved in the Soviet Jewry movement felt that the more publicity their plight received, the better their chances to emigrate, or to live the life they chose as Jews even while in the Soviet Union.

When your father returned, he went on a speaking tour to everywhere and everyone who was willing to listen. He made phone calls to Russia to show the Soviet secret police that the American public was aware and concerned with human rights there. Your father (assuming that the line was being tapped) told his friend that he would take this matter up with the President of the United States – no little *chutzpah* for an 18-year-old.

Your Uncle Allan was in Russia that year, too. He took with him money for the continuation of the dissident movement, brought in pictures from families who were separated, and brought vitamins disguised as candy. I think his work was so dangerous we could have lost him, and no one would have been able to help. What I think about it is, your uncle is one of the most righteous men we Jews can be proud of. But if his father and I had known in advance what he was planning for that trip, we would have locked him in his room for the summer.

Allan was arrested seven times for demonstrating in front of the Soviet Embassy in Washington, D.C., to "let my people go." Not every parent is proud to call his son a jailbird. His father and I were proud.

During the 1973 trip, your father visited the mass graves at Babi Yar. In 1974, your Uncle Norman went to Russia and Poland. Norman's group visited Auschwitz-Birkenau. I had been open about my experiences with the boys. Perhaps I was more open to discussion than other survivors at that time. It was not shocking to me that they would be interested in seeing the sights from the war. It's part of their history and identity.

From your father's singing of "Hatikvah" in Red Square with dissidents, to Uncle Allan's involvement on behalf of other Jews by doing such things as calling newspapers and going on the radio to speak out, to Norman's deep connection with his heritage, I think we Jews have overcome the image of the Ghetto Jew who accepts every injustice from others as it is dished out. After a long, sad history and much anguish, we have become a proud people.

Uncle Allan attended the University of Rochester and was on the premed track. However, unknown to his father and me, he applied to the Jewish Theological Seminary and had early acceptance. At that point he dropped all the courses he could drop and concentrated on humanism. The one course he could not drop was microbiology. In those days it was very difficult to be admitted to American medical schools, and good grades were part of this intense competition that went on. Since his focus was already on spiritual matters, he got a B+. An A- was the minimum expected for medical school admission. He sat down to write his father and me a very serious letter telling us of his decision to change career paths. In a lifetime, one collects all sorts of trivia. Unfortunately, I cannot find this letter. The gist of it was that he was motivated by a sense of responsibility to the Jewish people and that he lived to make good on this statement. Every Sunday evening when he knew we would be at home, Allan called. The Sunday after the letter, his first question was whether we had read his letter. Then he went on to tell us that he saw his calling to the rabbinate as a sign from God, for if God had wanted him to be a doctor, He would have given him an A!

Love, Ruth

Passover lessons

Dear Ruth,

Do you remember when Uncle Allan and Aunt Robin hosted that huge Passover seder in Winnipeg? I was in middle school. You and I flew in from New Jersey to spend the week for the holiday. My aunt and uncle, as the rabbi and *rebbetzin*,[1] prepared their home like madmen to host at least 30 people from the congregation that night. Chaos abounded. I played with my cousins and had a great time with you helping to cook chicken soup with matzah balls.

Uncle Allan made the seder meaningful by making everyone think of how the Exodus story applied to their lives here today. He paused in

---

1. Wife of the rabbi (Yiddish).

between the passages being read in Hebrew to ask everyone to close their eyes and imagine what it must have been like to leave Egypt. Did you grab your favorite shirt? Did you take your pet dog? Did you have food cooking on the stove?

You are supposed to retell the Exodus story as though you personally had lived it, he told us. Close your eyes and remember what it was like to be a slave. Was it hot out? Did you sweat when carrying bricks on your back? How did the matzah taste? If our forefathers had not left Egypt, he told us, we would still be there today.

In your generation, the words of the Haggadah can be taken quite literally, that they rose up against us to annihilate us. Passover was a particularly difficult time for you. It was Erev Pesach 1943 that your family was called for deportation, so it was the last time your family was all together. I think you felt a sense of uneasiness and discomfort at Passover, but you tried to get it out of your mind by staying busy with the cooking, cleaning, and other preparations for the holiday.

Albeit difficult to do, I tried to imagine what it was like leaving Egypt and moving from slavery to freedom. Yet, here you were with me – someone who had experienced imprisonment and liberation in her lifetime – so my cousins and I asked you to explain to us what it was *really* like.

What was it like to have been deported to Auschwitz on the first day of this holiday that celebrates our freedom from Egypt? Does celebrating Passover make you think of your own liberation?

Love, Lauren

Dear Lauren,

On Pesach I often find myself thinking of my own experience of deportation, imprisonment, and liberation. It takes a lot of living to take a small step toward understanding.

When I was a child going to school in Frankfurt, our required courses were Hebrew language, Jewish history, customs, prayers, holidays – in short, every aspect of Jewish life.

When we studied the Ten Commandments, the last eight were easy to understand. You shall not do this, or you must do that. But the first commandment, and by extension the second, seemed not even like commandments. But life is the best educator.

I have come closer to understanding God's meaning: "I am the Lord your God who brought you out of the land of Egypt, out of the house of bondage. You shall have no other God before me..."

You cannot idolize another God (for there is no other), and you must not deify a tyrant, or any human for that matter.

How galling it must have been for Moses to have just received this declaration of human freedom and proudly brought it to the people, only to be greeted by the sight of an idol. Since these commandments were given, wars for individual liberty have been based on this greatest of liberating declarations.

How arrogant for Hitler to declare himself *Der Führer* – the leader of the country, the head of the master race. He saw himself as the redeemer of Germany, a god-like man to be idolized and worshipped. By law his image was required in every public place, and it was to be hung higher than the crucifix in that Christian country.

He was their golden calf, their savior! How wicked for the German people to follow him like God. They followed him as though he was the messiah. They followed blindly for the 12 years of the Third Reich.

The Haggadah tells us that in every generation an evil one will arise to try to destroy us, a tyrant who will challenge our liberties and try to wrest authority from God and appropriate it for himself. (But God in His wisdom makes it easy for us: He conveniently supplies us in every generation with this enemy.) And in every generation, we must fight anew to preserve the rights of the individual, and so by extension the rights of the community. And after every struggle, we see the strength of God emerging victorious over the enemy.

We read in the Haggadah that every Jew must consider himself or herself personally to have been redeemed from Egypt, to have been personally present at the receiving of the law. Because we were there personally, the law is as valid for us today as it was then.

"I am the God who brought you out of Egypt... you shall have no other God before me." Honor only *Hashem*. Do not idolize any man or tyrant who pretends to be Him. I lived through what can happen when man disobeys this commandment and worships a tyrant as a deity, so I have come to learn the significance that I had never quite grasped as a child.

Knowing our history will sensitize you. It will keep you aware. It will make you appreciate your Jewish heritage as something precious, as something worth fighting to keep alive. Our rich Jewish identity is something that must not be taken lightly or cheaply as others attempt to destroy us and, in the process, defame humanity.

Love, Ruth

THE FATE OF OUR FRIENDS AND FAMILY

Zev's experience

Dear Lauren,

We learned Zev's whereabouts from the American soldier who collected information on people from Frankfurt.

Zev survived Auschwitz-Birkenau and the death march out of Birkenau. He survived Sachsenhausen and Mauthausen concentration camps. After being liberated at Mauthausen, the British Army's Jewish Brigade, which was made up of Jews from British-mandate Palestine, collected the orphaned children and took them to a DP camp in Bari, Italy. In Italy, they made a bar mitzvah for all the young boys around age 13, including my brother, who had just turned 12 in May 1945.

The Jewish Brigade was connected with underground Jewish military operations in Palestine, and they were anxious to get the children to Palestine. Zev was taken with the other Jewish boys from Italy to Palestine by boat. Zev traveled on a ship named *Francis Katon* and arrived in Palestine on November 8, 1945. The British were still highly restricting the movement of survivors to British-mandate Palestine. The orphaned minors were the only ones the British were allowing in legally. They were excluded from the British quota system.

We later learned about Zev's experiences in the last two years of the war and in Palestine, which became Israel in 1948.

Zev had just turned 11 years old in the spring of 1944, when the SS transferred him from the women's camp, where he was with our mother and me, to the children's barracks in the men's camp at Birkenau. We believed that, by then, our father was no longer alive and no longer in the men's camp.

In the children's barracks, Zev was with many children and teenagers who had been in the Lodz ghetto in Poland. The children were given work moving items around the camp. They had to pull a wagon, collect junk and garbage, and move it all around the camp, all while starving and looking for food from other prisoners.

Zev remembered going to seek food in the block of the *Sonderkommando*, the group of Jews forced to work in the crematoria burning the bodies. They often had enough food to spare a little for Zev. He later told us about a man in the *Sonderkommando* who gave him a little bit of vodka, and he became slightly intoxicated. The prisoners had to take off their hats every time they passed a German. The punishment for not taking your hat off on time was 10 or 15 lashes. Zev went back to his block and passed an SS officer along the way. He only just managed to take his hat off as required. During his stay in the men's camp, three times he received a beating of three lashes but does not recall why.

He remembered some of the non-Jewish Polish prisoners in the camp. He thought that the children's relationship with the Polish prisoners was quite good. On one occasion, a Polish prisoner, seeing him, lashed out at the Germans, using some choice Polish obscenities in the process, for keeping children as prisoners in the camp.

In the summer of 1944, the Germans hung the Polish head of a barracks. Rumor had it that he was in contact with the Polish underground. All prisoners had to be present at the execution. Zev told us that the children were excluded from attending the hanging – ironically, given that they were exposed to everything else.

Zev told us that children were exempt from roll call, but there was still a selection process for them. The children from the block had to pass under a rope. If they were shorter than roughly a meter forty (four feet seven inches), they would be exterminated. Those who did not reach the height of the rope were taken out of the children's barracks to the gas chamber.

In the summer of 1944, another boy and Zev were the only two selected. They were too short, so they were slated for extermination. Zev started to cry. One of the two SS sergeants in charge returned him to the rest of the children. He did not know why and thought perhaps it was because he spoke German. The other child was sent to his death.

Zev clearly remembered another two events in Birkenau. One was the gassing of the inmates of the Roma camp in August 1944. The other was the uprising of the Sonderkommando in October 1944.

Sometime toward the end of 1944, Zev got an infection in his arm that caused bone damage. He was sent to the infirmary. Normally patients in the infirmary did not get treatment and did not get better but instead were sent with the next group to the gas chambers. Surprisingly, they treated him in the hospital. A Jewish doctor who was also a prisoner performed surgery on his arm, with an ether anesthetic and all, to cut out the infection. The infection healed right away, and he was sent back into the children's barrack.

Zev remained in Auschwitz-Birkenau until January 1945, when the Nazis evacuated the prisoners as the Soviet troops approached from the east. Zev survived this death march. After days of forced marching, the group of boys he was with from the children's barrack arrived at Gleiwitz, Poland. From there they went by train to Sachsenhausen, a concentration camp near Berlin. They spent a few days at that camp. One of the Polish prisoners, by the name of Yane, who must have held a privileged position, took a group of the children under his wing and somehow provided them with food.

From Sachsenhausen, Zev continued by cattle car trains to Mauthausen concentration camp in Austria. During this leg of the trip, when the train stopped in Czechoslovakia, citizens standing behind the guards threw food to the prisoners. This was something that did not happen while they traveled through Germany and Austria.

In Mauthausen, conditions got progressively worse. The prisoners received even less food than in Birkenau. They had to sit outside the barracks for hours. It was cold, and they were shivering.

Later – it must have been early April 1945 – the Germans in charge at Mauthausen drafted all the German inmates for military service. The German inmates were probably political prisoners or common criminals. The SS took that motley crew, gave them wooden guns, and marched them around singing military songs. The story was that they were training to go to Yugoslavia to fight the partisans. According to my brother, this scene tells us something about the German mind. The Nazis were a few weeks away from final defeat, and they were focused on training prisoners to go fight partisans.

All the Jewish prisoners were put into a big tent outside the main camp. Conditions got even worse. One day, an Allied plane bombed the camp. The guards started to run around screaming. It was later reported by survivors that some prisoners cannibalized the victims of the bombing.

Zev stayed in Mauthausen until April 1945. He was then marched to a subcamp called Gunskirchen, which was in the woods. There the prisoners were placed in overcrowded barracks. One day the German guards gave the prisoners food packages that had been provided by the Canadian Red Cross.

A few days after being taken to Gunskirchen, Zev heard shooting early in the morning. Suddenly, the Germans guards were gone. He walked out in one direction of the highway. American troops appeared from the opposite direction. Zev was freed by these US Forces in early May 1945, just a week or so before his 12th birthday.

When Zev arrived in Palestine in November 1945, at age 12, he was able to meet up with our father's brother Uncle Abba and his wife, Rachel. Uncle Abba found him. Zev was too young to have remembered our uncle from before the war. I remembered Abba – he was the opera singer who ate raw eggs. He had been dismissed from his job in 1933, the year Zev was born, and he left for Palestine in 1936.

Zev didn't live with Uncle Abba, but they spent holidays together. Zev lived in the places where the Jewish Agency[1] put him. The Youth Aliyah Department of the Jewish Agency placed him in Mossad Yakir, then Mossad Aliyah, and then Sdeh Eliahu Youth III. He lived with other children on a kibbutz organized through B'nai Brith and went to school. At first Zev was part of a nonreligious kibbutz and later a religious one. At that time, the emphasis was not on learning. It was on building a state and feeding the population.

In 1948, Israel fought the British for independence and then the neighboring Arab countries, which attacked the newly independent Jewish state. During this time, Zev lived on a children's kibbutz in Petah Tikvah. The children worked and helped with the war effort during the War of Independence. During that war, they were

---

1. The Jewish Agency for Israel, known at the time as the Jewish Agency for Palestine, was an organization established in 1929 under the British Mandate to promote Jewish immigration as part of the creation of a Jewish national homeland and to serve as the Jewish liaison for affairs in that homeland. They were active in resettling Jewish refugees in Palestine after the Holocaust.

evacuated from the kibbutz and taken to a safe house. Zev remembered the enemy army bombing and shelling the area, so many children had to hide in trenches. During this evacuation, Zev stayed behind as a means to show his resistance because he felt the need for a Jewish state so strongly.

After Zev's studies at the kibbutz concluded, he worked for a while.

In 1951, he joined the Israeli Army. He belonged to a combat unit, although no major combat took place at the time. He was a combat engineer and was trained in building bridges and other infrastructure.

However, since he had been hurt in Auschwitz and had surgery on his arm, he could not lift that arm above shoulder height. Unfortunately, the army considered my brother to be disabled because of the limited mobility in his shoulder. In 1953, the army sent him to a convalescent home, where he said he pretty much did nothing all day long. They performed a reparative surgery on his shoulder to try to increase the mobility. By 1954, he was disqualified and discharged. After being discharged, my brother felt out of place in Israel, since everyone else his age served in the army.

Zev left Israel in 1954 at the age of 21 and joined us in the United States. He later said he would have just come to the United States for a visit with family, but at the time it was expensive to go back and forth.

Our reunion in 1954 was the first time my mother and I had seen Zev since we were separated. The journey from Israel to the United States was very long in those days. Zev went by plane, but flights took several days. He finally arrived, and it was a much-anticipated reunion!

At first Zev lived with me, Harry, and little Allan. After a short while he went to live in Passaic with Mutti instead. Before the war, we had spoken German at home, but we also knew some Polish and Yiddish.

None of us wanted to speak German anymore. We spoke Yiddish instead. Eventually we switched to speaking English at home.

Zev was too old for high school, so he studied for a high school equivalency diploma, similar to today's GED. For most topics he was just able to read a textbook, study for an exam, and pass; however, he took a course on elementary algebra to pass that test. Ironically, he once failed a German test because, although he could speak and understand the language, his grammar was poor. His elementary school education at the Philanthropin had been cut short.

Zev received his high school equivalency diploma in 1959 and began college at night at Seton Hall University. He started as a non-matriculated student, got good grades, and was then able to be a matriculated student. However, after completing about two years of coursework, he did not continue his studies. He began to work instead.

His first job was teaching Hebrew at a Jewish Center in Clifton, but he admittedly could not discipline the students or handle the class well. Later he taught at a different school in Perth Amboy for the Jewish community. Again, he felt ill-suited for teaching. He held some odd jobs after that. By 1975, Zev decided to start his own business selling candies, and he established Zev's Candy LLC. He had candy supplies delivered to him, and he did wholesale distribution. He was a self-employed businessman for the remainder of his career.

One day in 1962, Zev saw an ad in the Jewish newspaper for a dance in Manhattan at B'nai Jeshurun Synagogue. He decided to go all by himself. There he met his wife Sylvia. They married on my 34th birthday, June 23, 1963. Their son, Yitzhak David, was born on May 10, 1964, and their daughter, Rina, was born on January 31, 1981. They settled in Highland Park, New Jersey, and followed Modern Orthodox tradition.

Love, Ruth

Dear Ruth,

When telling his story, Zev was always proud that he arrived in Palestine legally. He would say that he was not part of Aliya Bet.[2] But the legality of Zev's immigration was questionable to me. Most survivors were moved to British-mandate Palestine illegally and had to pass British patrols when doing so. The Jewish Brigade was known to have acted without official authorization. As it turns out, my suspicions were confirmed. Israeli government records show that the *Francis Katon* brought passengers clandestinely. This means it was not legal according to the British law that was in effect at the time. I suppose the people in charge must have told the children otherwise, perhaps not to worry them, or perhaps because they did not recognize the authority of the British.

Did Zev ever receive the letter that you and Mutti wrote to him when he was in Bari, Italy? Did he know you were alive at the time he left for Palestine? You said you wrote to him in the fall of 1945, but he arrived in Palestine on November 8, 1945, meaning he left Italy around October 1945.

This detail seems lost to history. Most likely the letter never got there, or by the time it arrived, Zev had already embarked on the journey to Palestine.

But what if it had gotten to him? Would the people in charge have sent him to Palestine rather than reunite him with his mother and sister? I think it is unlikely. Would Zev have chosen to go to Israel anyway? Rina is not sure what he would have chosen to do in that situation but knows that he always felt strongly Zionistic. He

---

2. Clandestine immigration of 100,000 Jews to Palestine between 1920 and 1948, including 70,000 Holocaust survivors after World War II; "illegal immigration" under British law.

believed in a Jewish state for the Jewish people. Like many survivors, he may have yearned to go to Palestine with all his heart.

Ten years seems like an incredibly long time to take to reunite. You and Mutti were already reestablishing your lives in the United States while Zev did the same in Israel. It is hard for me to fathom how difficult it must have been to be apart, knowing he was alive, especially for Mutti. What was the process of trying to see one another? Did you and Mutti consider moving to Israel once it became a state? Zev was very much a believer in Zionism, so that may explain why he stayed in Israel and joined the army rather than leaving sooner for the United States.

Love, Lauren

Aunts and uncles

Dear Lauren,

Immediately after the war and in the following years, Mutti and I tried to find out as much information as we could about the fate of our relatives by placing advertisements in the Jewish newspapers. Everyone was doing this. There was a whole section of each newspaper devoted to family members looking for one another. We survivors had to rely on lists of names printed in local newspapers and on bulletin boards listing names at community centers. There were also radio programs where survivor names were read aloud.

On my paternal side my father's siblings were Lina, Abraham (Abba), Julius (Isidor), Mollie, Selma, and Fanny. Julius was dead; we had learned of his fate from his fiancée when we were in Frankfurt before our deportation. Selma also did not survive; I do not know how she died. Abba was in Palestine as I mentioned before. Lina, Mollie, and

Fanny also lived, because they had left for the United States before the war. We were able to get in touch with them after the war.

On my maternal side my mother's siblings were Mendel, Gitman, Cyma, Rifka, Malka, Moishe, and Bella. Mendel, Gitman, and Cyma, along with my mother's uncle, Moishe David, who was the one who originally took my mother from Poland to Germany in 1918, all lived because they had left Europe before the war for Argentina, Canada, Uruguay, and Israel respectively. Moishe, Rifka, and Malka were murdered in the Holocaust. I have no details.

Aunt Bella was the only one remaining in Europe to survive, although just barely. You'll recall Bella was the sister too squeamish to become a midwife like her mother. Bella lost her entire immediate family during the war, including her husband, a niece they had been raising as their own, and their two sons, ages six and two. Bella hid in the woods, fought with the partisans, and escaped from the Russian army. After the war, in a displaced persons camp Bella met Leon Radzelli. His name sounds Italian, but he was Jewish. He, too, had lost his entire family. Bella and Leon were married in the DP camp, where they had a daughter whom they named Gloria, after Bella's mother Gitl.

We knew that one of my mother's brothers, Gitman, had made his way to Toronto, Canada, before the war. By 1948, we decided to post an ad in the local newspaper there to look for him. Someone saw the ad. We received a phone call at our home in New Jersey. My mother answered and nearly fainted! The voice sounded like her father, although her father had died before the war.

It turned out to be Bella! Bella had a deep voice that resembled their father's. It was the first time that my mother had heard her sister's voice since my mother had left Poland for Germany in 1918. Amazingly enough, Bella informed us that their brother Mendel, who had been in Argentina, was also in Toronto!

That is how my mother found her brothers and sister, and they were reunited. It was exciting to learn that I had a cousin. And I must say, all the stories that I know of my mother's family, I learned from overhearing my mother and my Aunt Bella when they visited each other. They would exile my Uncle Leon out of his side of the bed and stay up all night reminiscing. This is, by all accepted standards, true research!

Love, Ruth

Sisters reunite

Dear Gloria,

Pease tell me the story of how Bella and Mutti found one another after the war.

Love, Lauren

Dear Lauren,

As your grandma probably told you, I am not a Holocaust survivor, but I was born "stateless" in a displaced persons camp in 1946. All survivors in the DP camps were considered stateless. They no longer had the citizenship of the countries from which they had originated. Survivors went as refugees, often to the United States and Canada, but were not considered citizens of those countries until the paperwork was complete.

My parents lost their immediate families in the war. They did not like to talk about it much when I was little. Their life before the war was considered a separate life, a distinct time and place, different from the here and now. My mother had two sons before the war. The older one was named Gitman after grandma Gitl, who I am also named after. I do not even know the name of the younger one. Someone once asked me if I have ever said anything in my brothers' memory during the Yizkor[3] service. I have not; my mother never presented them to me as my brothers or half-brothers; rather, they were her sons before the war.

After my parents married and I was born, we went to Canada in May 1948. They were able to get back in touch with my mother's brother Gitman, who had left for Canada in the 1920s.

A few months after we arrived, my parents saw an ad in the Jewish newspaper in the section where relatives were looking for one another. It seemed like someone in New Jersey was looking for my Uncle Gitman. My mother answered the ad. We all gathered together and called the phone number listed. It appeared to be my mother's sister Chana!

I was very young and just remember that everyone in the room was crying on the phone. No one could even speak. Neither Gitman, nor my parents, nor my aunt on the other end of the phone, could get out any words. Everyone was just in shock. We were amazed that the others were alive and had survived. "You survived!?" I remember my mother was uttering in disbelief between her sobs to her older sister.

After finding one another, my mother and her sister kept in touch. It was not until my parents and I were Canadian citizens in 1954 that we could travel. We embarked on our trip to New Jersey to see my Aunt Chana and my cousins, Ruth and Zev. I was eight years old when we traveled from Canada to New York by train. It was around Christmastime. The train ride must have been 12 hours or so, and I remember it being a very long ride.

I was worried at that time that my mother and aunt would not be able

---

3. Memorial service held on certain holidays for deceased parents and relatives.

to recognize one another. They had last seen each other when my aunt was 17 years old and my mother was just five. As it turned out, although my mother was taller, they were practically identical; they certainly looked like sisters.

We arrived at Grand Central Station in New York. My Aunt Chana, my cousin Ruth, and Ruth's husband, Harry, and little Allan, were supposed to meet us there. There was some mishap or miscommunication, and the train was delayed. We emerged from the train station with our luggage. The crowd seemed to disperse. Our family must have come and gone, because no one was at the train station to greet us when we arrived. Since we had their family address, my mother must have decided that we should try to make our way to New Jersey.

Some other people who had been on the same train were taking a taxi to the bus station, so we shared a cab. It must have been one o'clock in the morning. We had no idea how to get to Fair Lawn, New Jersey, but we were intent on figuring it out.

We boarded a bus to New Jersey. My mother spoke to the bus driver and gave him the address of where we were going. I remember dozing off over the suitcases and not being so worried.

When the bus arrived in Fair Lawn, the bus driver explained that he could not detour to the street we needed, but he pointed out to us how to get there. He said to go straight down the road. If it wasn't correct, there was a taxi stand at the end.

We were walking down the street carrying all our heavy luggage, with no idea where we were going, when suddenly we heard someone yell, "Bella!" Someone was calling my mother! It was her sister!

It must have been two at night at this point. Our relatives were outside on the street looking for us. They had been at the train station earlier but seeing as we were not there had returned home by car and arrived just before us. Apparently, they had telephoned someone back in Toronto to ask what we were wearing so that they could recognize us. It was not common to place international calls in the 1950s.

Once we were all reunited as a family, everyone just started talking all at once. As a kid, I found it all very exciting!

That first night of their reunion in 1954, after not having seen one another in 36 years, my mother and aunt stayed up all night talking. After some two hours I must have fallen asleep. When I awoke at 8:00 a.m., my mother and aunt were still talking!

It was a wonderful reunion. This was also just two days after Zev had arrived from Israel, so it was all very exciting.

After this, my mother and aunt would visit each other regularly. They had lots of years of talking to catch up on. My father used to say that when they stayed up all night talking, one would talk while the other would sleep, and then they would switch. I used to try to stay up to listen to it all.

Years later, my mother asked her sister what had taken so long for them to place an ad in the Toronto newspaper to look for Gitman. They had arrived in the United States in 1947 but waited a whole year to place the ad. Why wait?

I remember Chana's answer being very indicative of her personality. In 1947 she had just arrived as a survivor with a child. She did not want anyone to think she could not function on her own or was looking for a handout. She did not want to seem desperate or needy. By 1948 she felt much more financially secure and in a better position to reach out. Chana had a very independent character.

Although they looked alike, my mother and my aunt had different personalities. They even had different accents because my mother's accent was Polish, while Chana's sounded more like German. My mother was crazy about her sister. My mother had a more serious personality, while Chana really had a sense of humor. She was funny, very warm, and a terrific cook. She always looked so put together and had a certain graceful elegance about her.

Your grandma Ruth had a different personality than her mother and didn't physically resemble her very much. Ruth seemed more energetic. I think that growing up in Nazi Germany and spending all those years in Auschwitz at her age, even though she was with her mother, had really affected her. She was imprisoned during her formative years, so it shaped her identity more than it did my parents and aunt, who had lived many years of their lives before the war. Ruth became very strong.

Love, Gloria

Finding Harvey Saalberg

2006

Dear Ruth,

After the war, you reunited with one of your elementary school classmates, Harvey Saalberg. As far as you were aware, Harvey was the only other surviving classmate from the Philanthropin School. Please tell me about Harvey and how you found each other.

Love, Lauren

2006

Dear Lauren,

Harvey Saalberg was born in Frankfurt am Main on April 7, 1929, making him almost three months older than me. His mother was

Lutheran, and his father was Jewish. According to Nazi racial theory, this made him a *Mischling* [mixed-blooded] but still considered a Jew under Nazi German law. Like other Jews, he was not allowed to attend public school, so he attended the Philanthropin School.

Throughout 1942–1943, Harvey performed forced labor, cleaning the streets of Frankfurt and removing debris from bombings. His family lost everything in the mass bombings of Frankfurt on October 3–4, 1943.

Harvey's paternal grandparents were deported and murdered in concentration camps. Although Harvey and his father were originally protected by his mother's status, their turn came in February 1945 to follow their family and friends to the concentration camps. Harvey and his father spent four months in Theresienstadt until May 1945. Harvey was tasked with building barracks and moving corpses from one location to another.

After the liberation on May 5, 1945, he and his father were reunited with Harvey's mother in Frankfurt. The family left Germany for the United States in 1946. Having only a seventh-grade education at age 17, Harvey worked minimum wage jobs and attended high school at night. He began college and was drafted into the United States Army. He served in Korea.

On March 20, 1951, Harvey married Gloria Ann Ellis at the Grace Episcopalian Church in New York. They had three daughters and later seven grandsons and a great-granddaughter. Gloria was Christian, and Harvey did not practice or identify with any religion after the Holocaust. He decided to disassociate from Judaism. His family was raised in the Christian tradition, as was his wife's preference. Being half-Jewish and half-Christian to begin with, my impression is that, it must have been easier for him to choose Christianity.

Harvey finished college, earned a master's degree, and became a high school teacher. Then he earned a PhD at the University of Missouri. He became a college professor.

Harvey was a professor at Kent State University and was there on May 4, 1970, when the Ohio National Guard shot at unarmed students, killing four students in an event that is now known as the Kent State Massacre. He was interviewed and quoted in a book written about the event, *Kent State: What Happened and Why,* by James A. Michener.

I bought a copy of the book. While reading it, I came across Harvey's name and immediately recognized it as my former classmate. I contacted the publisher, then the author, and finally got Harvey's contact information. Harvey and I were able to meet up and exchange stories. We kept in touch for many years and became good friends.

He wrote to me once about taking his daughter Julie to see Steven Spielberg's *Schindler's List* on opening night. The poor girl cried through almost the entire film.

Once he retired, Harvey began to speak on the Holocaust. He felt compelled to do so despite the difficulty of it. We even compiled a list of classmates' names and submitted them to the Shoah Victims Database.

Love, Ruth

2017

Dear Ruth,

I am writing you this letter in the year 2017, and you are no longer here. I am writing to express things I wish I could tell you but cannot.

In October 2012, I was fortunate enough to meet Harvey and his family. Harvey showed signs of Alzheimer's disease and could not speak much.

Harvey had written his life story in a manuscript for his family to keep. He still had some of the items from his war years. This includes his Theresienstadt ration cards and the Star of David with *Jude* on it that he was required to wear. It also includes Theresienstadt fake "Jewish" money picturing antisemitic images of a rabbi with a big nose counting coins.

The most memorable part of the visit was hearing Harvey's recollections of your friendship with Irma. He recalled that you and she were inseparable.

Harvey passed away on September 30, 2013. He was survived by his wife and daughters.

Love, Lauren

Seeking any trace of Uncle Julius

2006

Dear Lauren,

"What did you expect to find?" My mother's words from many years before came back to my mind. Yes, what did I expect to find?

After the Iron Curtain fell, I hoped to be able to obtain any information from the Czech government about my uncle's fate. Yet, it seemed no one could provide me with any information. In 1998 I traveled to Pilsen in the Czech Republic, hoping to find a part of my Uncle Julius.

I had not seen him since I was four. In the evenings after work, he came to his married brother's house for dinner and a romp with his only niece. Julius wrote for a local newspaper. What did he write? Was he good at what he did? I was only four and did not know then that I would not see my uncle again. I never would. One day, he was gone. His fiancée had informed us that he was hurt in a motorcycle chase with the SS, taken to a hospital, and then shot by the SS.

Pilsen did not yield what I had hoped, against my better knowledge. Since my uncle was shot there, I had hoped to find his grave. But the office listed him as deported, as well as Mr. Lederer, the man whom my father met several times at the park to discuss plans to help Jews get out of Germany.

Now I know Uncle Julius was killed somewhere else. No other trace is left. Learning he had been deported, and most likely killed in a concentration camp, was not only contrary to the information we had received from his fiancée at the time but also the opposite of what I had traveled there hoped to find. I felt extremely saddened by this newly discovered information.

I walked the streets of Pilsen, where I imagined he once had walked with the woman he was engaged to, holding hands and hoping that the madness called Nazism would go away, play itself out, and restore Europe to normal times filled with all the everyday things that make up life. I wished for their sakes that they were able to grab as much from life as this miserable existence permitted.

Only a few Jews of Pilsen survived. The remaining survivors were probably scattered to the four corners of the world. The Jewish population of the city was a fraction of what it once used to be.

The government of the Czech Republic has restored Jewish cemeteries, houses, and synagogues. The synagogue in Pilsen is one humongous building. I was told it had been the largest in Europe.

There is a *bimah*,[4] where once a *chazan*[5] or even a professional conductor led the chorus. I could imagine the worshippers of the past, their lofty prayers garbed in music and accompanied by a million tears of the devoted. The walls of the synagogue are clad halfway up in marble, as befits such a prestigious house of worship.

I was the only visitor to the synagogue that summer day. I stood in silence, unable to form a thought or even to bring up any emotion. The next day I left, but with the nagging feeling that there was something I did not find, and I did not know where to look or what it would mean. After the experience of Pilsen, I left Europe two days early, very depressed.

In my dreams soon after I returned to Pilsen, to the synagogue. I could feel the presence of the Jews of Pilsen. I did not hear them, but I knew they were there, surrounding me, not clawing at me, not crowding me. It was Simchat Torah, and they were dancing with the Torah scrolls and thanking God for the gift of Torah, for the love of family, and for the pleasure of just being alive. Souls, thousands of them... no, millions. Silently surrounding me, showing me the treasure that they held in their arms. I could sense Uncle Julius among them. I stood near to him. How long were we thus united? I do not know how long I stood, lost in the past, pleasured by his presence. I awoke filled with a sense of accomplishment.

Love, Ruth

Dear Ruth,

I have researched the fate of Uncle Julius to learn whether there was any more information on his writing or his death. Unfortunately, I

---

4. Altar in a synagogue (Hebrew).
5. Cantor, person who leads the congregation in prayers through singing (Hebrew).

have some unsettling news. At the age of 43 he died in Auschwitz-Birkenau after two months of imprisonment. Three sources corroborate Julius's fate: the Shoah Victims Database, the Theresienstadt Museum, and the Auschwitz Office for Information on Former Prisoners. The official history, kept so pristinely by the Nazis in the Auschwitz Death Books, is as follows:

Name: Isidor Krautwirth

Born: January 22, 1899 in Frankfurt a. M., son of Jacob and Rosa (maiden name Wertheim)

Place of Residence before Deportation: Pilsen, Mansfeldgasse 1

Deportation: From Pilsen to the Ghetto Theresienstadt, October 24, 1942

Deportation: From the Ghetto Theresienstadt to Auschwitz, October 26, 1942

Death: Auschwitz, January 4, 1943

Official Cause of Death: Heart insufficiency with influenza

Prisoner Number: 71133

This information certainly puts him in Pilsen at the time of his deportation to Auschwitz via the transit camp Theresienstadt. The Auschwitz camp records also show him as having been admitted to room 7 of Auschwitz block 28, the so-called internal medicine ward for sick patients. The cause of death listed, "heart muscle insufficiency" was the same so-called reason given as your father. The archivist said that the Nazis frequently used this description without greater detail to hide the nature of the crime. I asked if she knew the real cause. Did he die of the flu, or a heart attack, or was he selected for the gas chambers? She did not.

Love, Lauren

A lifetime of longing for Poppie

Dear Lauren,

When I read Shakespeare's *Hamlet*, part of my coursework toward earning a master's degree in English literature, I so clearly understood Hamlet's emotions and found a common link with him. He, too, had returned to find his past obliterated, his values turned upside down, and his emotions without an outlet and invalidated, all because of the workings of unexplained evil.

Hamlet, having been absent in the last days of his father's life, wills himself to see his father's apparition. So strong is his yearning, his need to be near this beloved man, that he even calls the guards and his friend Horatio to testify to the ghost's existence. So much had remained undone and so much left unsaid between father and son that it spilled over from the unconscious and showed itself in the only way possible for nescient man. This scene is the essence of the play; the rest, as Hillel famously said, is commentary.

Some students in my English literature class struggled with the relevance of the ghost scenes. I, on the other hand, understood and found meaning in Hamlet's search for just one more meeting with his beloved murdered father.

Here is the story I wrote for that class based on the ghost scene of Hamlet, set in what is now Oświęcim, Poland. I've titled it "Longing for Poppie."

All day the wind had raged through the spare clusters of trees. Most of the visitors had chosen to leave this eerie place and seek the greater comfort of nearby cities. Really, there was not much to be seen anymore. Some long, restored wooden houses not lived in for 50 years, and an old railroad line with patches of snow, stray clusters of weeds interspersed with chunks of rock and old wood. And the arched gate with foreign words facing the incredulous. I could not tell if their tears were from sorrow or recoil, or simply the result of this unrelenting windstorm. This side trip had become perfunctory. They seemed to be more concerned with blowing some warmth into their fingertips and keeping their ears from freezing than with immersing themselves in the past. By the time I had returned to the tour bus, most of the passengers had boarded and decided among themselves to continue on to whatever large city on their itinerary would have a comfortable hotel. Only I could not enter the bus. I was fastened to the place. I had really not seriously considered leaving, and now there was no power within me – or outside – that would move me. The driver, sensing my decision, pointed a finger toward the inn a few feet's distance from the bus stop. There would be a panorama of desolate fields and a view of four separate ruins with loose rock strewn about them, together with one recreated chimney as it was seen some 50 years ago.

The innkeeper had expected a bigger crowd, but when he saw at least one customer, he adjusted somewhat and offered me his best room, ready for use: veranda, private bath, wood-burning stove, and a thermos of hot tea. The room was chilled, but by the time I washed and looked at my surroundings a pleasant warmth overcame me. I settled drowsily into the overstuffed chair and watched the clouds being driven rapidly across the moon. Then I heard the knock. The glass door leading to the outside shook slightly, and he entered.

I had been here before. Many years ago. When I was a child. I had learned not to fear the dead, but to pity the unrelenting stream of corpses passing through the barracks every day. And I had learned to hate the treachery of the living. The dead were the innocent, and our living masters, robust and cruel, were the loathsome ones. These thoughts comforted me as I walked daily among the corpses.

Now, just as then, I felt as if in the presence of the dead. No fear, just a great pity, and then the puzzlement that after so many years I would feel this way again.

My father came through the door silently. He was dressed in the clothes I had liked him in best: gray slacks, blue blazer, gray-striped tie. Only the over-starched collar was from an earlier decade. He was younger than I am now, 45 when I last saw him. I am now a grandmother.

I wanted to run to him, if only to feel his light touch on my hair once again. But just sitting in this soft chair and letting his presence comfort me seemed enough. My hands motioned him to make himself at ease, as I do with the many guests who enter my house.

He did not speak but eyed me curiously. And I knew that words shaped by our lips were not necessary. We transferred our thoughts into each other's consciousness. And anyway, small talk seemed a sacrilege.

On the last day of his life, he was on one of the four trucks that wound their way toward the gas chambers. As the first truck came within sight of the chimneys, the men began to sing "Hatikvah." The men in each of the following trucks picked up the anthem. As the first truck entered the compound, the sound grew weaker until it stopped with the last truck. Then we saw the flames leaving the chimneys, smelled the sweetish scent of the cyanide, heard the jarring noise of the fire grates as the ashes were emptied. And then nothing.

But he had not come to remind me of those days. He was instead eager to tell me, to make me understand, only I did not know yet what. He began slowly, "The Hatikvah... you heard me sing... the final recognition that my life was dedicated to the wrong premise... I was deluded by hope... I had thought the antisemitism of the past had finally been buried. I had fought in the army of the Empire; I saw the Jewish men die – for their country, they thought. I should have known when a census of Jewish soldiers was taken; I should have known... betrayed by the veneer of civility until even this civility, this thin scab, ruptured and turned into crass brutality..."

Still the civilized man. His emotions were at a breaking point, yet his voice was not raised by one decibel.

How I loved him. All the years of yearning for just one more moment of his presence, one look into his beloved face; it was finally granted me, and I sat bathed in this aura of his being, aware of this special gift. I wanted to hold the sun back from rising, and I was thankful for the storm that had brought us together. I did not want it to end.

"We are the spiritual nation, our unique gift... trampled and burned... I beg your forgiveness. Please..."

This plea, so wrenching, so urgent, it seemed incongruous. Mother, brother, and I had survived, and he was the only one not to return. We had picked up our lives, not fully and eagerly, yet it was as we made it, and we missed him and spoke to him each in his own way when sadness struck or happiness came.

But it had not been as he perceived it. The ideology of "survival of the fittest" had risen long before he was born. The fittest were those who believed themselves to be the inheritors of the land by the logic of longevity on that soil.

Many Jews in Europe after Emancipation were so eager to assimilate, so eager to please, and so anxious to practice their polite social code. With damnable apologetics as leaders, they had not spoken up vigorously enough for their natural rights. In the intervening years, these Jews counted on their civility and meritoriousness as the common glue that would afford them their place in this society. But no matter how often they declared their loyalty, they were forever the alien, the other race. And Hitler, mesmerizing the ignorant and the desperate, had finally succeeded where every rational person would have thought it impossible.

Father was visibly spent. The ordeal he had feared and faced with his usual braveness had come and was finally overcome. He sank into the chair, exhausted by the events of the past few minutes. "...And how is it with my people, the ones we forged with the singing of Hatikvah?"

My nod reassured him, and he finally sat back the way he always had, relaxed and cordial. "You know," he continued, only now he was calm, and I saw again the slight smile that played across his face as I remembered when he was in conversation with friends. "I will not spoil our visit with tales of betrayal."

"We have overcome it," I told him. "We cannot be fooled anymore. We have learned. We are vigilant. Please be at rest." I seemed so sure. Could I seem the naive child to him?

For me, the emptiness I had called my soul was now filled with the warmth of his nearness, his breath, the zest for all that was of value in his world. He must have known this, too, for he was still and at ease. We had lost count of time.

And then I noticed that the wind had let up, the moon had moved, the clouds were banished. In the East the tint of a new day slowly drove away the darkness, and I became aware that soon the sun would be restored to the sky, and he would fade.

Indeed, he rose and noiselessly made his way to the sliding door. I wanted to run to him but was again held in place by some miraculous force outside ourselves. He turned once, and I saw him full face for a long moment.

And this was for me the culmination of a lifetime of longing.

My dear Lauren, not having been present in my father's last hours, I must use any means to bring him close. My ghost's image is held in two or three snapshots clandestinely saved by an old greengrocer woman in an alley near our former house.

Never again will I be able to discuss the fine points of difference between Plato and Aristotle, or have explained a difficult logarithm, or share a moment of music, family pictures, the joys of a quiet walk in the meadow.

Never again will I discuss a section of Talmud with him.

Never again will I feel the light hand of approval on my head and the love of a parent.

I am now 77 years old. I had my father for the first 13 years of my life. I have spent the following 64 years missing him. I will continue to miss him for the remainder of my days.

I have never adjusted.

I have never forgotten.

I can never forgive.

Love, Ruth

THE WORLD GATHERING OF JEWISH HOLOCAUST SURVIVORS

Deciding to tell my story

2006

Dear Ruth,

Dad told me that when he was a kid he did not think to ask you or Mutti too much about the war. He knew you were both survivors and had tattoos on your arms. He knew there was no family left in Europe and that they had all been killed. As a child, he never realized that you and his grandmother would not be around forever to speak about the past later. Dad said there were many survivors in the community at the time when he was growing up so that the experience itself seemed commonplace rather than unique. There were also so many war veterans that his father did not speak about fighting in the US Army or liberating Ohrdruf. There was no pressing urgency or need to talk about the war. He says you did not bring it up that much either. In contrast, you spoke about it often with your grandchildren. We loved hearing the liberation story about the noodles!

Did recalling the past make you feel like you were reliving it? Did you not want to scare your children or pass the trauma on to them? Did the past secretly haunt you in your thoughts or nightmares?

It was a conference that you attended in 1981 – the World Gathering of Jewish Holocaust Survivors – that made you realize you must tell your story. All your writings on the Holocaust were done in the 1980s, 1990s, and 2000s. In these decades, you became an active Holocaust educator, telling your story to schools, synagogues, and, most importantly, your grandchildren.

Please tell me about that conference and what prompted you to speak about your experiences.

Love, Lauren

Dear Lauren,

I attended the World Gathering of Jewish Holocaust Survivors in Israel on June 14–18, 1981. I was 51 years old at the time, and our sons were grown and married, but we did not yet have grandchildren.

Before the conference, I had gone about daily life trying not to think about the past too much. I thought, better to have my children (and later my grandchildren) create Jewish identities not based solely on the Holocaust.

The conference was a momentous event that brought so many memories and thoughts to mind. The event made me realize that I should tell my story. I must write it down as best I can and tell my sons and later my grandchildren.

I will tell you about the impact of this conference on me. These are my deepest thoughts and perspectives on the Holocaust – my quest to find meaning after all these years.

The men and women who arrived in Israel in June 1981 looked no different than other tourists; only the white and green tags of the Holocaust conference set them apart. But their permanent baggage was different – the sparsely concealed wounds of the memories of the ultimate horror.

The theme of the conference was "From Holocaust to Rebirth, *fon churban zum oifkum, mishoah l'ktumah*." It was not designed as a memorial service. For that, Nisan 27 is set aside annually. That date coincides with the first day of the Warsaw Ghetto Uprising, tangible evidence of the destruction – and of the resistance. Nor was the conference a cry for revenge – that is not the Jewish way – but this does not mean naive forgiveness or blank forgetfulness. We were there in Israel not to mourn, but to commemorate and look toward the future. We came to the Gathering of Holocaust Survivors to declare to the world that, incomprehensible as it still is, there really was such a hell called "The Holocaust."

We had come to this World Gathering from 23 countries, speaking many languages, united in our intention to give our testimony before all the living witnesses were gone. Notably absent from the conference were those Jews who resided in the Eastern European countries behind the Iron Curtain. How ironic that from those countries that had suffered most, no one was permitted to attend.

We went to Israel for the conference hoping that future generations of Jews would be aware of what the Jewish people have gone through, of what it means to be a Jew, and will search for (and find) the inner strength that gave our people the possibility of hope and strength to fight against all odds. We hope our descendants will find the same strength that we had with us in the 2,000 years of the *Galut*[1] so that they too can make a Jewish life for themselves, their children, and the future generations.

---

1. Jewish exile from the Land of Israel (Hebrew).

On a personal level, we came to meet the other survivors and their children. We came to find friends with whom we had shared those bitter years in the camps, since the extended families and roots we once had are gone. We rejoiced in the progress each had made, and we asked about all the things that had happened to one another since the war. The journey was, for all of us, a reaching out for the comfort of shared experiences. It soon developed the tone of a family reunion. The tattooed numbers, designed to shame us, now served to identify the time and place of our imprisonment. We asked, like all concerned family members: Where were you liberated? How have you fared since then? What thoughts occupy you now? What about children, husbands, wives?

Sometimes small miracles would occur. There were shrieks, kisses, hugs, the total gamut of emotions. One of the women recognized a former neighbor she had not seen since before the war. Each had been deported as a teenager. Walking behind her friend and remembering her voice, she called her by her name.

The opening ceremony in the Tel Aviv Sports Arena included a presentation of a Ladino melody of love for Zion. Sung by a men's choir of Greek Auschwitz survivors, it brought vividly back to my mind the memory of Mimi and the Greek girls. The Greek Jewish girls were charming, beautiful, multilingual, and musically talented. Very few survived. During a ceremony at Yad Vashem, a family from Greece was conversing in several languages. They translated for me a Ladino cradlesong performed by a young woman who could easily have been the daughter of my dear friend Mimi, had she survived.

Immediately following World War II, we survivors mourned the deaths of family and friends. Only 36 years later had we come to recognize the full impact of the loss of community: our institutions, our way of life, our seats of learning, and the lost potential of the unborn generations.

Those of us who are now Americans were proud to say that from this destruction the largest viable Jewish community in the Diaspora has learned to actively seek out and try to combat dangers to the Jewish people.

We feel it is important to stress that we are living witnesses to the destruction that outside forces, the neo-Nazis and the old antisemites, are trying to deny. Our eyewitness declarations are significant in combating the evil lies of the neo-Nazis and all those revisionists who claim that the Holocaust is an invention, a ploy to create sympathy for Israel or concocted by Jews for some other nefarious reason.

Other times we feel that while it is critical to combat such lies, ultimately their denial of our history is just an external manifestation coming from a place of ignorance. Perhaps we should refocus our efforts, for it is a useless task to try to combat antisemites. What will ever open the mind of a bigot?

Ultimately, we have decided that we must be at the forefront of guarding against Holocaust denial. We should remember that there was such a place as Auschwitz. Remember that it happened. It is within many cultures to displace their aggression and to scapegoat. It can happen again if we are not careful. We must guard against the idea of human sacrifice and the need to "clean the world" of anyone unworthy. We survivors must speak out now, for there may be a time that comes when an indifferent and often belligerent world makes a mockery of our history.

Our motto is "Never Again"; our goal is to prevent another Holocaust. I tremble at the thought of the need for us Jews to sacrifice again. We were urged to let remembrance serve as a warning that future Holocausts are indeed possible, and that within the rise of the new antisemitism and in denials of the horror can be the beginnings of another attempt at destruction. As was told to us by speaker after speaker, most notably by Professor Yehuda Bauer,[2] it would be in the interest of all the peoples of the world to prevent another Shoah, for it begins with aggression against the Jews and quickly spreads to other victims: from the Unique to the Universal.

The conference in Jerusalem was a momentous event. Many of us survivors felt that the symposium stimulated our internal analysis of the meaning of our own survival. Our thoughts on this topic needed time to become assimilated into the mind. There were many thoughts that came to me after the Jerusalem conference.

What came out of the conference was our common goal for the survival and strength of the Jewish people. We are driven, as survivors, to combat the denial of the Holocaust, to strengthen our ties to one another, and to rebuild our lives and our communities. We left the conference with the pride that we are rebuilding the Jewish people as a people with dignity, with a national, religious, and ethnic purpose.

With all my heart, I wished we would not have needed to meet there at that time.

Love, Ruth

Survivor guilt

Dear Lauren,

As does any momentous event, the conference brought many thoughts and ideas to mind. One of the ever-present ideas bandied about was the question of survivor guilt. I am not a psychologist, but enough is known that I feel I should speak about it.

---

2. Holocaust historian and professor at the Institute of Contemporary Jewry at the Hebrew University.

Ever since Bruno Bettelheim[3] described life among the concentration camp inmates, the mere act of survival has become suspect, as though it was accomplished over the bodies of other human beings. We must tread carefully for I fear the repercussions of what is said will negatively impact the minds of survivors. Further, if not careful, our enemies will, as it suits them, spout the primitive psychology of the late 19th century, which held the victim to be as responsible as the perpetrator. It is a disservice to the Jewish people as a whole – and to the six million – to discuss this phenomenon without proper explanation. Survival was random. Excesses on the part of the prisoners did occur once in a while under conditions in which no human being should be tested.

This is not the guilt of which people generally speak when they refer to survivor guilt. The meaning spoken of is the all-pervading guilt that lives with Jews who survived the war years, whether they lived through a camp or ghetto or weathered it out in hiding or in relative freedom. It is a guilt we harbor because we lived while others died.

We think, *Why did I survive? Why me and not the others?* Many are the sole survivors of their entire families or even entire communities. Why us? It did not come down to survival skills, for anyone could have died of starvation or typhus, or could have been chosen in the next selection to the gas chambers. It was pure chance whether you were admitted to a concentration camp on arrival, where maybe you might have a chance to live, or went directly to a death camp like Treblinka, where there was almost zero chance of survival.

Do we have some purpose in this world that the others did not? I do not think so.

I could see at the conference that survivors carry a unique mission.

---

3. Jewish psychoanalyst and concentration camp survivor who wrote controversial opinions about how specific actions could determine life or death, including that many of the Holocaust victims were complacent and unwilling to defend themselves.

Having survived, without understanding why or how, gives us both a huge burden and, at the same time, an important responsibility and purpose.

We look for ways to make our survival and our lives meaningful. We use our very existence while still on this earth to bear witness before it is too late. We survivors feel aware that our presence signifies the affirmation of life, the triumph over Hitler's attempt to banish the Jewish people from this world. We feel that we were called upon to give hope to the Jewish people because even after almost total destruction, Judaism can grow. We have not come by this awareness easily, nor always by choice.

Love, Ruth

The second generation

Dear Lauren,

I know just some of the many different nightmares haunting survivors. Does our pain stem from witnessing the unspeakable horror, or from living with the guilt of surviving when so many others did not? The trauma of those times still affects us, only some people had the ability to adjust better than others. I saw the survivor's trauma in Jerusalem, but perhaps not at its worst, because I think that those who wanted to reach out came, whereas others simply stayed home.

I had gone to Israel in the assurance that my personal private grief must, for my own good, be put aside, that it was time to become detached, to submerge in the normalcy and routine of daily life. All my assumptions were destroyed when I learned that trauma is handed down to the second generation. I was struck by the damage done to some of our children. I found real tragedy in the sad outcries of those in the second generation who are traumatized – it seems to me almost beyond repair – by their parents' inability to articulate, even after all these years, to expose the "inner person," as one agonized young man said.

It was piteous to see so many young people scarred by their parents' inability to communicate their experiences and feelings. This parental silence extends even to the life they knew before Hitler. These parents simply avoid any discussion of the past, and while not speaking of the Holocaust, they also do not speak of life before the war, of their families and friends and community. The unspeakable horror has become a living tomb from which all dialogue is repulsed. Thus, their children are doubly cheated: they lose their sense of family and identity, with the implied security of roots, as well as the meaning of our rich Jewish heritage, and with it the assurance of a Jewish future.

We cannot afford the additional loss, yet what is to be done? Today we know that we must try to mitigate the effects of imprisonment and torture, which continue to traumatize the survivors. For children, the real sadness is for the loss of years, which could have been spent in building and sharing and celebrating new life. It is with an awareness of such traumas that many of the survivors I met felt the need to relate their experiences. We must tell our stories, for no matter how painful for us to recall, the alternative is worse.

At the conference, we, the first generation, were barred from attending the second-generation workshops, but I spoke to as many of the adult children of survivors as I could reach. Not all children of survivors are so affected. Like my own three sons, most seem to be well adjusted, loving, and empathetic. They are proud of their parents' ability to live through, to adjust and begin anew, proud of their accomplishments and their claim to life. Many of these children are concerned with Jewish survival and universal problems. All mourned the loss of extended family, the absence of the experience of sharing secrets with cousins, of feeling the loving hands of grandparents. They fantasize a family life they have never known, a family they could have had. They have dreams of vibrant communities, which in their imaginations are rosy and ideal. Among their school friends, they felt different. This is the catastrophe imposed on that generation by the war. This in itself is not all bad, for it spurs these young people to invest in families of their own and to make their communities the best possible places to live in.

The conference ended with an impressive charge to the second generation. Children of the survivors were given the duty of keeping the memories of the Holocaust alive with its terrible manifestations and results. In a solemn ceremony at the Western Wall, we enlisted the second generation as active partners, passing onto them the awesome responsibility to continue the task we have set for ourselves: to alert the world to the danger of all potential holocausts. The children of survivors pledged to tell the chronicles of their parents, to draw analogies from the past, to keep vigil over the future.

New groups are being formed worldwide with the express purpose of keeping history alive, to prepare for a Jewish future, and to fight antisemitism. Survivors' children are in the forefront of recognizing the need for these causes. At the Western Wall the survivors' children accepted this responsibility fervently and seriously. They seem determined to see to it that there will never be another Shoah.

Through this conference, I have increased awareness of the impact on the second generation. My own prayer would be that the children of survivors love their parents for the strength of survival, that they seek out and try to prevent persecutions wherever they might find them, and that they should always be prepared to strengthen the Jewish people. And finally, as in the "Song of the Partisans" – *Mirzaynen do!* We are here! This will be our ultimate triumph.

Love, Ruth

Searching for an elusive god

Dear Ruth,

I know that you maintained your belief in God both during and after the Holocaust. How?

I have read books written by survivors describing how the people in the camps who were on the brink of death seem to die a bit more quickly if they felt abandoned by God or lost faith in His existence. I remember you confirmed this, based on your own experience. You told me that in Auschwitz, the people who lost faith and who had lost all hope of survival were the ones who died more readily. Everyone struggled to survive. Those who felt God had abandoned them, who were already torn from their families and alone in the world, did not see the purpose of living any longer. As you've always said, survival was a matter of chance. Death came to both the religious Jews and the secular Jews in the camps. Given the situation, I understand how maintaining some sort of faith or hope despite the conditions could give someone extra motivation to continue the struggle for life.

I have read Victor Frankel's *Man's Search for Meaning*, which explores the psychology of the concentration camp inmates. The author was a medical doctor, a psychiatrist who survived the Holocaust. He wrote that the inmates sought to find meaning in their suffering and a purpose to their lives. If they could find such meaning, whether it was to live for a spouse or child who might be alive and waiting for them, or an unpublished manuscript or other life's work waiting to be completed, then the camp inmate was better able to withstand the conditions and perhaps ultimately survive. I strongly believe that because you and Mutti were together, you were able to find the meaning that was so important for survival. You survived for one another. I suppose the same logic of Frankel's theory could apply to someone who felt God was still present.

The Holocaust made some people reject their religion or belief system, while others clung more closely to it. I know it has never been your position to say that the existence of evil is proof that God does not exist. But how else can the Holocaust be explained? How could God have allowed the Holocaust to happen?

Love, Lauren

Dear Lauren,

I have always maintained my belief in God. I recall reciting just one prayer over and over in Auschwitz. It was the *Shemoneh Esrei*.[4] I didn't remember any other prayers by heart; this was the one prayer I could remember without a *siddur* [prayer book]. It served me as the ultimate prayer. Being able to say a prayer gave me a sense of identity and strength. I vowed then that I would live as a Jew as much as I could.

Even while in Auschwitz, I saw the Holocaust as a vast theological occurrence. Without success, I searched for the *Av Ha-Rachamim* [Merciful Father] that I had learned of in my childhood.

I continue to see the Holocaust within a theological framework. People will always seek scapegoats, but can there be no ethical constraint? Who is this god – or is it Beelzebub[5] – who insatiably demands burnt offerings?

For the Gathering of Survivors Conference there could not have been a more gracious host than the State of Israel. Every day I thank God for the State of Israel, and I am so proud of the Law of Return, which gives every Jew the right to live in his or her own country

---

4. A central prayer in Judaism, also called the Amidah (Hebrew).
5. Christian Testament name of a devil, similar to Satan; Hebrew Bible epithet for the Canaanite god Ba'al.

when other nations prove fickle. The guides were gentle, the officials solicitous, the ceremonies impressive and imbued with just the right amount of emotion.

I do not know how many of us came for more. I know I did. I wanted answers. We learned the history of antisemitism but not the reason why a seemingly sane society turns to human sacrifice at intervals in history. I wanted to hear opinions on God's role in this tragedy. Notably absent from all the symposia, speeches, and ceremonies were any attempts at a religious explanation.

Ever since the war, I have wanted to confront the God of the Holocaust, but He remains elusive. I have no answers to your question on how the Holocaust can be explained. There have been many attempts at a religious explanation.

Elie Wiesel's play *The Trial of God* was based on his experience in Auschwitz. While in the camp, Wiesel witnessed a *Bet Din* [rabbinic court] put God on trial and find Him guilty of having broken His covenant with the Jewish people by allowing the Germans to commit genocide. But I think God is not guilty; the prosecution did not place the defendant at the scene of the crime.

His book *Night* puts forth the belief that God died in Auschwitz. I could never muster Wiesel's anger.

Martin Buber's *God in Eclipse* suggested that God was inexplicably absent for reasons unknown to us. By refusing to reveal his face, God could not see the world. But I think that God is omniscient and should have seen. I looked up at the stars, cold and uncaring... Was God above? Did God make the Earth and then retire to bigger and better things? Possibly let humans use their ability for doing good or evil? I see Buber's eclipse as a convenient contrivance.

In 1974, I attended the International Symposium on the Holocaust in New York City. I heard Emil Fackenheim discuss the theory that the Holocaust represented the birth pangs of the Messiah. The theory is that the destruction led to the establishment of the State of Israel, which was the dawn of our messianic redemption. Apocalypse to Redemption. My mind absolutely refuses to accept six million stepping stones.

Despite my quest for answers, I think that we as humans can never fully comprehend the enormity of the evil, nor could we ever understand God's role in it.

I thank God, not for six million dead, but for the survival of Jews in Israel and England, where the Nazi grasp did not reach, as well as for stopping Rommel in El Alamein. Eretz Israel became a refuge for escaping European Jews. If the forces of Montgomery had not broken the German forces of Rommel at El Alamein, which is just a few hundred miles away in Egypt, Eretz Israel would have been destroyed again, and the remnant of our heritage, our holy places, would have been obliterated. Perhaps I rationalize the destruction, try to see a purpose where actually there was none. I must find meaning in the meaningless.

I had gone to the 1981 Gathering in Jerusalem searching for the God who would gently make His reason clear. There was a touching ceremony at the Great Synagogue, yet my God remained elusive, playing a hide-and-seek game.

Did I meet Him in Mea Shearim,[6] where little yeshiva *bochurim* [religious students] earnestly studied the Torah? Perhaps in the green fields of Israel? The strong bodies surfing in the coastal waters of Tel Aviv? The crowds going about their daily business in Jerusalem? Perhaps. Perhaps it is enough to feel the love and care of our people during this conference, to see Israel strong and vibrant, and to see the little children playing.

---

6. A Haredi (Ultra-Orthodox) Jewish neighborhood in Jerusalem.

In the closing ceremony at the *Kotel*,[7] Ernest Michel, an organizer of the conference, thanked God for the achievement of being in Israel at this time, and for our strength to meet the challenges of our lives. We left determined that our generation and every generation will be told of the Holocaust as a triumph of the Jewish spirit.

These experiences give me hope for a new beginning, yet my mind and soul are bound to the past, and still I search for answers.

Love, Ruth

---

7. "Western Wall" of the ancient Jerusalem Temple, the most holy site in the world for the Jewish people (Hebrew).

PERSPECTIVES

German collective guilt

Dear Ruth,

How do you feel about Germany and the Germans today? Do you believe in the collective guilt of the German people, a topic they have struggled with after the war? Germany acknowledges and takes accountability for the atrocities committed during the Holocaust, unlike other nations who have committed genocide but deny responsibility.

I know that you receive a small sum of reparations from Germany every month as part of the Claims Conference.[1] The money is nowhere close to the equivalent of what was taken from your family. I remember your joking how ironic it was that you were in favor of a strong *Deutschmark* (later a strong Euro) in comparison to the dollar so that the value of the payments would go up. Is it strange for you

---

1. The Conference on Jewish Material Claims Against Germany is an organization that seeks compensation and restitution for victims of Nazi persecution.

even to accept money from Germany, as though this could undo what they did?

Throughout Germany there are many Holocaust museums and memorials. Streets are lined with little plaques, *Stolpersteine*, bearing the names of Jewish families who once lived there but were deported, serving as a constant reminder of the past and ensuring that the Holocaust is not forgotten. I have heard that there is extensive Holocaust education in German public schools. Germany funds the maintenance and upkeep of the concentration camps as museums so they can be preserved for historic memory to combat Holocaust denial. Today Germany seems to be an ally of Israel and of the Jewish people.

I once wrote a paper for an International Criminal Law class about the Nuremburg Trials. I asked you if you thought justice was done there. Although Nazis were convicted of genocide and crimes against humanity, you did not think that justice was achieved in Nuremberg. Only a select few of the upper echelons of the Nazi party were punished, but many more should have been. Many Nazis were let go and were able to live the rest of their lives in freedom. Many of them were not brought to justice, either in Nuremburg or later. You thought that the American principle of "innocent until proven guilty" should not have been used. The Nazi criminals should have been judged under the same standards as German Law, 1933–1945. During the Third Reich, if one disgraced Germany, one would be killed. These Nazi criminals who disgraced Germany should have been punished by the same logic.

Please let me know how you feel about Germany.

Love, Lauren

Dear Lauren,

On the whole, the German people who were adults during the Third Reich, supported and loved their *Führer*, and so they are guilty. The vast majority of German society during that time supported Nazism and all its aims.

Consider this analogy to the laws of kashrut: when one boils chicken soup and a drop of milk accidentally falls into the pot, but the texture, the chemistry of the soup, remains unchanged and the broth remains clear, the soup is considered kosher. There were just not enough well-meaning German citizens to affect the outcome of the looming tragedy. Standing by just to shake one's head, while doing nothing, does not count. There may have been some political dissidents. There were some who helped save Jews and can be considered Righteous among the Nations. But these types were a very small minority. You may have heard the argument that people feared for their lives if they spoke out. They could be killed for hiding Jews. Yes, this is true. But even the people who wanted to help, but did not out of fear, were still very few and far between. Germans had always looked for a scapegoat. First, they blamed the Treaty of Versailles. Then they blamed the Jews. The deep entrenchment of antisemitism in German society made the inhumanity of the Holocaust possible.

Some Germans and others just don't want to hear us talk about the Holocaust anymore. The Germans don't want us to remind them of 2,000 years of persecution. What should we do? Ignore the wrong done to us? Why should we ignore it? Doesn't a murderer need to be brought to justice, even if his wife swears to his insanity? The only things we can do are continue to remember their guilt and continue to advocate for bringing anyone left to justice. Any remaining perpetrator, anyone who played any role in the state apparatus that made the Holocaust possible, should be brought to justice. There can be no statute of limitations on the crime of genocide, for which each individual who played a role was personally responsible.

The reparation money does not undo the past, but it is better for the German government to take responsibility and financially support survivors in Israel and abroad than to do nothing at all.

The collective guilt of the German people during 1933–1945 does not extend to the descendants of the perpetrators or to the entirety of the German people today. Part of the Nazi racial theory was to go back into the ancestry of a people, find a collective fault – whatever it might be – enlarge on it, and burden past and future generations with this presumed flaw. The children of Nazis should not be considered guilty; doing so would make them fall subject to such Nazi tactics. Those who were not there at that time cannot be held responsible for the crimes of their parents and grandparents.

Many of the younger generation of Germans today have made great advances toward reconciliation. I think there are now enough responsible young Germans to create a better image and a better resolve. It is up to the next generations of Germans to effect change in their society. They are responsible for not letting another Holocaust happen again to anyone.

The great-grandson of Richard Wagner is one such example. In the summer of 1999, Allan gave me a book that made quite an impression: *The Twilight of the Wagners* [*Die Götterdammerung der Wagners*]. This great-grandson, Gottfried Wagner, broke with the family tradition of antisemitism. He hates every aspect of his forebears. Now Gottfried Wagner travels the globe trying to make amends with Jews in Israel and in other parts of the world and is active in a group promoting understanding (as far as that is possible, probably only with the second-generation). He is outspoken against the neo-Nazis who are still entrenched in the estates along the North Sea and the Baltic. (It is frightening to realize that they still celebrate

Hitler's birthday on April 20, and they use the code word U.S.A. for *Unser Seliger Adolf* – Our Blessed Adolf.)

When Gottfried Wagner was scheduled to speak at Fairleigh Dickenson University, I skipped class and went to hear him. I spoke a few words to him, and then something strange happened for a few seconds. There was recognition – a meeting of the souls. I cannot explain it. Here was the great-grandson of one of the most notorious antisemites, meeting the descendant of a rabbinic family and sensing a common humanity.

Additionally, I have been in touch with a man who was the son of Nazis. I was put in touch with him through my daughter-in-law Robin when he came to Allan's congregation seeking reconciliation with Jewish survivors. He is an attorney, married with three sons and now living in Canada. He was born in Germany a few years before the end of the war. He takes on the guilt of his nation and spends his time in agony. He never knew his father but assumes he was killed in the last days of the war after being recruited to defend Berlin. This man wrote to me that the only purpose for his birth was to become a soldier for the Third Reich. What a heavy load to bear in a lifetime. Not only was he conceived to serve as cannon fodder, but also it came about from the horrible and ugly custom in which Nazi soldiers of special Aryan appearance were mated with equally Aryan-looking women for the express purpose of propagation of the master race.

It is such a shame that he spends his life trying to live down his parents' past, taking on the guilt of crimes for which he cannot possibly be personally responsible. This way of thinking almost seems like the racial policies of the Nazis, who postulated that traits can be traced back into many preceding generations. How can one console such a suffering soul? I have exchanged written correspondences with him, and I empathize with his plight. Yet, I am hesitant to meet him.

Many years ago, I wrote a story about my childhood friend Erika Schmidt. You'll recall that her father refused to call a Jewish doctor for her, and she died of peritonitis. At the time that I wrote it, I was friends with a minister in Paterson. After he read the tale, his critique was what I would have given, at that time, my two thumbs to avoid: "You make it sound as though the Germans suffered, too." Now, after corresponding with the unfortunate man in Canada who finds it hard to live with himself and is searching for something that he himself cannot define, I've come full circle. The German people from 1933–1945 were collectively responsible – and collectively guilty – but I can acknowledge that some of their own suffered too as a result of their actions.

The German people of 1933–1945 deserved to be brought to justice, but not their children. Like Gottfried Wagner, the descendants of the Nazis have a great opportunity and a great responsibility to try to combat Holocaust denial and fight antisemitism.

Love, Ruth

Zev's thoughts on German cruelty

Dear Zev,

You showed me your copy of the 1845 children's book *Der Struwwelpeter* by Heinrich Hoffmann about the disastrous fate that would become of children who misbehaved. To you, this book epitomized the culture of the German people – their obsession with obedience, cruelty, punishment, and death.

What are your thoughts on Germany?

Love, Lauren

Dear Lauren,

In response to your question, I'd like to explain to you my theory on cruelty as a basic component of the German national culture and which in part enabled the rise of the Nazis and the Holocaust. I would like to express my opinion as to why the Holocaust began specifically in Germany.

I use the term "Germans" and not "Nazis." The culture of cruelty was deeply engrained in the German mindset over centuries and was not limited only to the 12-year existence of the Nazi regime.

While it is true that only a small percentage of the German population was actively engaged in the implementation of the Final Solution, and notwithstanding the fact that most Germans were not personally involved, I believe that the blame must be placed squarely on German society. It seems to me that cruelty was an integral part of German society and German national character at the time.

Had you randomly picked out 100 Germans, giving them guns and some defenseless people, the results in all probability would have been predictable. I say "in all probability" to leave open the possibility that at times Germans in an official capacity acted in a humane manner. However, it was never enough to tilt the situation the other way.

We, the Jews, were the primary, but by no means the only, victims of German cruelty. There were also the Roma, Russian prisoners of war, and non-Jewish citizens of occupied countries.

It was the character of German society that produced death camps. By comparison, some Jews in Italy were also put into detention centers. However, it is known that conditions in the Italian camps were more bearable. The character of Italian society produced camps where prisoners were treated in a relatively more humane manner.

Here are my thoughts on the Holocaust and the Church. One well-known position is that centuries of Christianity and historic Jew-hatred based on religious reasons[2] laid the groundwork for the antisemitism that led to the Holocaust. Another position is nearly the opposite, that Christianity tamed German ferocity, and, with the decline of Christianity under Nazi rule, the Holocaust became possible. I do not think that either theory captures the complexity of the relationship between the Church, the Jews, and the Germans during the Holocaust.

During the war, in some countries, Christian clergy of various denominations came to Jews' aid in a variety of ways. Meanwhile, the clergy in Germany and Austria were silent.[3] One could also criticize the Christian clergy for being silent when the victims were non-Jews.

It was the character of German society, and that of other nations participating in the genocide, and not their religious affiliation, that could explain their unique responsibility for the genocide.

Had Europe, instead of adopting Christianity, adopted or been forced to adopt Islam, which almost occurred, and had all else been equal, then Germans who would have happened to be Muslims still would have perpetrated the same crimes as Germans who were Christians. Germans of any other religion would be the same.

In terms of the future, the end of World War II, in my opinion, marked the end of the age of nationalism in the industrial world, and therefore the end of the glorification of war.

The Germans today admit what the previous generations did, and the younger generation does a lot of soul searching. In fact, there has been much reconciliation between Germans and Jews, and today Germany and Israel are allies even working together on medical advancements. I firmly believe that in many ways we now live in a better world. The existence of the State of Israel has eliminated many

---

2. This refers to the Christian belief that "the Jews" killed Jesus, which led to persecution and "Other-ing" of Jews on religious grounds.
3. Notable exceptions were Dietrich Bonhoeffer and Martin Niemöller.

of the dangers faced by the Jewish people in the past – or so one hopes.

Love, Zev

Traveling to Frankfurt

Dear Ruth,

Frankfurt, having been decimated during the war, was completely rebuilt and transformed into a modern city.

I remember you told me about going with Harry and the boys to Germany in the 1970s to the Frankfurt Fur Fair. You said you felt nothing for the city, no connection. Visiting Germany held no meaning for you. It felt like a completely different city than the one of your childhood.

You traveled to Germany with my cousin Ayelet in 2001. I regret not joining you on this trip. Back at home, I remember my father receiving an unexpected phone call from you. You and Ayelet had taken a train, and you were pickpocketed. Your wallet with all your cash and credit cards was gone.

Ayelet told me later about what happened next. You proceeded to the police station to report the robbery. You were wearing a short-sleeve shirt, so your tattoo was not hidden. While reporting the crime, the policeman, who had never seen an Auschwitz tattoo before, started asking you all sorts of questions and even apologized on behalf of his generation of Germans. Ayelet said you were in no mood to tell your life story to this curious stranger after having just been robbed.

Please tell me more about what it was like for you to travel back to Germany. What do you think of Jewish life in Frankfurt today?

Love, Lauren

Dear Lauren,

Every so often in the past few decades I have gone back to the city where I was born. Strange, to have been born in a city and grown up there and not once call it my *hometown*. I guess because *home* means warmth and love and welcome back. We travel to Frankfurt because of the family business to attend the Frankfurt Fur Fair several times.

Germany seems to be a place of contradictions. Once while I was there, the left-wing Grüne Partei formed a coalition with the rightist Republicans. Both are antisemitic for their own reasons. Yet, on the street one can see graffiti saying, "*Nazis Raus* [Nazis Get Out]." On the 50th anniversary of Kristallnacht, in 1988, the city of Berlin taped a broad satire on life during the Third Reich, showing how the burning of books led to the burning of people. What is one to think of a people who show on public TV a wonderful lecture on the Kabbalah and an anti-Nazi film in the same evening, and yet I have not ever been on a plane going to Germany without meeting some old-time Nazi or a neo-Nazi?

I must admit, very grudgingly, that Frankfurt is charming, and I can see why our ancestors fought to remain part of it. I return to seek answers to questions that cannot even be asked. I am searching for ghosts. I am haunted by the last home where my friends lived. I cross and re-cross the streets, remembering incidents, faces, hopes, but mostly despair. I stand in front of Irma's home daydreaming about her, as though she might emerge from inside her home and we could share stories of our grandchildren over cookies, but then my memory of the last time I saw her cuts into my mind like a knife and I relive that agony. Every time I return to Frankfurt, I tell my sons to cut up my passport if I should speak of going again.

I visit the cemeteries. The three Jewish cemeteries of Frankfurt – the Ancient, the Old, and the New – were not bombed. Today the state pays for the upkeep of the three Frankfurt cemeteries and for some of the sites that have been declared historic.

The Ancient Cemetery is located on Battonnstrasse. It was desecrated by Nazis during the war. They dug up some of the tombstones and left them in a pile. Those that remain somewhat intact are now placed along the inner part of the outer cemetery wall. The cemetery has been restored as much as possible. On the outside of the cemetery wall is the Holocaust Memorial, where there are embedded thousands of rectangular boxes, each about two inches long. They contain the names of all the Jews of Frankfurt who were deported – all that remains of them.

When the Jews were driven out of Frankfurt in the medieval period, the Ancient Cemetery was robbed. Two stones from 1260 were used to build the altar of the Frankfurt Cathedral, the *Frankfurter Dom*. They were found when the church's damage was restored after World War II. Who knows what else could have been found if the church had gotten more bombings?

The land adjacent to the Ancient Cemetery is where our Börneplatz Synagogue once stood, which was on the outskirts of the medieval ghetto. During excavation, a 16th-century *mikveh* [bath used for ritual purification] was discovered. People took notice; the city promised to keep this a protected area. Today the Museum Judengasse stands there. It explains medieval Jewish life in Frankfurt and contains important archeological excavations. There is a memorial plague for our synagogue, explaining that it was destroyed during Kristallnacht.

I visit the graves of my grandparents in the Old Cemetery on Rat-Beil-Strasse, where my grandmother Rosa Wertheim and several baby aunts and uncles are buried.

I also walk to the New Cemetery on the Eckenheimer Landstrasse. In one section are the graves of teachers, parents of friends, and friends of my parents, who took their own lives when the betrayal of their very existence by the Nazis became evident. These were the suicides that occurred just before the person was scheduled for "resettlement," which meant death in a cattle wagon or worse. You do not see graves dated 1943 or 1944. There are no graves for those who died during these years of the war. Our people died in places like Majdanek, Buchenwald, and Auschwitz.

A worthwhile side trip is to the city of Worms, where you can find the grave of Rabbi Meir of Rothenberg and walk along the steps and synagogue where Rashi[4] once walked. Back in Frankfurt, the Jewish Museum documents the full history of Jewish life in Frankfurt and is a must-see.

Based on a few weeks' visit, it would not be fair to make a complete appraisal of Jewish life in Frankfurt today. I can only give my impressions. I wish I could say that the *kehillah* [local Jewish community] arose like the Phoenix out of its own ashes. It did not.

The people in Frankfurt today have no connection with the historic, the religious, the communal fiber that made up Jewish life in Frankfurt before the war. The city was once home to nearly 30,000 of us; today, about 7,000 Jews live there. Many are Russian Jews who came in the 1990s. The community today is, for the most part, well-to-do. They continue their projects of charity for those in the community who are not wealthy. There is a Jewish home for the aged. Some of the old buildings, such as a nursery, the orphanage, and my former school building, have remained. There is a new building complex that contains two school classrooms and holds lecture series, makes socials for retirees, and holds the offices for the rabbinate. It is designed in such a way as to signify that amid the well-constructed house, we remember the destruction of the perfect home, the Temple in Jerusalem. The new community complex has no sentimental attachment for me.

The community seems self-consciously Jewish. The question of

---

4. Medieval rabbi and biblical commentator.

young Jewish men being drafted into the German army is an obscene notion. Yet, the old accusation of having double or divided loyalty arises to haunt. The Jewish community today sends money to Israel and supports Jewish causes worldwide. They educate their children as Jewish as possible.

I went to the West End Synagogue on Shavuot[5] for Yizkor. The West End Synagogue is the only prewar synagogue that remains. It has been restored. Today services take place for the very religious – Haredi men in *shtreimlech* [fur hats] and kaftans. There are several *shtiblach* [small rooms for communal Jewish prayer] in addition to the main synagogue. You can hear many languages just attending services.

I attended a lecture by a Swiss woman on Isaac Bashevis Singer, and one by Emil Fackenheim on the political stance of Israel. Sometimes these lectures are also attended by non-Jewish educators and others. A few days later, in the Hotel Intercontinental, there was a very elegant kosher dinner and fundraiser for Keren Hayesod.[6] Yet, a few days after my return, I read that a bomb had exploded outside of the community building, which is better protected than Fort Knox, with a security system that is unbelievably complicated.

So why should Jews live under such conditions in a country that at best was always ambivalent and for the most part hostile? Several years ago, a play by an avowed antisemite made its way onto the stage. It was called: *The Garbage, the City and Death*. There was a worldwide outcry, but neither the authorities nor the actors themselves were willing to ban the play. On opening night, members of the Jewish community marched themselves onto the stage and physically prevented the performance of this filth. They are there to remind, to show and lead with a moral tenor, and they are there

---
5. Jewish holiday celebrating the giving of the Law (Torah) at Mount Sinai.
6. United Israel Appeal; the main fundraising organization for Israel throughout the world (Hebrew).

because not to be there would give Hitler one more victory. To live there is not for everyone. But since they are Jews, stubborn and vocal and vigilant, we must wish them well.

Love, Ruth

2017

Dear Ruth,

I am writing you this letter in the year 2017, when you are no longer here. I am writing to express the things I wish I could tell you but cannot.

My parents and I traveled to Frankfurt together to visit the important Jewish heritage sites. We went to the places that were important to you, including your grandmother's grave, the Philanthropin School, and your old address. It was profoundly moving.

The most impactful was going to the site where the Börneplatz Synagogue had stood. We walked around the memorial of names of 11,000 Jews who had been deported from Frankfurt and found the names of Isidor Krautwirth, Yitzhak Krautwirth, Irma Stern and her family, and Harvey Saalberg's relatives.

We had been traveling throughout Poland and Germany to see the sights of the Holocaust, and so it felt personal yet almost surreal to conclude the trip with finding my family's names on a memorial wall in a foreign country.

Love, Lauren

American Jewry

Dear Lauren,

One of the gallows humor sayings circulating during the war was "the world *verhandelt* while Hitler *handelt*," meaning that the world negotiated while Hitler went about with his plans.

Many have asked me what my thoughts are on whether Jews abroad could have done more to help their European brethren during the Holocaust, as the nations of the world largely ignored the plight of the Jews.

Do the Jews of America share in responsibility for the Holocaust? Could the Jews of America have done more to help or to save the Jews of Europe? And what about their children – should they, too, feel responsible? What could the average American Jew have done?

Your father, our son Mark, who at 16 had returned from helping the Soviet Jewry movement in Russia, spoke of his commitment to Russian Jewry, of never wanting to be part of a generation that could be accused of inaction while six million Jews were destroyed. He took on the burden of collective responsibility and extended guilt. He said this even though his father had been out there fighting Germans and helping to liberate the concentration camp of Ohrdruf.

The accusation Mark made has often been heard from other sources, and often shrilly. Yet, not all the facts are generally known.

Just when I thought every statistic on the Holocaust had been published, and my challenge had gone out to philosophers and rabbis to bring their conclusions, my daughter-in-law Robin and son Allan left on my desk Yehuda Bauer's *American Jewry and the Holocaust: The American Joint Distribution Committee 1939–1945*. The sight brought a mental groan. Not again. How often in a lifetime must one human relive the horror?

According to Bauer, the American-Jewish community at the time had barely emerged from the Depression, was deliberately uninformed by the State Department, and had not divested itself of the ghetto mentality that dictated: "Do not upset things, do not call attention to your own people, wait for negotiations, trust and depend on diplomacy, and if the Allies win the war, Jews will be liberated together with others."

With very few resources, with every possible shortage, and – ironic as it might seem to those idealists who refuse to equate the value of human life with mundane cash flow – yes, even with a lack of funds, the workers of the American Jewish Joint Distribution Committee, with great love and concern, went in there and saved people. They cheated the Germans, arranged for the few available passages, and generally did well. If a few could accomplish so much, the mind reels at the possibility of total recruitment.

Professor Bauer finds a Jewish community that could possibly have coped with what he calls a "normal disaster" but was totally unprepared for the magnitude and ferocity of the Shoah. It fell into the category of "abnormal disaster," and for that no one was prepared.

Books on this topic should be required reading for all fellow Jewish grandparents whose grandchildren will someday ask, "And what did you do while six million..." Yet, the question is not fair. It would take the combined Allied armies, including 550,000 Jewish American soldiers, four years of hard fighting to expunge Hitler.

Palliatives for rescue were proposed: mass emigration to Madagascar, some little-known country, in exchange for payoffs to some greedy tyrant, or some number of Jews in exchange for trucks or money. (Those "idealistic" Nazis would deal for money in the best gangster fashion.) The real chance to stop Hitler, through negotiation or a confined war, was passed up in 1935, when he renounced the armament provision of the Treaty of Versailles, or in 1936, when he invaded the Rhineland. But here our investigations are hindered by that proverbial, torturous, perfect hindsight.

World Jewry, divided in many respects, could never have imagined the unbelievable horror awaiting European Jews. American Jewry, barely emerging from its lower-class status, plagued by the ravages of the Depression, and fighting its own American antisemitism but thoroughly convinced of the democratic process implied in the Constitution, put too much confidence into the civilizing effect of the 20th century. Yet, even the victims, some until their last minutes, closed their minds to the possibility of total destruction.

The rebirth of Jewry after the war has been impressive. Where once during World War II the American Jewish Community was passive and too timid to rock the boat, keeping quiet even in the face of American antisemitism, today we have marched as one before the Six-Day War, we demonstrate for Soviet Jewry, we lobby against the sale of Airborne Warning and Control System (AWACS) jets to Saudi Arabia,[7] and we show our humanity in the Raoul Wallenberg case.[8]

American Jewry has come a long way in divesting itself of the ghetto mentality that centuries of oppression fostered in us. A new, free consciousness is evident among our people – not in total perfection but definitely in evidence. For if anything deserved to die in Auschwitz, it was this ghetto mentality.

Love, Ruth

---

7. Controversial arms sale of aircraft from the United States to Saudi Arabia in 1986, which was largely opposed because it meant providing state-of-the-art aircraft to Saudi Arabia, potentially threatening Israeli security.

8. Raoul Wallenberg was a Swedish diplomat who saved thousands of Hungarian Jews and is considered Righteous Among the Nations. He disappeared at the end of the war. This reference is to the international pressure exerted by the Jewish community for investigations into his fate and attempts to discover whether he was imprisoned or executed by the Soviet Union at the end of World War II.

Jewish resistance

Dear Lauren,

I am sometimes asked why Jews went to the slaughter as the proverbial sheep and why they did not resist. Let's debunk this myth once and for all. Here are my thoughts on resistance as I saw it on a personal level, both the passive and active resistance that occurred throughout the war.

First, we must examine the nature of resistance. A case can be made that, for the most part, revolutions, uprisings, and riots are not effective. Except for the American Revolution, nothing much changes after the mob presides. The most telling example is the Russian Revolution, where only the name of the leadership changed.

A story can be told of two congregations headed by two different rabbis along the same railroad line connecting two little towns in Poland. Jews were rounded up, taken to the train, and pushed into cattle cars. The rabbi of the first congregation became so enraged that he grabbed the gun out of the holster of the nearest soldier, killed him, and in the process was killed himself. The congregation was deported to their deaths. The second rabbi calmed his people, lined them up in an orderly manner, and even though they now knew they were doomed, they faced their dreadful ordeal with dignity. They too were deported and killed. Can we say one rabbi or one congregation was braver than the other? It took tremendous courage to grab the gun, but it also took great courage to remain calm and keep one's humanity and dignity in the most inhumane situation people were ever forced to undergo.

As soon as the Nazis came to power in Germany, they pronounced a boycott of Jewish stores and businesses, doctors, lawyers, movies, theaters, and more. Jews outside Germany urged a counter boycott of

German goods. The question was raised as to whether it would be more effective for Jews worldwide to confront Hitler or to negotiate with Hitler. As it turned out, within Germany the Nazis stopped any pro-Jewish demonstrations and intimidated the Jewish participants by beating them, chasing them from the demonstration sites, and so forth. A counter boycott of Germany from Jews in other countries did not move forward. The leaders called them off, fearing worse retributions against their brethren in Germany. We cannot judge them as cowards, for we do not know what we would have done in their situation. Ultimately their genteel actions were no match for the murderous, crude hordes they faced. The Nazis seemed so ridiculous with their wild leader and their idiotic goose-stepping marches. There was no reason to expect them to exist for 12 years.

Our home became a hub for young people escaping from Austria after that country was annexed by Germany in 1938. They were trying to make their way to western countries: England, the United States, Holland, and so on. As you know, we lived atop a Nazi. Every little step we took could be heard downstairs. Yet, risking their lives and that of their children, my parents gave these refugees shelter, food, clothing, money, and when possible, arranged for legitimate visas to other places.

My father knew his way around officialdom and was no stranger to the art of bribery when required. He was able to have reinstated many visas of people who had been in Argentina but had left because life there was tough, and who now needed to return when no other country opened its doors. I only hope that the people my parents helped remained free and alive. It all seemed so natural to me at the time. One simply helped other Jews when they were in danger. You must picture the air of fear that hung over everything in those times. This was a tremendous act of courage.

Passive resistance occurred within each population, wherever there was oppression. As soon as the Nazis came to power, the right to privacy ceased to exist. The Gestapo would come and go into Jewish homes like wild animals let out of a cage.

Yet, in every ghetto in Poland, schooling went on with the very limited resources still available. Teachers were in class one day and gone the next. Students needed to scrape together whatever food they could find for their starving families. Starvation and filth were everywhere. Still, classes went on as much as possible: music, drama, medical school subjects, and the sciences. Holidays were observed with the limited foods and wine and perhaps no prayer books. This was the day-to-day passive resistance of our people desperately trying to preserve our lives and – above all – our humanity. If we read "Yellow Butterfly," by Pavel Friedman, we learn that even under the most horrible conditions the human mind created – in spite of the German torturers.[9]

Another form of passive resistance, although less apparent and less dramatic than active resistance, was never compromising or abandoning our faith. Morality was the guide to Jewish conduct throughout centuries of persecutions. We have, for instance, many verified cases of rabbis who, when brought to the last place of assembly and faced with certain death, found reason and solace in the Scriptures for themselves and their people. Many passages from the Torah, the Psalms, and everyday prayers were the tools of these pious men as they tried to ease the terrible fate facing their people. We must remember this courage, this calm, this dignity, and find peace in this memory.

One form of resistance that I remember well happened in Auschwitz on December 25, 1943. Four trucks with condemned prisoners were driven to the crematoria in Birkenau. As they came within sight of the chimneys, they broke into "Hatikvah." This act of courage at that

---

9. Hana Volavkova, ed., *...I never saw another butterfly... Children's Drawings and Poems from Terezin Concentration Camp, 1942–1944*, 2nd ed (Schocken: New York, 1993).

time was to me a sign of the oneness of the Jewish people – the Jewish nation – and the future of Israel. We believed my father was among them.

During this time, Jews in Israel (then Palestine) were prepared to fight the Germans if Field Marshal Rommel were to bring his Afrika Korps close to the borders of Israel. From Israel, Jews like Hannah Senesh parachuted into Hungary to attempt to rescue Jews. She was captured and executed in jail.

Active resistance, meanwhile, took place in many of the ghettos and camps in Poland, once it became known that there would be no help from the outside. The Allied armies would not come in time to liberate us. We clearly were completely abandoned. Any onetime attempts at liberation were unsuccessful, with weaponry that could not compare to the enemy's. The Sonderkommando in Auschwitz also once tried a revolt. They hoped to make contact with the non-Jewish partisans outside of the camp. No one came to help, and they were killed the same day.

The most famous case of active resistance was the Warsaw Ghetto Uprising, which took place on April 19, 1943. The revolt proved to be out of absolute necessity; it occurred only when it was clear that there was not a single opportunity left for life and survival. This resistance happened in response to the mass murder and deportations to Treblinka. The Warsaw Ghetto Uprising was almost the first civilian uprising in occupied Europe. It was an event with predictable results. A few bottles of gasoline, some outdated guns, emaciated fighters with almost no outside help. We can trace the events in the Warsaw Ghetto: the hunger, the degradations, the indifference of the outside world, and finally the uprising, the heroically tragic actions of a few men and women, without armaments, facing the highly equipped army of the Third Reich – they wrote a glorious chapter in Jewish history. What would have been a birthday present for Hitler, an easy victory for the strongest army in Europe, became instead the watershed event of Jewish consciousness. We can always refer to this uprising and prove that indeed we were brave; we can be proud.

The Warsaw Ghetto Uprising holds for the Jewish people a special meaning and poignancy. It destroys the stereotype of the Jew as the complacent victim. And so, when we adopt as Holocaust Remembrance Day the first day of the Ghetto Uprising, Nisan 27, April 19, 1943, to extend to all those days of terror, we not only memorialize the fighters of Warsaw, but every one of the six million. We memorialize this very visible and courageous resistance.

Remember, Lauren, you must always be proud. Staying united as Jews may give us the power to resist any other attempt on our religion, our nation, our moral standards, and our teachings. Our people have maintained our humanity despite the worst conditions imaginable. I maintained my humanity even in Auschwitz, the most inhumane place on this Earth. Preserve this legacy. Stay strong! I love you.

Love, Ruth

PHOTOS

Ruth and Chana resettling in New Jersey and
resuming their love of music, 1947.

Ruth and her husband, Harry Meyerowitz, on their wedding day, New Jersey, December 5, 1948.

Ruth and Chana with Ruth's eldest son Allan, New Jersey 1952.

Zev Krautwirth in Israel around 1948.

Zev and his wife, Sylvia, on their wedding day, June 23, 1963, in New Jersey. Top row from left: Chana, Zev, Sylvia, Ruth, and Harry. Bottom row from left: Norman, Mark, and Allan (Ruth and Harry's sons).

Ruth's mother, Chana Krautwirth, in New Jersey around 1965. Although widowed, she wears a wedding band. On her left arm is her Auschwitz-Birkenau prisoner number. She was given number 42715 and a triangle (half Star of David) to indicate she was Jewish.

Chana with her brother and sister in Canada, around 1960.

Ruth and Harry's three sons. From left to right: Allan, Norman, and Mark, New Jersey, around 1975.

Ruth and Harry celebrating at their son Allan's wedding, December 23, 1979.

Ruth (bottom left) with her cousin Gloria (bottom right), and Gloria's parents, Bella (Chana's sister) and Leon around 1990.

POSTSCRIPT

RUTH'S FINAL YEARS AND HER LEGACY

New Jersey, United States
2006–2009

As told by Lauren, 2025

THE FINAL YEARS

The fourth generation

2025

Dear Ruth,

I am writing you this letter in the year 2025, but you are no longer here. I am writing to express the things I wish I could tell you but cannot.

I married my wonderful husband, Jonathan Port, on November 23, 2019. We have two daughters.

Our first daughter Anna Ruth was born on December 30, 2020. Just like you said to me when I was named for your mother, she has a strong namesake in you. At four years old, she is bright, inquisitive, caring and sweet.

Our second daughter Julia Hayley was born February 27, 2024. At a year old, she is precious, charming, and lights up the room wherever she goes.

They are part of the fourth generation, the great-grandchildren of Holocaust survivors. I see so much potential in the fourth generation to bring brightness and love into this world. We hope that they learn their family story, cherish it, and continue your legacy.

You would be so proud. I miss you.

Love, Lauren

Recent events

2025

I often wonder what Ruth would think if she were still with us.

The proverbial torch has been passed to the third generation (3G), the grandchildren of survivors, to preserve the memory of the Holocaust and combat anti-semitism and hatred in all forms. There is much work to be done. Antisemitism is on the rise. I suppose it has always been there, but it has not been so in-your-face in my lifetime. When I was younger, I was never aware of any antisemitism. It seemed a thing of the past, something of Ruth's time. I became more aware, and it has gotten worse in recent years.

During the COVID pandemic, there was much controversy about policies for masking and isolating. There were different opinions on what the government should do – shut things down, harming people's livelihoods and wellbeing, yet for the purpose of keeping the general population safe and alive. I disliked so many of the Holocaust references made at that time because they were so trivializing. We were not living in a police state, even if businesses were closed for some time, masking was mandated, and vaccination encouraged. As I was going rather stir crazy stuck at home for so long, I tried to gather courage by thinking about the people who were in hiding during the Holocaust.

Zev passed away from complications from COVID on July 18, 2020. It was upsetting that hospital visitations were kept to a minimum. I did not attend the funeral since it was during the midst of the pandemic, with so many unknown issues related to transmission, causes and effects, and we were expecting our first child.

My cousins Yael and Ayelet live in Israel now with their families. What happened there on October 7, 2023, is horrifying. The aftermath is horrifying. My cousins and their families regularly hide in bomb shelters for safety. It is traumatic for them. Is this the life Ruth would have envisioned for her descendants in the holy land? Despite the latest atrocities, my cousins remain steadfast and dedicated to leading Jewish lives in Israel. Ruth would be so proud to see them living such purpose-filled Jewish lives.

Back in New York, post October 7 and the resulting war against Hamas in Gaza, the antisemitism was in-your-face. I had never actually seen swastika graffiti with my own eyes in my own neighborhood before. The local synagogue was vandalized. Our apartment building was vandalized. Everything was cleaned up quickly, but I will not forget. There were posters of the Israeli hostages of all ages pinned out around our neighborhood, but those were regularly torn down, only to be pinned up again and torn down again, over and over. What would Ruth think of all this?

I wish I could speak with Ruth about it. What advice would she give me? How do I use what I've learned from her already to make the world a better place? The whole thing just makes me feel overwhelmed, but I must try.

I resolve to continue to tell her story, just as she did. My steadfast commitment to "never again" is reach a widespread audience. My work is far from over. I have my purpose, my mission, and, in Ruth's memory, I will carry it on.

Ruth's final years

Ruth suffered greatly in the final years of her life. The genocide that she survived in her youth impacted her until the very end.

Her decline began with the loss of vision and hearing. She had diabetes which was hard to manage. The back pain she had experienced ever since her time in Auschwitz worsened.

She was diagnosed with dementia and lost her short-term memory. It became increasingly difficult for her to recognize family members. While losing her memory of when she had last eaten, Ruth worried about where the next meal would come from.

Ruth tried to convince us that she was fine and nothing was wrong. She insisted that there was no reason to take her to a doctor or hospital. She demonstrated a deep mistrust of doctors and medical institutions in her final years. In her childhood she'd had to prove she was in a state of health so as not to be selected by physicians for the gas chambers. In her elder years she could not comprehend that doctors were there to help, to improve her health and reduce her suffering. Rather than admit to having pain or illness, she denied any weakness. Sometimes she would call 911 if she experienced any pain and could not get in touch with my father, but then she would adamantly refuse to be taken to the hospital.

As I worked on compiling Ruth's stories to write her biography, she still wanted to help me, to share with me the last thing while she still could – her memories. My parents encouraged me to ask questions to keep her mind engaged and to make sure I had all the details I needed. Yet, as her condition worsened, I wanted to be careful not to upset her or cause more anxiety by making her recall the atrocities of her past.

Ruth remained in her home despite her diminishing independence. Eventually we hired full-time help to take care of her. Distrustful of anyone who was not family, Ruth fired the caretakers on multiple occasions.

Old age became a torment for Ruth as old traumas came to the surface. She sought to answer the unanswerable. "The world is vicious and indifferent," she would say. "So now my father is dead, and Irma is dead. No one is left. Why did the Nazis have to kill? Why did they kill everyone? Kill, kill, kill. Why do people kill? Why did they do this to us?"

I listened as she mourned deaths from decades earlier. The wounds had never fully healed. The trauma had been suppressed for many years. I reminded her that she now had a big, loving family with three sons and daughters-in-law and seven grandchildren... but this was no solution to her depression.

Ruth used to host Shabbat dinner. Throughout my life, Friday night dinner with Ruth was special. In those last years, my parents and I continued to go to Ruth's home, but she could no longer prepare the meal, so I cooked or we ordered take-out. We made sure Ruth still attended all the family events. One Thanksgiving it was a two-hour ordeal just to bring her from her house to our house a mile away.

Dad framed a photograph of Mutti to put by Ruth's bedside. She had been so close with her mother that we thought the photo would bring her some joy. While Ruth was happy that she looked like her mother in her old age, the picture made her suffer more. She was reminded of her parents. As she cried out to them in the night, she prayed out loud to be with them again. Soon we moved the picture to a less prominent spot, since it was too painful of a reminder of the past.

One time I gave Ruth a bath. As I gently touched Ruth's arm to clean it, I found myself staring at her tattoo. She could feel me looking at it. "It doesn't go away with soap. It's there permanently." Her words were not curt, nor meant to be condescending, but rather just matter of fact. She had lived with the tattoo for practically her whole life. When I apologized for staring, she asked me if I had any questions about it. I asked if she had ever tried to have it removed later in life. She had looked into it but decided against it. Even in her final months, Ruth was willing to answer my questions.

We eventually moved Ruth into the Jewish nursing home Daughters of Israel. They could best take care of her with round-the-clock attention and medical care. It was an extremely difficult decision since she was adamant about not leaving her home. Yet, her quality of life at home had deteriorated so much that she required better care than we could offer. We took turns visiting. I would visit on Saturdays and one or two weeknights. Norman went on Sundays. My dad was there every single day. We switched the location of Shabbat dinner on Friday evening to the nursing home. We never stopped this beautiful tradition.

Ruth lost some of her long-term memory in addition to her short-term memory. Unfortunately, her childhood war memories stayed with her, while she essentially forgot who her children and grandchildren were. The antisemitism, deportation, Nazi brutality, and Auschwitz were deeply ingrained in her long-term memory and would not be erased. It was incredibly painful to witness how she forgot who I was, yet she remembered Nazi brutality in Birkenau.

Each time we saw Ruth in the nursing home, she asked when she would be going home. So as not to cause greater agitation, we would fib and always say "on Tuesday." She would then ask us what day of the week it was. If it was Friday dinner, I showed her gently that we were eating freshly baked challah. She still had enough long-term memory to know that this meant it was Friday.

One Shabbat dinner, she said that she never expected to grow old or have children or grandchildren of her own. "I thought for sure I would die in Auschwitz. My mother also thought I would die. She did everything she could to keep me out of danger. She also treated my typhus." "How did she do that?" I recall asking, even though I had heard this story before. "Not with medicine or anything. We didn't have medicine. She held my hand and wiped my forehead until I got better." Like Mutti, I did our best to comfort Ruth in her old age.

Yael and Simcha's Wedding

Ruth's oldest granddaughter, my cousin Yael, was married to Simcha on a festive Tuesday evening in Brooklyn. To me, this was at the start of the time of Ruth's decline.

I flew in from Michigan for the wedding. I had missed Ruth while I was away at college, so I wanted to spend my time at home and at the wedding with her. She seemed to be deteriorating. During the wedding reception, I sat next to Ruth at the table. Most of the guests were up and about dancing, but I preferred staying seated to keep my grandmother company. She got a real kick out of it when my cousins Yael, Ayelet, and Chana starting dancing around her at our table!

We sat together while the others chatted and laughed. Between the loud music and losing her hearing, it was difficult for Ruth to partake in conversation. I held her hand, partially listening to the conversation going on around us and partially updating her on what everybody was talking about. Sometimes we just sat quietly and held hands. It was not an awkward silence, but rather a peaceful one. We enjoyed each other's company.

Ruth was aware that we were celebrating a Jewish wedding. I had to remind her a few times that it was Yael's wedding. She was hoping to see Zev, but he could not attend due to a last-minute emergency.

In one of the quiet moments, Ruth became pensive. She said to me: "Lauren, I know this may sound crazy, but I still fear, after all these years, that right now the Nazis could just storm in here and start rounding up people and shooting. I know there are no Nazis anymore, and that it is from a time past, but in my head I can still see it happen. I can just picture it. Please let's leave soon, and don't forget to drive me home with you. Please don't leave me here by myself." She repeated, "Do not abandon me in my old age," in reference to Psalm 71:9, "*Do not send me off at the season of old age; as my powers diminish, do not abandon me.*" She made me promise that we wouldn't leave without her. Her long-term memory and the trauma of her youth were very much intact. Aunt Robin once told me that Ruth had said the same thing to her at a wedding in the 1980s.

What could I say to comfort her? There was really nothing to say. Could I confidently assure her that this would not happen because it was New York in the 21st century? Her subconscious fear would ever be present. Maybe it was post-traumatic stress disorder. I just nodded my head, letting her know that I understood. I held her hand and stayed closeby.

Meeting baby Aliza

My cousin Ayelet had her first child, a daughter named Aliza, born on December 28, 2007. Aliza became Ruth's second great-grandchild. Ayelet and her husband, Raffy, lived in Brooklyn at the time and did not have a car to come visit Ruth. Public transportation with an infant was not an option. I drove round trip from New Jersey to Brooklyn twice in one day to bring Ayelet and the baby to visit Ruth. Ruth met her great-granddaughter Aliza on January 22, 2008, when Aliza was just three weeks old.

Aliza was adorable – so tiny and precious! She already looked just like the other girls in the Meyerowitz family, with a fair complexion, green eyes, and a head full of dark brown hair. She did not open her eyes much yet. She slept peacefully most of the day.

When we put little baby Aliza into Ruth's arms, Ruth's face lit up. I had never seen such a genuinely happy smile on Ruth's face. She grinned from cheek to cheek, being so happy to see such a precious infant. She held little Aliza in her arms and couldn't get enough of her. It must have been just like little Yael visiting Mutti, as Ruth had written to me about.

Ruth knew she was holding the newest member of our family, a beautiful Jewish newborn baby. Having this infant girl sleep on her shoulder brought Ruth so much joy, so much *nachas*.[1] Aliza was the next link in the continuity of Ruth's family and of our people.

Then Ruth closed her eyes and remembered. She thought of the babies who were killed in Auschwitz, the babies who were killed before they had any chance of life, the ones she found suffocated in blankets, the baby boy who was born and who died on Christmas Day and whose body was disintegrated in streams of acid water in Birkenau, diminishing any hope of the Messiah or a liberating army coming soon. That trauma was deeply embedded in her mind. Babies are to be cherished as little miracles from God – they are not meant to be killed by suffocation or poison gas. As Ruth used to say, it is dismal to speak of children dying in a world made by adults.

Ruth made a promise to Aliza that day. "Baby Girl," she said aloud, "the Nazis will never do to you what they did to other infants. I won't let them. No one will ever do to you what the Nazis did. God, protect this baby."

A sense of sadness filled the room as Ayelet and I looked at each other, and our eyes filled with tears. Ruth had always felt mixed emotions at happy events. Here was the birth of a baby, an event which makes most people feel pure joy, and yet, her gladness was tainted by the wounds of her past. She was forever marked by her experience of seeing the horror inflicted on infants by the Nazis that

---

1. Pride, pleasure, and satisfaction, especially from the achievements of one's children (Yiddish).

she could never see another infant without remembering the little ones whose murder she witnessed.

Even with the celebration of a new life, the memory of the Holocaust lingered in Ruth's heart.

Nightmares

I lived with my parents in New Jersey for a short while after graduating from Michigan while working on a master's degree. During this time, Ruth was admitted to the hospital. When she was discharged, the social workers said she could no longer live independently, so we brought her to my parents' home. She had difficulty with stairs, so she slept in the living room downstairs. This was not long before she moved to the nursing home.

I remember her screaming in the night, night after night after night... It was mostly just shrieks, but there were some words and phrases mixed in. I couldn't tell what she was saying. She screamed in German. I had never heard her speak German before. It is not a beautiful language to me and it sounded even more terrifying when yelled in the middle of the night. Dad recalled that Mutti had also screamed during the night in her final years.

My parents and I heard Ruth from upstairs. I think we tried to wait a few minutes in the hope that she would become quiet again soon. That usually did not work. One of us would get up in the middle of the night to comfort her.

One night, around 2:00 a.m., I stood in the entrance to the living room, and she saw my silhouette at a distance.

"Mutti, Mutti, is that you?" she called out.

Had she forgotten her mother was dead? What year did she think it was? Was she having a bad dream, or was she awake? Had her mind taken her back in time? She must be awake, I thought.

"No, Ruthie, it's Lauren. Is everything okay? You've been screaming." I slowly approached her and sat down next to her on the bed, where she was sitting upright.

"Lauren, where is Mutti?"

"I'm sorry Ruthie... Mutti is in heaven. She has been there ever since a few months before I was born, since December 1985."

She became quiet. Her nightmares had brought her back to Auschwitz. I could sense her confusion, but she was calming down a little. Her agitation subsided. She mumbled that she was hungry. It couldn't be. We had eaten a big dinner. Maybe she was thirsty from the diabetes. I brought her a glass of water. Then I held her hand.

"What year is it, Lauren?"

"It's 2008. The war has been over for a very long time. Why don't you try to get some rest? Close your eyes." I hugged her.

"When am I going to see Mutti again?" The thought of being separated from Mutti was causing her anxiety.

I struggled with how to reply. "I don't know. Maybe soon. Try to get some rest."

She lay down, and I continued to sit next to her and gently rub her head and arm. I gave her a kiss on the forehead. She seemed slowly to fall asleep again. I stayed with her another ten minutes before heading back upstairs to bed.

The nightmares never stopped. They transported her back to the years of the Holocaust, night after night. Back to Auschwitz. I was mostly helpless to comfort her.

The subsequent year brought Ruth even more torment, as her body and mind were failing her. It was not fair for her to suffer like this. Hadn't she suffered enough in one lifetime? She missed her mother, father, and Irma. She missed her husband. I wondered if it would be immoral of me to hope for her finally to be at peace and to be reunited with her loved ones in heaven.

The death of my grandma

Ruth passed away on the morning of Tuesday, February 3, 2009, at the age of 79. Many years have passed since then, but sometimes it feels like just yesterday. The suffering she experienced in her final years came to an end. In our grief, Dad and I noted that indeed she went home on a Tuesday.

When I arrived home from my graduate school that day, Dad told me that Ruth had passed away that morning. For the very first instant I did not believe it, but then, realizing it was true, I fell to the ground in shock. We broke into tears together.

Mom had prepared a light dinner, but I could not eat. I spent the whole night crying. I knew it was Ruth's time and that now she was no longer in pain, but I felt an incredible loss like nothing I had ever felt before. It was the first time I could remember that someone in my family had died, so I experienced how permanent a loss can feel. To think that I would never see my grandma again was devastating.

I thought of the losses Ruth had suffered and mourned all those years. Although it is in the normal order of life events for a grandchild to lose a grandparent, I still felt my world was shattered. To try to make myself feel better, I had to remind myself that the agony she had been in was over. I had previously thought her death might bring a small sense of relief, an end to her suffering, but it was just too drastic a change for her to be here one day and then suddenly gone the next. The day Ruth died was the worst day of my life.

The next day we made the plans for the burial. I spent many hours shoveling snow off the driveway to prepare for the funeral and *shiva* [week-long period of mourning], which was held at my parents' home. The following day, on a freezing cold morning, we buried Ruth in between her husband and her mother.

Aunt Robin had been in Israel and booked the first flight home when she learned of Ruth's death. Coming straight from the airport to the funeral home, she saw my Uncle Allan, and they began to sob as they embraced. We eulogized Ruth and spoke about her difficult life, as well as about how wonderful a mother and grandmother she had been.

In my eulogy, I recalled asking her questions about the Holocaust. I swore to all in attendance that although she was gone, her memories would not be forgotten. I made a promise to her then, in that moment. I have made the same promise to her in my heart every day since that day. I promised her that I would always remember her story.

Ruth's legacy and the future

Ruth was determined to pass her story onto her grandchildren. Recalling the events of the past caused Ruth to relive the horror, but despite this difficulty, she told her story. What was her goal, her mission? What did she want us to learn from this?

In her first letter to me as a baby, she says she must tell us her story because, if not, it would be as Emil Fackenheim says, to hand Hitler and his cohorts the final victory. Fackenheim was known for his

"614th Commandment," that Jews are forbidden to hand Hitler posthumous victories and must keep Judaism alive.

In line with his theory, Ruth believed that the most important lesson we can take from the Holocaust is that Judaism and the Jewish people must live on. We must not be Jewish *because* of Hitler, but rather *despite* him. We are Jewish for many reasons: because of our belief in one God, our adherence to Torah, our love of Israel, our value system, or because we are born into Jewish families with a rich heritage and beautiful traditions. We choose Judaism as our religion, our identity, our way of life.

Now we, Ruth's children, grandchildren, and great-grandchildren, are the future and must carry on Ruth's wishes for the survival and strength of the Jewish people. We express our Judaism in our own way just as she would have wanted. We have the obligation to learn and teach the lessons of the past and to do everything in our power to ensure there is never a recurrence of genocide against our people or any other people.

Throughout Ruth's lifetime, she mourned the lost potential of the unborn generations. She mourned the vibrant prewar Frankfurt Jewish community of which she was among the few surviving members. She mourned for countless friends and family members who were destroyed. She mourned for Mimi as she remembered her heroism. She mourned for Irma as she failed to understand the rationale behind why or how the Nazis could murder an innocent little girl. With unspeakable grief, Ruth mourned for her father.

Despite these devastating losses, Ruth looked toward the future and the continuity of the Jewish people. She bore witness to the genocide of our people but also to the establishment and successes of the State of Israel and the rebirth and growth of new Jewish communities in the postwar world. She created her own family with three sons, seven grandchildren, and now many great-grandchildren, including precious little girls Nechama Rus, Ruti, Anna Ruth, and Temima Rut, who are named for her.

Ruth became a Holocaust educator. She gave her audiences and her family a sense of purpose and identity by telling us her story. She wanted to make sure we appreciated our heritage, and we do. She did her part to ensure the vibrant future of the Jewish people.

With love and gratitude in my heart for hearing her story, I strive to carry on Ruth's legacy. It is my hope that this book will serve to make us remember and honor the six million Jews who perished in the Shoah. This book serves to make Ruth's children, grandchildren, great-grandchildren, and future descendants know and remember her story. It is because of Ruth's survival that we are here.

I hope that I have conveyed Ruth life's story as a story of the triumph of the Jewish spirit over hate, destruction, and inhumanity. It is my sincere prayer that I have done it justice.

PHOTOS

Ruth with her son Mark, daughter-in-law Nancy, and grandchildren Jeff and Lauren, at Lauren's Bat Mitzvah, West Orange, New Jersey, April 10, 1999.

Yael's wedding, Brooklyn, New York, October 17, 2006. Top row from left: Shai, Robin, Yael, Allan, Chana Bottom row from left: Ruth, Ayelet.

Ruth meeting her first grandchild, Lauren's older brother Jeff, with whom she shares a birthday (June 23), New Jersey, 1983.

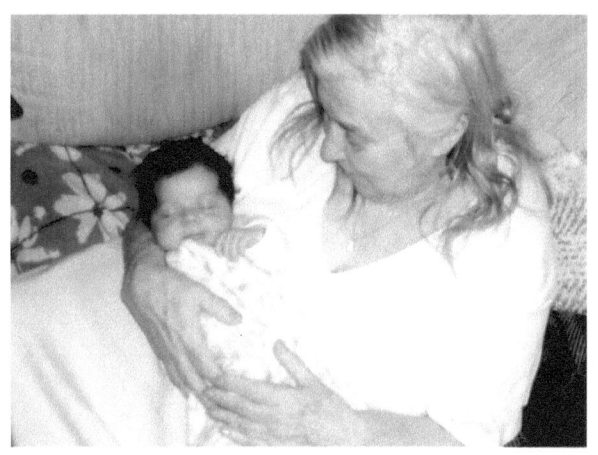

Ruth meeting her great grand-daughter Aliza, January 2008.

Ruth and Lauren after discussing Lauren's plan to write Ruth's biography, New Jersey, 2006.

ACKNOWLEDGMENTS

This book would not be possible had my grandmother Ruth Krautwirth Meyerowitz not given her testimony to schools, museums, and family. Thank you to all my relatives who encouraged her to speak to us grandchildren. The first time I ever heard Ruth's story in its entirely was to a class of students at a school where my aunt Robin taught. Thank you to her brother Zev Krautwirth, for providing additional stories. Thank to Gloria Shapero, for the details about the maternal side of the family before the war and the fate of those relatives. Also, Zev's daughter, Rina Krautwirth, for sharing the primary sources that were in her possession.

Additional thanks go to: Tina Tahir, for translations; Birthright Israel, for it was during the visit to Yad Vashem that the idea to write a book came to my mind; Olami Manhattan (formerly JEC), for the trip to Poland; 3GNY for the "WEDU" speaker training; Bonnie Gurewitsch, Elizabeth Edelstein with the Museum of Jewish Heritage for guidance through the Heritage Testimonies program. It is an honor to share Ruth's story as part of the Museum of Jewish Heritage's Speaker Bureau.

I must deeply thank my editor, Carol Wise, from Writes of Passage. Carol brought not only her expertise in writing and editing to the table but also her vast knowledge in the areas of Holocaust history and Judaic studies.

Finally, thank you to my parents, Mark and Nancy, and my husband,

Jonathan, for their enduring support, love and encouragement to write over the years.

If Ruth's story has inspired you, please consider a donation to the Blue Card (http://www.bluecardfund.org/), to support impoverished Holocaust survivors today, in her memory.

ABOUT THE AUTHOR

Lauren Meyerowitz Port grew up learning about the Holocaust from her grandmother. She holds a Master of Arts in Diplomacy and International Relations and a Bachelor of Arts in Spanish. She works in the field of international trade and resides in New York City with her husband and two daughters.

AMSTERDAM PUBLISHERS HOLOCAUST LIBRARY

The series **Holocaust Survivor Memoirs World War II** consists of the following autobiographies of survivors:

Outcry. Holocaust Memoirs, by Manny Steinberg

Hank Brodt Holocaust Memoirs. A Candle and a Promise, by Deborah Donnelly

The Dead Years. Holocaust Memoirs, by Joseph Schupack

Rescued from the Ashes. The Diary of Leokadia Schmidt, Survivor of the Warsaw Ghetto, by Leokadia Schmidt

My Lvov. Holocaust Memoir of a twelve-year-old Girl, by Janina Hescheles

Remembering Ravensbrück. From Holocaust to Healing, by Natalie Hess

Wolf. A Story of Hate, by Zeev Scheinwald with Ella Scheinwald

Save my Children. An Astonishing Tale of Survival and its Unlikely Hero, by Leon Kleiner with Edwin Stepp

Holocaust Memoirs of a Bergen-Belsen Survivor & Classmate of Anne Frank, by Nanette Blitz Konig

Defiant German - Defiant Jew. A Holocaust Memoir from inside the Third Reich, by Walter Leopold with Les Leopold

In a Land of Forest and Darkness. The Holocaust Story of two Jewish Partisans, by Sara Lustigman Omelinski

Holocaust Memories. Annihilation and Survival in Slovakia, by Paul Davidovits

From Auschwitz with Love. The Inspiring Memoir of Two Sisters' Survival, Devotion and Triumph Told by Manci Grunberger Beran & Ruth Grunberger Mermelstein, by Daniel Seymour

Remetz. Resistance Fighter and Survivor of the Warsaw Ghetto, by Jan Yohay Remetz

My March Through Hell. A Young Girl's Terrifying Journey to Survival, by Halina Kleiner with Edwin Stepp

Roman's Journey, by Roman Halter

Beyond Borders. Escaping the Holocaust and Fighting the Nazis. 1938-1948, by Rudi Haymann

The Engineers. A memoir of survival through World War II in Poland and Hungary, by Henry Reiss

Spark of Hope. An Autobiography, by Luba Wrobel Goldberg

Footnote to History. From Hungary to America. The Memoir of a Holocaust Survivor, by Andrew Laszlo

Farewell Atlantis. Recollections, by Valentīna Freimane

The Courtyard. A memoir, by Ben Parket and Alexa Morris

Run, Mendel Run, by Milton H. Schwartz

The series **Holocaust Survivor True Stories**
consists of the following biographies:

Among the Reeds. The true story of how a family survived the Holocaust, by Tammy Bottner

A Holocaust Memoir of Love & Resilience. Mama's Survival from Lithuania to America, by Ettie Zilber

Living among the Dead. My Grandmother's Holocaust Survival Story of Love and Strength, by Adena Bernstein Astrowsky

Heart Songs. A Holocaust Memoir, by Barbara Gilford

Shoes of the Shoah. The Tomorrow of Yesterday, by Dorothy Pierce

Hidden in Berlin. A Holocaust Memoir, by Evelyn Joseph Grossman

Separated Together. The Incredible True WWII Story of Soulmates Stranded an Ocean Apart, by Kenneth P. Price, Ph.D.

The Man Across the River. The incredible story of one man's will to survive the Holocaust, by Zvi Wiesenfeld

If Anyone Calls, Tell Them I Died. A Memoir, by Emanuel (Manu) Rosen

The House on Thrömerstrasse. A Story of Rebirth and Renewal in the Wake of the Holocaust, by Ron Vincent

Dancing with my Father. His hidden past. Her quest for truth. How Nazi Vienna shaped a family's identity, by Jo Sorochinsky

The Story Keeper. Weaving the Threads of Time and Memory - A Memoir, by Fred Feldman

Krisia's Silence. The Girl who was not on Schindler's List, by Ronny Hein

Defying Death on the Danube. A Holocaust Survival Story, by Debbie J. Callahan with Henry Stern

A Doorway to Heroism. A decorated German-Jewish Soldier who became an American Hero, by W. Jack Romberg

The Shoemaker's Son. The Life of a Holocaust Resister, by Laura Beth Bakst

The Redhead of Auschwitz. A True Story, by Nechama Birnbaum

Land of Many Bridges. My Father's Story, by Bela Ruth Samuel Tenenholtz

Creating Beauty from the Abyss. The Amazing Story of Sam Herciger, Auschwitz Survivor and Artist, by Lesley Ann Richardson

On Sunny Days We Sang. A Holocaust Story of Survival and Resilience, by Jeannette Grunhaus de Gelman

Painful Joy. A Holocaust Family Memoir, by Max J. Friedman

I Give You My Heart. A True Story of Courage and Survival, by Wendy Holden

In the Time of Madmen, by Mark A. Prelas

Monsters and Miracles. Horror, Heroes and the Holocaust, by Ira Wesley Kitmacher

Flower of Vlora. Growing up Jewish in Communist Albania, by Anna Kohen

Aftermath: Coming of Age on Three Continents. A Memoir, by Annette Libeskind Berkovits

Not a real Enemy. The True Story of a Hungarian Jewish Man's Fight for Freedom, by Robert Wolf

Zaidy's War. Four Armies, Three Continents, Two Brothers. One Man's Impossible Story of Endurance, by Martin Bodek

The Glassmaker's Son. Looking for the World my Father left behind in Nazi Germany, by Peter Kupfer

The Apprentice of Buchenwald. The True Story of the Teenage Boy Who Sabotaged Hitler's War Machine, by Oren Schneider

Good for a Single Journey, by Helen Joyce

Burying the Ghosts. She escaped Nazi Germany only to have her life torn apart by the woman she saved from the camps: her mother, by Sonia Case

American Wolf. From Nazi Refugee to American Spy. A True Story, by Audrey Birnbaum

Bipolar Refugee. A Saga of Survival and Resilience, by Peter Wiesner

In the Wake of Madness. My Family's Escape from the Nazis, by Bettie Lennett Denny

Before the Beginning and After the End, by Hymie Anisman

I Will Give Them an Everlasting Name. Jacksonville's Stories of the Holocaust, by Samuel Cox

Hiding in Holland. A Resistance Memoir, by Shulamit Reinharz

The Ghosts on the Wall. A Grandson's Memoir of the Holocaust, by Kenneth D. Wald

Thirteen in Auschwitz. My grandmother's fight to stay human, by Lauren Meyerowitz Port

The series **Jewish Children in the Holocaust** consists of the following autobiographies of Jewish children hidden during WWII in the Netherlands:

Searching for Home. The Impact of WWII on a Hidden Child, by Joseph Gosler

Sounds from Silence. Reflections of a Child Holocaust Survivor, Psychiatrist and Teacher, by Robert Krell

Sabine's Odyssey. A Hidden Child and her Dutch Rescuers, by Agnes Schipper

The Journey of a Hidden Child, by Harry Pila and Robin Black

The series **New Jewish Fiction** consists of the following novels, written by Jewish authors. All novels are set in the time during or after the Holocaust.

The Corset Maker. A Novel, by Annette Libeskind Berkovits

Escaping the Whale. The Holocaust is over. But is it ever over for the next generation? by Ruth Rotkowitz

When the Music Stopped. Willy Rosen's Holocaust, by Casey Hayes

Hands of Gold. One Man's Quest to Find the Silver Lining in Misfortune, by Roni Robbins

The Girl Who Counted Numbers. A Novel, by Roslyn Bernstein

There was a garden in Nuremberg. A Novel, by Navina Michal Clemerson

The Butterfly and the Axe, by Omer Bartov

To Live Another Day. A Novel, by Elizabeth Rosenberg

The Right to Happiness. After all they went through. Stories, by Helen Schary Motro

Five Amber Beads, by Richard Aronowitz

To Love Another Day. A Novel, by Elizabeth Rosenberg

Cursing the Darkness. A Novel about Loss and Recovery, by Joanna Rosenthall

The series **Holocaust Heritage** consists of the following memoirs by 2G:

The Cello Still Sings. A Generational Story of the Holocaust and of the Transformative Power of Music, by Janet Horvath

The Fire and the Bonfire. A Journey into Memory, by Ardyn Halter

The Silk Factory: Finding Threads of My Family's True Holocaust Story, by Michael Hickins

Winter Light. The Memoir of a Child of Holocaust Survivors, by Grace Feuerverger

Out from the Shadows. Growing up with Holocaust Survivor Parents, by Willie Handler

Hidden in Plain Sight. A Family Memoir and the Untold Story of the Holocaust in Serbia, by Julie Brill

The Unspeakable. Breaking my family's silence surrounding the Holocaust, by Nicola Hanefeld

Eighteen for Life. Surviving the Holocaust, by Helen Schamroth

Austrian Again. Reclaiming a Lost Legacy, by Anne Hand

The series **Holocaust Books for Young Adults** consists of the following novels, based on true stories:

The Boy behind the Door. How Salomon Kool Escaped the Nazis. Inspired by a True Story, by David Tabatsky

Running for Shelter. A True Story, by Suzette Sheft

The Precious Few. An Inspirational Saga of Courage based on True Stories, by David Twain with Art Twain

Dark Shadows Hover, by Jordan Steven Sher

The Sun will Shine on You again one Day, by Cynthia Monsour

The series **WWII Historical Fiction** consists of the following novels, some of which are based on true stories:

Mendelevski's Box. A Heartwarming and Heartbreaking Jewish Survivor's Story, by Roger Swindells

A Quiet Genocide. The Untold Holocaust of Disabled Children in WWII Germany, by Glenn Bryant

The Knife-Edge Path, by Patrick T. Leahy

Brave Face. The Inspiring WWII Memoir of a Dutch/German Child, by I. Caroline Crocker and Meta A. Evenbly

When We Had Wings. The Gripping Story of an Orphan in Janusz Korczak's Orphanage. A Historical Novel, by Tami Shem-Tov

Jacob's Courage. Romance and Survival amidst the Horrors of War, by Charles S. Weinblatt

A Semblance of Justice. Based on true Holocaust experiences, by Wolf Holles

Under the Pink Triangle. Where forbidden love meets unspeakable evil, by Katie Moore

Amsterdam Publishers Newsletter

Subscribe to our Newsletter by selecting the menu at the top (right) of **amsterdampublishers.com** or scan the QR-code below.

www.ingramcontent.com/pod-product-compliance
Lightning Source LLC
LaVergne TN
LVHW091713070526
838199LV00050B/2377